OUT OF EGYPT

Paul J Davis

A journey from the captivity of the past to a new life in Christ

Or, you can take the new Christian out of their 'old life'.
But can you get the 'old life' out of the new Christian?

Published for Revd. Paul J Davis by
Verité CM Limited, 124 Sea Place, Worthing, West Sussex BN12 4BG
+44 (0) 1903 241975

email: enquiries@veritecm.com
Web: www.veritecm.com

British Library Cataloguing in Publication Data

A catalogue record for this book is available from the British Library

ISBN: 978-1-910719-82-4

Design and Print Management by Verité CM Ltd
www.veritecm.com

Printed in England

ACKNOWLEDGEMENTS

The idea for this book came after prayer and I have continued to seek the Lord through all the hours I have spent on this book; I thank Him for His grace.

I am very grateful for the help and support I have received from Chris Powell and Pete Goddard at Verité CM Ltd. Also, to all at Verité without whom this book would still be an idea and the spelling and grammar would render it unreadable.

I am particularly grateful to my friend and former Pastor James Glass that in the midst of his exacting schedule he took time to read the book. I really appreciate his perceptive, knowledgeable and encouraging comments. Equally I really appreciated my friend Nigel Fawcett-Jones insightful comments I liked his way of looking at things. I also would like to thank the Friday morning ladies prayer group for their ongoing prayer support and commitment. Nor could I ignore the encouragement from my friend Nevil, a wise godly man always encouraging people to be all they can be.

Finally, a very special thank you to my children Peter and Sarah who have supported me throughout the writing of the book; occasionally rightfully and helpfully challenged my thinking but always both have encouraged me to 'go for it'.

I could not be prouder of my children. Even more so as I can join with the writer of 3 John 1:4 *I have no greater joy than to hear that my children walk in truth.*

Finally, to those who I have not mentioned by name but have encouraged me, Thank you.

Revd. Paul J Davis February 2020

CONTENTS

PREFACE

What is the relevance of the Jewish nations escape from captivity in Egypt to the 21st Century Christian?

The Christian in today's world is a member of a world-wide multi-denominational Church with in excess of 2.2 billion fellow members making it the largest religious group in the world. (www.reference.com/Christianity).

In this book we are going to focus on the original Jewish nation, its captivity and struggles in Egypt and explore how God led them out of captivity.

WHY?

If there are only an estimated 14 Million Jewish people in the world today, why should we explore their ancestor's experiences? This a good question and the question several people will ask?

The history of the Jewish nation is of great importance to the Christian today, Christians ignore their Jewish roots at their peril. The Bible is very clear that Jesus is a descendant of Abraham and King David, that's a very strong Jewish lineage.

Derek Prince in his book Why Israel?[1] quotes Exodus 19:6 Where God tells Moses to tell, the people of Israel, *'You shall be to Me a Kingdom of Priests and a Holy Nation'.*

God has not said this to any other Nation.

In Genesis 17 God made a covenant with Abraham that he would be the Father of many nations, this ties in with many prophecies in the scriptures.

Derek Prince goes onto say *'Without the Jews, we would have no patriarchs, no apostles, no Bible and no Saviour!*

---

1 *Why Israel,* Derek Prince Ministries. www.derekprinceministries.com

'God predestined us for adoption to himself as sons through Jesus Christ, according to the purpose of his will, to the praise of his glorious grace, with which he has blessed us in the Beloved. In him we have redemption through his blood, the forgiveness of our trespasses, according to the riches of his grace'. (Ephesians 1:5 ESV).

So when we believe in Jesus and accept him as our Saviour, we are then adopted into his family: we become members of the family of God His chosen people. When we believe in Jesus we start to become more like him, as we are changed by God through the power of the Holy Spirit; to become the person God created us to be. To live a life that is pleasing to God. As we grow with God sometimes we find that what we do and what we say and the manner that we say and do things are contrary to God's ways.

This book will explore some of those issues.

If we are adopted, then we have the same rights of an heir in any family.

Good and bad.

Book of Psalms tells us 'we are his people and the sheep of his pasture'.

Therefore, whatever reward that will fall upon the Israelites will fall on us.

We therefore may also suffer as the Jewish people have suffered and as Christ himself suffered.

As we follow the journey of the Israelites out of captivity, their battles, fears, hopes, successes, failures: together with the teaching they received from the Patriarchs and the prophets. We can draw parallels to today's Christians and the journey made from a life without God to getting to know God and to discover what is important to him.

We then find the promises that God makes to us can become challenges of living as a Christian; but above all that God has a plan for us to grow in him and become more like him as we journey from our former captivity: our lives lived away from God, was like being a captive in a foreign land.

Can we as Christians follow Jesus and be all he wants us to be whilst we are still in many ways captive to our old lives? Do we need to be set free?

We will also consider how did we get into captivity?

How did God get the Israelites out of captivity in Egypt and how can God get 'Egypt' (or the things that hold us captive) out of us?

Now we start to learn the language and lifestyle of Christian Living.

We read in Micah 6:8 what God requires of us:

> *He has told you, O man, what is good:*
> *and what does the Lord require of you*
> *but to do justice, and to love kindness,*
> *and to walk humbly with your God?*

As we explore the Israelites journey from Captivity, we will better understand the relevance of this verse to us.

We will see that on our Journey from Non-Christian to Christian and then following Jesus, that many of the experiences the Israelites had: we will experience the same or similar: at the end we will also achieve the same outcome. We will enter into God 's promised land; for a us a land flowing in milk and honey.

Finally, when the day comes for us when our time on earth is finished Jesus will come and take us home to his Father's house where there will be a special place for us.

I pray that this book will help you on your journey, it will be informative and encouraging as you seek to live a life pleasing to God.

God loves to walk with us, may you know his grace, forgiveness, peace, love and joy as you daily walk with Him.

Be blessed in Jesus name.

Paul J Davis

CHAPTER 1

Why did the Israelites end up in Captivity in Egypt?

God chose the Jewish nation to be his people, a people that would love him and forsake all other gods but walk with him and worship him.

The Bible says God created man in his own image, he wanted to fellowship with man, celebrate with them when it went well, perhaps encourage them if there were challenges, and it would appear from the beginning God did not put a life span on man. He did however warn man that if he ate of the Tree of Life he would surely die.

After the fall, (when Adam and Eve ate from the tree of Life that God had forbidden them to) God said 'man will die and return to the ground from which you were hewn'. (Gen 3:19)

God chose the Israelites to be his nation, now I don't profess to have a direct line to God or to know his mind, but I think God chose Israel for some or all of the following reasons.

- They were a Holy nation appointed by God. Deuteronomy 7:6 '*For you are a holy people to the LORD your God: the LORD your God has chosen you to be a people for Himself,* a special treasure above all the peoples on the face of the earth'.

- Speaking of the nation of Israel, Deuteronomy 7:7-9 tells us, '*The LORD did not set His affection on you and choose you because you were more numerous than other peoples, for you were the fewest of all peoples. But it was because the LORD loved you and kept the oath He swore to your forefathers that He brought you out with a mighty hand and redeemed you from the land of slavery, from the power of Pharaoh king of Egypt. Know therefore that the LORD your God is God: He is the faithful God, keeping His covenant of love to a thousand generations of those who love Him and keep His commands.'*

- Israel was to be a nation of priests, prophets, and missionaries to the world. God's intent was for Israel to be a distinct people, a nation who pointed others towards God and His promised provision of a Redeemer, Messiah, and Saviour.
- God wanted a lineage for his Son, he was already seeing how mankind was turning from him to worship other gods, how man was afraid to *walk with him in the cool of the evening.*
- How by one man's disobeying God (Adam) *'sin entered the world, by one-man sin entered into the world, and death by sin: and so death passed upon all men'* (Romans 5:12). God knew it would be necessary for one man to pay the price for all, *'so also one righteous act resulted in justification and life for all people'*. (Romans 5:18).
- God wanted a nation that would keep his law and the words of the prophets, his own nation, his people, he would show them favour
- The Israelites were good at remembering things, keeping copies of the law, the old scriptures.
- God chose Abraham because God believed Abraham would be faithful, he tested him even to the point of Abraham being willing to sacrifice his son in order to demonstrate that he would have faith in God and obey God, all the while believing that God would provide a solution. (Gen 22 1-18) God knew that Abraham would be a faithful forebear for Jesus.

- Abraham proved to be faithful, in a generation that followed idols and rebelled against God. Paul writes to the church at Rome (Rom 4:1-3) *'That Abraham's faith was credited to him as righteousness'.*

- There was within the Jewish people a tribe that was 'in touch' with God, that endeavored to honour God and do his will.

The Jewish nation was split into tribes, for example, the tribe of Aaron was a priestly tribe responsible for ensuring the nation of Israel kept the religious rules and duties of God. The Aaronic priests were there as the only people who could speak to God, but then only after rites of purification, could they enter into the Holy of Holies and plead with God on behalf of the people, only they could make sacrifices to God according to the Law strictly laid down.

- God wanted the words of his prophets kept so that at the right time man could see that what God said came true.

- God wanted his people to be a nation that told others how good God was and thereby to lead people back to meet with God.

- (Zac 8:20) This is what the Lord Almighty says: *'Many peoples and the inhabitants of many cities will yet come, and the inhabitants of one city will go to another and say, 'Let us go at once to entreat the Lord and seek the Lord Almighty. I myself am going.' And many peoples and powerful nations will come to Jerusalem to seek the Lord Almighty and to entreat him.'* And in Verse 23: This is what the Lord Almighty says: *'In those days ten people from all languages and nations will take firm hold of one Jew by the hem of his robe and say, 'Let us go with you, because we have heard that God is with you.''*

- God wanted the nations to see how he looked after his people when they followed him and to know the consequences of their actions when they disobeyed him.
- God gave them an inheritance: their Egyptian masters gave them gold and silver for the journey (The Exodus from Egypt), the Israelites had been gold and silver smiths in Egypt, it was a tremendously wealthy country. (Exodus 12 35-36)

The people of Israel had also done as Moses told them, for they had asked the Egyptians for silver and gold, jewellery and for clothing. Ex.12:36 *'And the Lord had given the people favor in the sight of the Egyptians, so that they let them have what they asked for'.*

Speaking of the nation of Israel, Deuteronomy 7:7-9 tells us, *'The LORD did not set His affection on you and choose you because you were more numerous than other peoples, for you were the fewest of all peoples. But it was because the LORD loved you and kept the oath He swore to your forefathers…' the LORD your God is God: He is the faithful God, keeping His covenant of love to a thousand generations of those who love Him and keep His commands.'*

After God had spoken to Abraham, he told him his descendants would be as many as the stars in the sky, he also told him that *'Know for certain that for four hundred years your descendants will be strangers in a country not their own and that they will be enslaved and mistreated there'.* (Genesis 15:13.NIV)

There was no doubt the Israelites would end up as slaves in a foreign land for many generations.

The Israelites did love God and throughout thousands of years have continued to serve him and honour him, however during this time many of their people have turned from God and worshiped other gods and Idols, additionally many of their leaders have argued about what is the right way to be Godly.

It has been said that the Jewish nation is a stubborn nation.

This can be a good character trait, one that has kept many of them following God from generation to generation even through terrible violent attacks and sufferings like the Holocaust. However, this same stubbornness has caused their Kings in history and many of the people to put themselves and their desires above God and not listen to reason (2 Kings 17:14) *'However, they did not listen, but stiffened their neck like their fathers, who did not believe in the LORD their God'.*

Jeremiah says of his people *'But this people has a stubborn and rebellious heart: They have turned aside and departed'.*[2]

Other translations say *Gone Away,* meaning *away from God.*

Whilst the following is a consideration for a further book, I wonder what we would do if God appeared to you or I today and told us our nation would end up in captivity for four hundred years?

- Would we just think we were having a bad day?
- Touch of indigestion?
- Watched too many movies?
- Would we believe that God was speaking to us or that we had too much happy juice last night?

Is God speaking to the church today?
Are we are ignoring his voice?
Does God speak to the church today?
Are we listening?
Are we bothered?
Does it matter?
How will God's voice affect me?

2 Jeremiah 5:23.

These are some of the questions Christians need to consider. It is not intended to give complete answers to each question raised in this book but I would encourage the reader to fully explore these questions.

However, the author believes that God is speaking to us today.

It could be argued that many in the church are not alert to hear what God says. Other people hear but don't understand; some hear and are unsure how to respond, so don't.

Jesus says to us all: 'Therefore be on the alert, for you do not know which day your Lord is coming'. Matthew 24:42. In many ways Christians are in captivity today, they are increasingly moving deeper into captivity, however, it is generally subtle and often Christians do not realise they have moved away from God.

Captivity creeps up on you, so slowly you don't realise you have gone off God's path, you fail to see your values are/ have changed, you say yes to things that yesterday you would have said no to. For some Christians being a Christian is a habit, possibly something they have done since childhood but without a real personal commitment to God. They often do not consider the implications of decisions that are made for them nor do they speak out, they are the silent majority. Church members are often unaware about different theologies or ideas like prosperity theology, residual anointing and kenosis theory that their church leadership may support, embrace or promote in their church.

Hopefully our church leaders have prayerfully considered these issues and embraced only sound biblical doctrine. However, church members should still be able to discuss these issues with the leaders and be confident that 'their church' is based on sound theology and biblical truths and not following some extreme ideologies.

It is in this state of mind that many Christians find themselves in captivity today, they are increasingly being drawn deeper into captivity, however it is generally subtle not being abused and battered as the Israelites were.

Often it's only the tiniest of things: in sport you only need to be half an inch or less off the target to lose. In Formula 1 you can lose a race by one thousands of a second I don't even know how long that is I can't count it!

Let's look at a simple church illustration:

Normal Sunday Service, all going well then the leader says, I won't preach today 'cos I got a cold', Ah. So we will have some extended music and a time of quiet reflection instead.

Sounds like a plan, after the service people say, 'you know really good we had that quiet time,' I would bring my friend to that type of service, good stuff Mr Leader we get so much noise in our modern world good to have quiet. We can read the Bible in our own times.

So based on that the church suspends preaching for a short while to be a reflective church listening to the voice of God. They don't hear much of anything, so they keep at it longer, they pray more fervently, but still no real improvement.

The Bible says *'So faith comes from hearing, and hearing through the word of Christ'*. Romans 10:17 ESV.

We need individually and collectively to hear the word of God, a church that does not hear the word of God regularly is missing out on hearing what God wants to say to his people. We need to hear the word of God not the word of man, you can hear that everyday anywhere but it won't guide you in the path of life.

In our illustration, eventually the church doesn't go back to preaching or reading the scripture because they 'have moved on', and they enjoy the quiet. Ultimately things start to go wrong and then church folds. They didn't move on they moved away from God. Not the same thing at all.

'Course couldn't happen in the real world?

Towards the end of the last century the church seemed to be growing, it moved from a place of preaching 'hell fire and condemnation' on every one, to being all things to all people:

We were living in a post-modernist society where it was ok to share your life story.

Many evangelists saw this as a great chance to preach the Gospel to tell the story of Christ and how He had set them free and would do the same for all listeners.

Post Modern thinking encouraged people to think of their story and capture it, to note it down for posterity. People's 'life stories' were important, special, not to be ignored and all of equal value.

The listener gave it a value, by the interest they showed and also when the Christian talked about their 'journey to faith' many listeners listened with genuine interest and were keen to have the same experience. The church tried to help people to understand the Christian faith, Alpha groups and meals seemed to be happening at each church in the town there was a sense that it was a great move, people coming to faith, asking the difficult questions, learning about fellowship, worship, the Holy Spirit. Many people were realising that the emptiness in their lives was their separation from God.

But the church tried to meet the needs of all, many in church leadership watered down the gospel, talked down the parts of the Bible that were tough to understand.

Even some church leaders said or implied the basic tenets of the Christian faith[3] were not relevant today.

3 Firstly Christianity is about having a relationship with Jesus Christ the Son of God. If you are unsure about the basics of your faith speak to your pastor or church leader. Each church will have on its's webpage details of its core values that should address the key issues including; The Trinity; God the Father, God the Son our Saviour and God the Holy Spirit. The Bible being the inspired, infallible word of God.

How can a leader of a Christian Church state that 'Jesus was the Son of God, was crucified, died, buried and after three days rose again and went to reign in heaven: 'but you don't have to believe that to be a Christian'?

That leader is denying what is written in the Bible the key book of the Christian faith. Denying key tenets of the Christian faith. When we do that we weaken the church, and allow people to become misled and misled people go astray, there is no power in their faith to help them through the tough times.

What do you have to believe? We live in an age where it appears to be ok to say take what you like from the basic tenets of the faith, and leave the rest, like it doesn't matter. It DOES.

Christians who have come to faith with this sort of incorrect and foolish teaching are suffering from only having half the message, I would suggest this is why many in the church are not living in the Power of Christ.

Additionally, the Church is not growing at present but the Secular church is, for many people the message of the Gospel being told them is incomplete, its missing some of the key parts.

It like having a burger without the meaty bits in the middle, or buying a car and finding it has no engine, it don't work, it is not ok. Relatively speaking it's a car, it looks like a car, but it's not a car the heart is missing but it don't work, it's a lump of metal.

I remember the phrase, 'If it looks like a duck, quacks like a duck and swims like a duck it probably is a duck'.

Can we say the same for the car with no engine it looks like a car, it it's the same size as a car, it doesn't drive like a car therefore it is not a car? It looks like a Christian church, it acts like a Christian church but it doesn't believe in God, or the main tenets of the Christian faith, therefore it is not a Christian church?

Salvation. God the soon and coming King. The Church, its's structure, offices and ordinances including Baptism. The Great Commission.

However, at the same time there is growing a different challenge to Christians today: outspoken minority groups who challenged the life stories as preaching and not true life stories although they were exactly that: stories of a person's life. Society now lives in an age of Spiritual Relativism

Many Christians are unsure what to believe in our modern world, how to react to situations.

The moral maze has become more complicated for today's Christian as we get sucked into our present day captivity in our Egypt.

The church often does not know what to say because it does not want to quote from the Bible for fear of offending someone, so it has watered down the message of the Bible: it has taken actions that appear to be against the Bible truths, therefore church leaders are unable to challenge the simple wrong issues because the more complex wrong issues have been accepted, they have been allowed.

Society has made judgements that the church should have stood against: it didn't, so now it has to support a belief structure that is taking it away from its own belief structure. Where the church stands up for the truth of the Bible it is being vigorously persecuted.

Questions are being asked: We are being held hostage to the sins of our Fathers, there is a spiritual famine in this land, we are trapped, if we speak out we open ourselves to attack. How can we say what we believe without hurting others?

How can we preach the gospel in a land that is constantly changing and wanting us to change our belief structure to a more relative theology[4] that tickles the ears of the listeners? A theology that says that man is equal to God, there is no place in our churches for the wages of **sin** to be preached. Its more

4 Theology, the function, activity, or charismatic endowment of a prophet or prophets.

about who has the best light show, band, which Pastor has the largest plane? For many people being in church is like being in a foreign land, where the message preached bears little resemblance to the Bible.

The Israelites had this very problem when they were in captivity, they cried out *'How can we sing the Lords song in a strange Land?'* (Psalm 137:4)

This land is changing, when I was a boy it was always described as a Christian land. Not all the things that it did were right but there was an overarching Christian philosophy and value band that was always there to monitor our actions and keep us moving forward.

England was a land where we tried to use Christian values and beliefs to set the moral tone for the land, where we taught children Christian family concepts and principles, our jurisprudence was based on Christian values.

The Ten Commandments was the back bone of the Law, many of these have now faded away.

Adultery is in many ways unimportant now, theft has changed, there are levels of theft, in some ways, taking odd items from work, pens, pads, paper etc. is ok.

It was always believed that people in special places of authority, i.e. church leaders were unimpeachable, their lives were to be an example to us all, how sadly that has changed. Our belief that priests, bishops, clergy, doctors, politicians, were without sin, they were the people to base our morals and life choices on has sadly at best been dented and in some cases, destroyed forever.

As a boy in the fifties we were taught values, rules, etiquette, it was part of the school day to show respect to teachers. I was taught to stand still at the side of the road if a funeral cortege passed by as a mark of respect. To open doors for ladies, offer seats to ladies or elderly on buses or trains: today one might get insulted by a 'lady' if you do that.

There are many good improvements in our world, but sadly we have removed some of the basics values and ways of life that enabled us to relate better to each other.

When I was in a children's home (thankfully for a short time) we were abused it was 'de rigueur' went with the territory. It continued into the foster home all covered over with a veneer of 'care'. Social workers turned a blind eye, the values then were different, now child abuse is flagged up there are more rules and procedures in place to try and prevent abuse, and to persecute the perpetrators. Yet it happens, as sadly does Elder abuse.

In my school days there were of course sadly teachers who abused their position, as happens today, however. it seemed to me there was some truth in the phrase *what came around went around*, bullying teachers seemed to suffer, to pay a price.

God speaks to his people, he wants us to know how to live: so that when we start to go wrong we don't suffer. It's best to stop something that is wrong right away, before it gets a momentum of its own and becomes almost impossible to stop.

God will tell us when we are going down the wrong path as well as he will affirm us as we go along the path that is right for us.

So if God appeared to you and told you what to say to the people. Then you went out and told people: God had spoken to us and told us 'our nation would end up in captivity'. How do you think people would react?

- Would they believe you?
- How would they react if they believed you?
- How would you react if they believed you?
- What would happen if they did not believe you?
- How would you feel?

Would you try and get a message to the nation's leaders, church leaders?

How would you go about spreading the message? Would they believe you?

Would we do as Johnny Enlow in his book the *Seven Mountain Prophecy* did?

He tells us how he prophesied good news to the leaders of Saposoa an isolated needy and destitute jungle city of Peru?

The city had suffered years of destruction from narco-terrorism and the government response: Johnny Enlow prophesied that 'God was going to help the city with its economy,' within eighteen months two salt mines, one thermal spring one scenic waterfall and a silver mine were discovered. Yet the area was not known for any of these things'.[5]

God is alive today and speaks to people, to individuals and church leaders, prophet's evangelists, worship leaders and many others.

He wants us to read the Bible and know of his plans, but he also appoints people to bring prophetic[6] words to us so we can be sure in the knowledge of his ways and walk in a manner pleasing to him.

---

5 *The Seven Mountain Prophecy,* Johnny Enlow, *Creation House A Strang Company,* Lake Mary Florida 32746

6 **Prophecy**

a. Inspired utterance of a prophet, viewed as a revelation of divine will.

b. A prediction of the future, made under divine inspiration.

c. Such an inspired message or prediction transmitted orally or written.

CHAPTER 2

Start the journey here

What is the relevance today for the modern Christian, of a series of events that took place nearly 4000 years ago?

What is the relevance to us today of events that took place nearly 4000 years ago other than as a nice historical story that would and has made a good movie? The fact that it has been made into a movie at least half a dozen times, or that in France a musical was made of `Moses and the story of the Israelites' suggests that it has a deeper significance in the lives of many people and that it is a piece of history that fascinates many and scares others.

Some may argue that there is no archaeological evidence to prove the Exodus, that it was merely a figment of imagination of some ancient Israelite priest.

I wonder why is it that many who are not Jewish are so willing to put down something that is an integral belief of the Jewish nation?

The Qur'an, The Torah and the Bible refer to the story of the Exodus these are key books in the three most widespread faith groups in the world.

In the Torah the story of Moses and the Exodus is a major foundational belief.

In the Qur'an the story is found in 4 chapters (Suras) namely 7, 10, 28, & 44.

The Bible tells the story in Old testament books Exodus, Leviticus, Numbers and Deuteronomy; additionally, referred to in the New Testament in many places referring to different aspects of Moses life and the time in the Wilderness.

There are approximately 2.5 billion Christians in the world and over 1.8 billion followers of Islam who believe much if not all of the story of the exodus and the key players God, Moses and Pharaoh.

So I would suggest the question is not did it happen or not, but what relevance does it have to us in our 21st century world today?

If it is part of the belief structure passed down from generation to generation for four thousand years and that large parts of the Jewish faith and theology are influenced by the story of the Exodus: we who are not Jewish should be advised by their spiritual leaders.

Additionally, most Bible believing Christians today believe that the Bible is the inspired, infallible word of God: that the history of the Bible is the history of the Christian: Christ was a descendant of Abraham and David: (David & Goliath fame), it may be argued that without David there would not have been Christ.

God made a covenant (an agreement between 2 or more people, usually formal), with Abraham: Christ came to fulfil that covenant: to ensure all that God had prepared for his people would be for his people, that Jesus was the promised Messiah and he came to the Jewish nation. The Bible tells us his own people 'knew him not'. [7]

Many of the Jewish nation ignored Jesus or chose to believe he was not the son of God, today many Jewish people are coming to believe Jesus was and is the Messiah or Saviour.

Christ died for the sins of many, in his death and resurrection God offered to the Jew first, then non-Jew the chance to become children of God, to be adopted into his

7 John 1:11

family. Those who own Christ as saviour are joint heirs with the Son[8], God welcomes us with open arms, our sins are forgiven and we can call him Abba (Father).We have the promise that when we die we will go to be with him in his' mansion', (in Heaven).

So to the Christian the story of the Israelites in captivity in Egypt and their release by God using Moses and Aaron and their journey to the promised land becomes our history, our heritage.

If it was true, as most believe, then it is vital we understand what its relevance is to today's Christian. If it is just folklore or a parable, then it is even more important we understand what the story is telling us and how we apply it today.

So let's journey together and make our own minds up at the end of the book.

The Exodus (time Israel left Egypt) took place around 1446 BC, there is much discussion regarding the exact date of the Exodus but many believe 1446 BC is a good date to use.[9] (Approximately three and a half thousand years ago).

The Israelites had been in captivity for over 400 years, therefore the Israelite nation went into captivity in 1876 BC

---

8 Romans 8:17

9 Usshers chronology places the date of Exodus in April of 1491 BC. His dates were published in the King James Authorized Bible as early as 1701 AD and are the ones used on the Bible History Timeline above. Thiele, a modern Biblical chronologist, calculates it to 1446 BC – a date often used by modern Evangelicals.Josephus relates it to the expulsion of the Hyskos from Egypt circa 1552 BC The Septuagint, on which the Catholic Bible is based, makes it 1512 BC That gives a hundred year range of dates. That's not bad when you consider how hard it is to date ancient history. For instance, Egyptologists suggest a 2300-year range of dates (from 2450 BC to 5004 BC) when trying to date the first Egyptian King, Menes. 'Reprinted with permission of Amazingbibletimeline.com'

approximately, 3891 years ago. Not really regarded as modern history, yet it is studied today and is relevant to the Jewish nation, Christians and other faith groups.

For the Jewish people being set free from captivity in Egypt was and is a foundational part of their history, theology and doctrine.

I live in 21st century England, as far away from 1400 BC Egypt as you can get. How will it help me to know what God did nearly 4000 years ago?

How can I apply to my life the things that happened then and does God answer in the same way? Is he still the same God? Oh yes he is!

One answer is to consider how God intervened in a time of major crisis and how ultimately he looked after his people in Egypt: starting at a time of major famine in the area, the Israelite people were invited to live in Egypt till, the famine was over:

- It was a practical solution to a major international problem: there was a famine in the land they were living in and the surrounding areas. It was a wise solution to move to Egypt where God had raised up Joseph (a Jew) who was anointed by God and prepared the Egyptian nation for the famine so that people had food and did not die.

God did not want his people to die, obviously there were no planes around to fly grain in from another part of the world, there were no man made foods that would fit the bill so God influenced circumstances, where he turned the bad intentions of Josephs' brothers and the natural crisis: together with the lack of planning of man, into an outcome that saved many people.

Joseph according to the Bible was sold by his brothers to slave traders who later sold him as a slave into slavery in

Egypt, to be a slave to Potiphar who was the Captain of the palace guard for Pharaoh.

However, God had a better plan: Joseph was God's chosen instrument to make sure that the Israelite people and people from the area did not die because of the famine that was going to come in around ten years' time.

God's desire was that if men followed God's plan: explained to the Egyptian Pharaoh and leaders by Joseph, there would be sufficient food for all people during the time of famine.

Joseph must have felt life was bad, sold into slavery by his brothers, he must have felt very rejected. Then sold as a slave to Potiphar, if that was not bad enough, he was accused by Potiphar's wife of rape even though he was innocent. She had tried to seduce him, but when he refused she cried rape. Joseph was wrongfully imprisoned but not executed: Yet God had big plans for Joseph. Read Genesis 38-41

In prison Joseph was given, by God, the interpretation of dreams for two men whom Pharaoh had imprisoned, his baker and Cup Bearer. God gave Joseph the interpretation of the dreams, which was accurate.

The cup bearer was returned to his job with Pharaoh, the baker hanged as Joseph stated. In prison Joseph was made the head over all the prisoners.

After two years in prison Joseph was brought out of prison to Pharaoh who had had a dream that no one in his household or in the land could interpret; none of the magicians or spiritual men understood the dream. (Genesis 41)

But God gave Joseph the interpretation that there would be seven years of plenty and seven years of famine, additionally God gave joseph a plan for survival through the famine.

Pharaoh was so pleased with Joseph and God gave him

favour so that Pharaoh appointed Joseph the number one person in the land with as much authority as Pharaoh. Genesis 41: 38-43 ESV.

And Pharaoh said to his servants, 'Can we find a man like this, in whom is the Spirit of God?' Then Pharaoh said to Joseph, *'Since God has shown you all this, there is none so discerning and wise as you are. You shall be over my house, and all my people shall order themselves as you command. Only as regards the throne will I be greater than you.'* And Pharaoh said to Joseph, *'See, I have set you over all the land of Egypt.'* Then Pharaoh took his signet ring from his hand and put it on Joseph's hand, and clothed him in garments of fine linen and put a gold chain about his neck. And he made him ride in his second chariot. And they called out before him, 'Bow the knee!' Thus he set him over all the land of Egypt.

Later on we read how God used this famine period to bring about reconciliation between Joseph and his brothers and reunion between Joseph and his Father.

That is great you may say, but what does it matter to me? I don't live in a desert area, I probably am better educated than most of the people at that time, I have greater access to food, I can store food much more easily than they could.

For many people in the 21st century to be starving appears to mean there isn't a Starbucks, Costa or McDonalds in my town: or its more than 2 hours since I was pumping my face full of goodies. Or maybe this food area does not have what I like, the refrigerator does not have the brand I like, I can't get the sweets I want.

It might be argued we are a spoilt people, we have available to us supermarkets that are open 24 hours per day, even the small corner shops are open 60% of each day, 365 days per year.

Four thousand years ago there was a real famine with no one around to help, there was no Super-Power, no special forces, no United Nations relief force or fund.

To visit today, a land ravaged by disaster. Wild fires, famine, hurricane or flood and see how paper thin our modern technologies and preparations are against the natural elements is very disturbing.

When the locust or famine came there was no quick answer. It was not a one season problem. Recently Californians have had and are battling with drought. It could be argued there probably would not be a water shortage if Californians change their lifestyles. It is estimated that their water usage can be reduced by over 36% if they stop watering their gardens, Golf courses and municipal verges

We hear today of areas of famine: we see some appalling moving views of thousands of people walking to neighbouring countries for safety and food. We do have the wherewithal in our world to feed them, we do send tons of grain for them, provide tents, blankets emergency first aid and experts to help their nation move out of famine. But the aid doesn't always reach the needy.

In the two-thirds world we are fortunate where we were born we can say with the psalmist (Psalm 16:66) the lines are fallen unto me in pleasant places: yea, I have a goodly heritage.

It is very moving to see the number of people that do support those who are in a land of famine: to see the work of many Charities including Christian Aid, BBC Children in Need, Comic Relief, International Christian Consulate and Billy Graham Samaritans Purse.

Today for me food and shelter are a given, a few years ago when I was homeless and had no money, I was fortunate to know people who gave me accommodation, there were others who fed me, and also I was entitled to benefit from the state, I relied on God for my provision, but there were lots of places and people for God to utilise to provide for me.

Whilst some may argue about the level of government benefits or pension we get today, we are far better off today than those who went before us and compared to 99% of the population 4000 years ago we are millionaires.

When I was homeless I may have felt insecure, I did, but there were many signs of God's love for me in the way his people reached out to me. I was never starving, I was not without medical care when I needed it, I didn't have anywhere to sleep although a council housing officer suggested I should sleep in the car, until a friend offered me a piece of their home office floor!

Our world in 21 century England is good for most of us: we have cars, motorbikes or scooters, a reasonably accessible public transport system that still offers transport for most of the day to most of the places you need to go. (Although there are some horror stories the basic system is there. It just needs sorting). A national/ international rail service, air services etc.

For the majority of the people we are able to talk to anyone without having to leave the comfort of our homes. We have iPad's and tablets, mobile phones, laptops, personal computers', we can if we wish communicate with anyone in the world who has a modern phone. If we do not have our own system, we can go to the library for the internet: or go to internet cafes. We can be in touch through Facebook, WhatsApp, Twitter, Instagram, Myspace, Facetime, Snapchat among the many ways of communicating available to us today.

In Egypt to pass a message was a long day or several days walk or camel ride, hoping the person you told the message too got through safely, remembered the message and was well received by the person the message was for. Today I e-mail someone on the other side of the world and as I am writing to them I can see them writing their answer.

Currently we have ships that can carry over 100 million gallons of oil at a time! Or hundreds of tons of grain, within five days the two thirds world can respond to major emergency thousands of miles away, if the political will is there to do so. Recently the Billy Graham Charity Samaritan's Purse dispatched physical aid (emergency shelters, food, water purification kits, blankets even mobile field hospitals and staff) to countries impacted by natural or man-made disasters, including famine.

In Egypt and surrounding areas if the people wanted to go anywhere it was on foot (most of the population) or if very rich possibly by camel or donkey. When Israel left Egypt the most oil they could carry was what they could put on their backs or maybe a camel, just a few gallons. The most Grain again was limited to what they could carry. When the Israelites entered Egypt it was at a time of famine so I guess they had little or no oil or grain to carry with them.

As I write the world's first eco plane is attempting to fly 8000 kilometres across a sea with just solar power for energy!

In our modern two thirds world there are nursing homes, care homes, home help, social services, meals on wheels, free bus pass, free medicines and dental care from the hospitals, GP's. Ambulances, Paramedics and emergency trained personnel for the sick, elderly and needy available 24 hours a day 365 days a year. For children who have special needs there are services geared towards their needs, not enough I hear you cry out... yet there are some.

Even in some of the worst places in the developing world there are many places where the conditions appear to be better than those that were prevailing 4000 years ago. It's hard to understand the situation then, the raw, brutal harsh way of life, the power wielded by the few, the lack of hygiene, health care, safety. Certainly not a 'nanny state' like many argue we have in the UK.

No, the poor were ignored, a world where there was an overriding sense of self-preservation, a world where only the strongest survived. To be born in the royal household could mean a life of great pleasure and comfort or violent and sudden death as a stronger person took your place.

It is a different world, climate conditions may be changing, even in the remotest parts of the world it is possible to keep up to date with the news and latest developments in the world. With radio, satellite communications, the world is so different to 4000 years ago why bother looking to then to find our help today?

No one today can really understand or imagine what life would be like as a slave in 1400 BC, Egypt. Today there are the eyes of the world watching what is going on. Countries where abuse of the people is going on is known throughout the world. Neighbouring countries will sometimes try and influence the Government of their neighbours: the United Nations will certainly discuss the situation and plan how to respond, by direct intervention, by sending an Envoy or another high-ranking diplomat.

The intervention is not always public, however there will be discussions and sanctions on the people leading the country be they, elected, rebels, militants, a religious group or a neighbouring state invading. Whilst there is no desire to send troops in or fight this has been a response from the UN. Countries have been 'taken over' by troops from UN and other allied countries.

In Egypt these scenarios were not on the cards, neither when the Israelites arrived or in their whole time of captivity.

The Jewish nation appears throughout history to have been the victim of some vicious attacks: there have been horrendous examples of anti-Semitism. Why one asks have the Jewish people attracted so much hatred and jealousy. Are they an easy target? Certainly Israel showed in the six days' war in 1967 they are not. After they left Egypt the Israelites were a force to be reckoned with, many were terrified of the Israelite army. That was then 4000 years ago so why worry about it now?

One answer is, it's a bit like a disaster movie when a beast from the past comes back to life and attacks the living people. The only answer is for a super hero or a super hero team to travel back in time to when the beast was born and first attacked the people and control it then so it is unable to have power now.

Now let me say before people jump up and down with the wrong conclusion. I am not saying or suggesting about Israel, the Jews Pharaoh, Egypt or any one or nation being a beast!

I am using it allegorically or figuratively: before we came to a new life in Christ, our lives were planned by us (if they were planned at all), directed by us doing those things that we enjoyed that were important to us. To a varying extent, we were all slaves to our former lives some more entrenched than others.

Our lives were dictated to by our lusts, desires, pleasures, pressures of daily life. The need for food and shelter was a major motivation, Maslow[10] in his initial paper *Hierarchy of*

10 Maslow, A.H. (1943). *A theory of human motivation.* Psychological Review 50 (4) 370-96. Retrieved from http://psychclassics.yorku.ca/Maslow/motivation.htm

Needs discusses how man is focused on providing for his basic needs, excluding all other things until these are met.

Man does not look toward his spiritual needs until that time when he has provided for all his needs, then he looks to be all he can be in self-actualising. Initially Maslow links love with spirituality in that stage in our lives where we are joining groups, looking outside of ourselves. Later in his *Critique*[11] he argues that self can only find actualisation in giving oneself to a higher power!

As Christians when we come to faith we start the process of being all we can be, being the person that God wants us to be.

That means we have to turn from our pasts, from our old life from the captivity that holds us restricted from living life to the full.[12]

The cage that allows us to see the hope of the new life but unable to reach out and grab hold of it.

I picture the old western Sheriffs offices with the steel bars for the jail, and the prisoner stretching his arm through the bars, fingers outstretched to try and get the keys so he can be free.

We can see freedom, the future but until the cage door is unlocked we can only see the future and freedom and hope.

Sometimes we are voluntary prisoners, we give our lives over to a habit, behaviour that we enjoy but ultimately will destroy us.

What are some of these cages?

When people start drinking with friends they don't do it expecting to become alcoholics, even though they may push the

11 A.H. Maslow, *'Critique of self-actualization theory'*, in: E. Hoffman (Ed.), Future visions: The unpublished papers of Abraham Maslow (Thousand Oaks, CA: Sage, 1996), pp. 26–32

12 John 10: 10.ESV *'I came that they may have life and have it abundantly'.*

boundaries as for as they can. People drink for fun, friendship, companionship, parties, celebrations, and holidays. Loads of good reasons, but for some individuals it is like signing a death certificate for themselves, they open a door that will entrap them for ever unless someone can set them free.

When we come to faith for the majority of us it is a journey, for years we have led a life that is not as God would want, indeed we have been far away from him. Some of our habits and behaviours beliefs and actions are incongruent with a God of love.

We might enjoy 'free love', one night stands, we may even be addicted to unusual sexual practices we can only share with other like-minded people, but for sure we could not tell someone we hardly knew.

We may be an aggressive person, beating people who would expect us to love them:

We might abuse our work position, 'fiddling the books'.

We may be a doctor abusing patients,

A politician milking their expense claims,

A mum or dad who hits their child a little too hard even though they are a being a really horrible child.

A police officer who takes advantage of a victim of crime.

All extreme cases you say, but in life people often say and do hurtful things to others. Sadly, we read of teenager's committing suicide because they have been bullied at school, been harmed by their teacher.

There are thousands of people young and older who self-harm, cut, pick, self ink and inject who abuse their own bodies in a range of different ways.

There are millions of examples daily where no matter how hard we try we all have sinned and fall short of the glory of God.[13]

---

13 Romans 3:23

It can be very tough to rationalise our behaviour with a God who is love, he is pure and free from all and any blemish, stain, mark or behaviour that is in any way not perfect.

Yet this very God wants to walk with us, he wants to meet with us in the cool of the evening breeze as he did all the thousands of years ago with Adam and Eve. (Then the man and his wife heard the sound of the Lord God as he was walking in the garden in the cool of the day).[14]

God wants to have a relationship with all he has created.

The Bible tells us why in Genesis 1:27 we read *'So God created mankind in his own image, in the image of God he created them: male and female he created them'.*

God wanted to meet and talk with his creation. Imagine if you had been the one that God walked with in the cool of the evening, chatting about the beauty of creation, about God, about us, what we like and dislike; our hopes and plans.

But mankind turned away from God to do what mankind wanted and became estranged from God. But He doesn't forget us

But it is not just the things that we have done wrong, the Bible calls them sin, these are the things we do that can stop us from fellowshipping with God and going on our Journey with Him to the promised land, 'cause that is where we as Christians are journeying to, to that place where we will be with Him forever, without fear, doubt, hate, persecution; that place a New Heaven and a New earth we see described so poetically for us in the book of Revelation.[15]

Things changed in Egypt and the Israelites became captive, they became slaves, then God through Moses set them

14 Genesis 3:8
15 Revelation 21

free and they started a journey to what was known as the promised land. A good land flowing with 'milk and honey.'[16]

When we become Christians we start a life growing closer to God: a life with a promise that one day we will go to be with him in heaven, one day we will be in the promised land. A life where all the things of the past that we did wrong (sins) are forgiven as though we had never done them, are no longer remembered by God.

This journey into the promised land will take many twists and turns, will teach us much about ourselves, but as long as we follow Jesus daily and trust him we will enter that perfect rest in heaven.

The Israelites had the same issues, if they followed God and did what he commanded them they would reach the promised land. God provided a pillar of cloud by day for them to follow and he also provided food.[17]

As we journey into our new lives as Christians we may see a pillar of cloud, as the Israelites did each day on their journey to the promised land; but unlikely because we have the Holy Spirit of God inside us to guide us.[18]

The things that hold us prisoner in our modern day 'Egypt' are not always the things we do to ourselves. Not just our sins, our weaknesses, our habits, our selfish ways.

For some people they suffer from and carry with them enormous pain both physical, mental and emotional trauma as a result of actions that have been taken against them.

---

16 Exodus 33:3 *'Go up to a land flowing with milk and honey'*

17 Exodus 13:21. ESV *'And the LORD went before them by day in a pillar of cloud to lead them along the way, and by night in a pillar of fire to give them light, that they might travel by day and by night'.*

18 1 Corinthians 3:16 ESV *'Do you not know that you are a temple of God and that the Spirit of God dwells in you'?*

The child rejected by the parent, the victim of rape, the parent of a child killed by a drunk driver, the battered wife or husband, someone divorced, the bankrupt, the victim of a road traffic accident, relatives of someone killed in an air crash. Victims of redundancy, crime, ageism, racism, sexism, and isolation so many different ways in which people suffer and are trapped in a 'foreign land'.

I was privileged to minister to some of the people affected by the Grenfell Tower fire.[19] The devastation in their lives that the fire has caused is immense for some they may never fully recover from the tragedy.

So many people who were just going about their business with no inkling that around the corner such a tragedy was going to affect them, that such a disaster would hit them. Not just immediate family members so many of the local community were affected by the fire. Churches, faith groups schools, social services, health services, emergency services, tradesmen and women, transport services, everyone was hugely impacted by the tragedy.

Sadly, in many places people are affected by major disaster, from bombings, shootings, natural disasters and man-made crisis all needing the hope that is available in Christ.

I don't believe these sufferings, crisis and disasters were in God's plan for mankind. The model we get in Genesis and in Revelation are of a pleasant land a time where men and women are in communion with God, enjoying each other's company and living in the shadow of the Almighty God protected by him and being blessed by him.

God made the world and mankind right first time, it was man who chose to disobey God or do what God advised them not to do. Man often thinks he is supreme there is no-one

19 A tragic fire in a housing block in London England caused 72 deaths. https://en.wikipedia.org/wiki/Grenfell_Tower_fire

greater than him—how painful when he falls.

When you see the new born baby you don't imagine any of these bad things happening to them, no of course you don't, you want the best for them. That's what God wants for us the best, but the evil and sin in the world mean that for many the life that God planned for them needs a restart. They need to escape and enter the promised land.

Sometimes it's hard to sing with the songwriter *'What a Wonderful World'* [20]

There are so many ways that life treats us badly and we will not feel wonderful. Divorce, redundancy, traffic accidents, slips, falls, burglaries, fraud.

Sadly, the list already appears endless and we haven't even started to consider people who are unwell, physically, mentally, emotionally, the person with a chronic disease, someone whose loved one has such a disease people who have been injured, in accidents, at work, at play, people injured by war, the impact on their lives and on the lives of those they love is at times incalculable.

So many things that ensnare, entangle and trap us that keep us prisoner in a strange land, because for many in times of suffering their bodies feel like a strange place, a foreign land. When we planned our lives it did not include ageing, debt, sorrow, loneliness, criminality, for others when they mapped out how their lives could be, they could not see on the horizon being disabled, the victim of an attack, losing the baby they had just had, or becoming dependant on alcohol and or drugs.

I was saddened at a recent documentary tracing the life of a famous person, who whilst celebrating the birth of their new child at day two, their older child aged 19 died.

20 *What a Wonderful World* by Bob Thiele and George David Weiss, recorded by Louis Armstrong 1967

I understand the circumstances were unusual, but how do you get free from such conflicting feelings? What an awful place to be held captive! What terrible circumstances for the new baby whose mother dies before they are five!

My mother put me in a children's home when I was four: she told me she would come back for me in a couple of weeks, I'm retired now and still waiting. I forgive her I don't know what was in her mind at the time, I have been told gossip, but I don't know.

I believe that God wanted a better childhood for me than the one I got, physical abuse in the children's home, and then violence and more physical abuse in the foster home, but that is what some women and men did and do to children. But God used it to give me an understanding of the terrible lives that others have had to suffer so that I can support them and minister to them and help them go forward into their promised land without the past holding them back, to be able to shake off the dust of captivity.

When faced with such cruel challenges in life there is only one way forward and that is to know God's love and grace, to feel him close to you.

The Israelites who were suffering greatly called out to God to set them free and he did.

But for many people in today's world they are too clever to need God, they have worked out ways to deal with their problems. 'Get over it' is very easy to say to someone very hard for them to do.

We live in a world relying on relativism, there are fewer and fewer absolutes, the church is watering down its message to appeal to the greater majority, decisions are being made on the hoof and then there is the challenge how does that fit into doctrine?

When homosexuality was decriminalised by the UK government in 1967,[21] the established church in the UK was rather caught out. Was there sufficient time for a debate? Did the church lead helpfully in the debate?

The church did not appear to have a policy or a voice to deal with the discussion and later decisions taken by the country's appointed government. Yet it was evident that the policy was against doctrine that the church had held onto for thousands of years. Were the church leadership silent, did they understand what was being considered?

Were in fact church leaders at that time caught up or imprisoned in views that limited them from freely expressing their real views, did all the church leaders support the decriminalization?

Or were church leaders those who were outspoken about the bill threatened with losing their jobs, or losing a promotion if they did not toe the party line? Or indeed was the church leadership united behind the decisions that decriminalisation of homosexuality was the right way forward? If the latter was true why was there no guidance given to the laity?

Decriminalization did not appear to be presented to the 'church'. It may be argued that if the church senior Leadership believed decriminalization was correct and the way forward and a robust case was presented to the church for the theology supporting decriminalisation, it is possible there would not have been the difficulty faced by the church some years later on whether it was doctrinally sound to appoint 'gay bishops'.

When decriminalisation of homosexuality was approved, it was obvious that there would be gay men and women wanting to enter the ministry. There appeared to be no

21 Sexual Offences Act 1967

consideration of how to support this?

You cannot differentiate between two people already on the same career path because of their sexuality, or their gender or any other discriminating factor that is at odds with your doctrine. If a person is at odds with the doctrine of the faith structure that should be explored before they start their employment.

These things must be considered before entry into the ministry. Do the person's belief and lifestyle exclude them from church leadership and lead them into conflict with the doctrine? Or does the candidate's lifestyle and interpretation of the doctrine support their entry into the ministry.

You can't let someone into such a role and then realise afterwards you're not sure if they qualify, if their beliefs are congruent with key tenets of the faith you espouse.

A different issue but same principle the Israelites were told it was wrong to worship golden idols, they had followed this practice in Egypt but it did not please God and was not a practice they were to continue. Simple!

But when Moses came down from the mountainside they had made a golden calf. Moses was angry, he told them with no uncertainty they were wrong, God told Moses he was angry.

Moses did not say well, tell you what well leave it for the moment and may be in a few years well think of a plan, no he burnt the golden calf.

When we get in a place where we are faced with tough decisions, we need Gods wisdom to know how to move forward and leaders willing to take tough decisions, avoiding knee-jerk reactions. There has been much pain in the world and the church because the church has not guided the people. It has not stood firm on its doctrine.

The church needs to lead and not follow man, it needs to be an example, if church is to be the salt then it needs to live its life and work as salt for the community.[22]

It is arguable the church could have been saved many hours of pain and debate if the leadership at the time had been more decisive and put in place a game plan that worked for the church and the community.

I wonder, have you ever made a model? When I was younger I used to make all-sorts of models with varying degrees of success. I made radio controlled cars, aeroplanes, motorbikes, ships. However good or bad they were they all had two things in common, I made them, I played with them.

I drove the cars on the road, in the park, on the grass, on the carpet, in the mud. I had a great time using or playing with them: I enjoyed the things I created. They were inanimate objects of plastic, rubber, steel and wood. But they were fun, I was proud of them, I showed them off, I challenged others who had made similar items to races, they were very important to me. But they were only objects if I could have made them talk, walk or react to me without pressing buttons, how good that would have been.

Today people shower their pets with toys and clothes they talk to them. I am told by some that their pet can understand them, 'knows what I am saying', they devote themselves to their pets spending hundreds and in some cases thousands of pounds per year on them.

If man will devote so much time and resources to toys and pets, how much more must God want to spend time with those he has created, human beings that can talk, walk, think,

22 Matt. 5:13 ESV *'You are the salt of the earth, but if salt has lost its taste, how shall its saltiness be restored? It is no longer good for anything except to be thrown out and trampled under people's feet.'*

rationalise. Able to love and be loved, able to enjoy the other things God has created. When God looks at his created man he sees people in his own image, aspects of himself. The Bible says that when God made man 'it was very Good'. (Genesis 1: 29) 'It was very good'; that was what God thought about man so for man, God also created, trees, grass, woods, birds, animals, sea, lakes, rivers fish.

The enduring picture I have from the Garden of Eden is of God walking in the garden with Adam and Eve in the cool of the evening, how many times did they do that, what a brilliant picture it captures, of intimacy, togetherness, Father with children, family just out together enjoying being together.

I have spent many a time walking with my children especially when they were younger, each eager to involve me with a ball game, a run, a discussion, share aspects of that days or recent experiences. Tell me their challenges, the things that weren't going well, fears, seeds of hope and ideas.

We would walk and talk, no agenda, no clear plan, hopefully a drink/ ice cream on route, didn't matter where we were: sea, woods, airport, town we had great times and great discussions. Sometimes we had to deal with painful or emotionally difficult issues while we walked.

When their mum was dying, going for a walk we could talk through things together without them having too big an impact or indeed before they had too big an impact, or if necessary to continue discussing those things that had had a huge impact.

When we told the children their Mum had been given a few months to live, you can't just drop it on them and walk away, they needed time, space, hugs, cuddles, someone to be angry with, to even fight with (mainly playful rough and tumble). Someone to swear at, to ask why, how?

When, what, if? How sure were we? What would happen? Could the doctors be wrong? Would they be there? Would God intervene? Where was God?

Walking and talking together was a good way to 'be there for them' in the midst of the stress, hospitals, doctors, medications, hospice, privations, doubts, fear, anxieties, there were so many things.

As the children got older we went for walks and they started telling me about things they had understood, new revelations, telling me 'what to believe'; fun times.

I'm sure many people in the spring really enjoy watching out for the new lambs, the buds on the trees, all things God has created. Imagine walking with God and telling him how good these things are, how much you like the way the baby lambs jump, or the bunnies run, or the vibrant colours of the trees.

But large numbers of mankind have rejected God, they have no need for their creator, they are self-sufficient and self-indulgent. They state there is no God, they joke about how good they are and how poor and powerless God is: or who He is?

'The worst moment for the atheist is when he is really thankful and has nobody to thank' (Dante Gabriel Rossetti, 1828 – 1882).

We see on reality TV, talent shows and commonly on YouTube, Facebook and other social networks the comment OMG (Oh My God) if challenged the people will strongly deny a belief in God, certainly no Christian faith yet they call out to God, man has called out to God throughout history in times of trouble.

There are those who hate God, Friedrich Nietzsche said 'I call Christianity the 'one' great curse, the 'one' great intrinsic depravity, the 'one' great instinct for revenge for which no expedient is sufficiently poisonous, secret, subterranean, 'petty' – I call it the 'one' mortal blemish of mankind.' (The Antichrist 1888).

The Bible says some day he and all those who use Gods name in vain or inappropriately will meet him face to face. In Ecclesiastes (3:17) we read *'I said to myself, 'God will judge both the righteous man and the wicked man'.*

Additionally in 2 Corinthians (2:10) we read *'For we must all appear before the judgment seat of Christ, so that each one may be recompensed for his deeds in the body, according to what he has done, whether good or bad.'*

For all those who have hoped in Christ there is promise he will bring us out of captivity (Egypt) into the Promised land and for those who have denied Christ there will be a day of reckoning, may God be merciful.

The author hopes this book will help those Christians who have come from a place of turmoil and suffering, who are new to the faith or who want to be the best they can be in the Lord.

Final thought for this chapter

After a time of crisis and challenge men and women need support, we need to rebuild our lives to press on toward our future.As Christians we look to Jesus as our hope, to our faith to take us through to a full life and then to our rest in heaven.

The Israelites believed in the same God as we who are Christians believe in today, they were before the time of Christ the Messiah although they believed the Messiah was coming. But they believed that God would save them that he would take them out of captivity and lead them to a promised land.

Their cause of suffering may have been different from ours today, but the feelings, the pain, the emotional hurt was as intense as ours is today and God helped them in the 'inner man' as well as practically leading them out of captivity. Their Journey out of darkness was as ours is, a journey of growth, enlightenment, a time to get closer to God and do the things and live a life he would have us live.

As we study the Exodus from Egypt: the Israelites journey to freedom, we find what God said to the Israelites and did for them all those years ago are relevant to us today, we can find guidance for today and ways to react in our exodus from captivity that will help us on our journey.

CHAPTER 3

As a Christian, what can we learn from Moses' experiences?

For the grace of God has appeared, bringing salvation for all people, training us to renounce ungodliness and worldly passions, and to live self-controlled, upright, and godly lives in the present age. 2 Titus 11-12 (ESV)

Before we can answer the question 'As a Christian what can we learn from Moses' experiences?' We have to first look at who was Moses, what did he do and why? Then how is this relevant to Christians today?

Who was Moses?

According to Exodus all the Bible tells us is: Moses was born in Egypt approximately 1526 BC. Moses was the son of a man of the tribe of Levi and his wife. (Many scholars believe their names were Amran, Father & Jochebed, Mother).

At the time of Moses' birth, the new King of Egypt (Pharaoh) was concerned that the Israelites were multiplying at too fast a rate[23] 'the Israelites have become far too numerous for us'. Pharaoh (believed to be either Amenemhet or Thutmose II) ordered that all boy babies under two years of age should be drowned in the River Nile.

The primary reason for this terrible act has been argued either as being due to the overpopulation of the Hebrew slaves or it had been foretold that there would rise up a man to free the slaves.

23 Exodus 1:8 NIV.

Moses was from the house of Levi a house of Priests who mainly served God in the priestly and or temple duties.

Moses' mother naturally did not want to kill her son, such a terrible thing for a parent to be forced to do.

So Moses' mother very bravely tried to protect her son and give him a future, obviously this was God's hand upon Moses life even as a little baby.

So Moses' mother decided to make a waterproof basket that would float and place her son in the basket and float him out in the reeds in front of Pharaohs daughter when she went to the river to bathe.

The river Nile at the time was populated with poisonous snakes and large crocodiles. What a scary place for a new baby to be.

What a different world to today; the King's daughter going to the river to bathe? Snakes, crocodiles, all manner of human waste that was thrown in together with rotting carcasses and insects, it was not going to be that clean in itself.

However, that was the practice in those days: Pharaoh's daughter whilst bathing hears the sound of the baby, spots the baby and feels sorry for the little baby.

She decides to look after the baby but can't take him back to Pharaohs palace because her Dad would have been very angry so while she is wondering what to do, Miriam Moses sister, pops up and says shall I get a Hebrew woman to nurse the baby for you, wet nursing was common practice in those days.[24] So Moses' sister brings Moses' mum to center stage.

24 When a woman breast-feeds someone else's baby it is called 'wet-nursing'. It was an ancient occupation mentioned in many early medical texts, including those by Aristotle and Ibn Sina. Wet nurses might act as foster parents for motherless babies or those whose mother was simply ill or not able to produce enough milk. V Fildes, *Wet Nursing from Antiquity to the Present* (New York: Basil Blackwell, 1988)

Great solution for Pharaohs daughter.

So Moses' mother looks after him until he is old enough to be presented to Pharaohs daughter to bring him up in the royal palace. Moses became a son of Pharaohs daughter a highly privileged position.

So God had saved Moses from being drowned in the river, and had brought him into the palace of the Pharaoh to understand the language, customs, and be educated in all things Egyptian, as the son of Pharaoh's daughter, a highly exclusive place in Egyptian society.

Why was Moses important? The Israelites were becoming a threat to the Egyptian leaders, they were multiplying, they would have been consuming lots of food. The leaders were worried that the Hebrew slaves (Israelite Nation) may become a force against them. They feared the slaves may side with the Egyptian enemies and bring about the fall of Egypt.

Pharaoh had a simple response. In Exodus 1 we read that the slave masters were told to oppress the Israelites, to give them the harshest work, they were to be brutal to them, to drive them mercilessly, even so it says, the Israelites continued to multiply and spread and the Egyptians dreaded the Israelites.

Whilst all this was going on the Israelites were pleading with God, set us free save us from captivity, from being slaves, from being treated so harshly.

They believed if they prayed and cried out to God he would hear their call, he would not ignore them, that he would act.[25]

---

25 Exodus 1:23-25 *During that long period, the king of Egypt died. The Israelites groaned in their slavery and cried out, and their cry for help because of their slavery went up to God. 24 God heard their groaning and he remembered his covenant with Abraham, with Isaac and with Jacob. 25 So God looked on the Israelites and was concerned about them.*

God indeed heard their cry and decided to get 'his people' out of Egypt.

God had a plan that was already taking place, he had a man of influence, Moses, already in the Egyptian camp!

- The first thing we need to learn today from this whole episode is that God is a listening God, he listened to the Israelites pleas, even before they asked he had a plan to rescue them.[26]
- Today for us long before we call to God for help he has a plan in place to help us.
- Many of us don't wait for his plan to outwork but rather we 'sort it' ourselves and end up in a bigger mess.

Some Learning points for us

1. God listens
2. God is interested in our situation
3. God answers
4. God answers in his way and his time
5. His time is the right time
6. Give time for Gods plan to outwork
7. Don't listen to the doubts stand in faith and watch what God will do!

God is attuned to the thoughts, feelings and prayers of all people especially more so of those he loves and who love him Romans 8:28 *'And we know that in all things God works for the good of those who love him'*.

26 Exodus 2:23-24. *'During that long period, the king of Egypt died. The Israelites groaned in their slavery and cried out, and their cry for help because of their slavery went up to God.'*

As Christians we have an advocate, Jesus, who sits at the right hand of God the Father Almighty: talking to God the Father about us but more than talking he is interceding.

He is acting on our behalf in our dispute with God: But I'm not in dispute with God you say!

However, every time we sin whether intentionally or accidentally, whether by commission or omission we become estranged from God, we go into the opposite camp, God is pure and sinless, he cannot sin. He does love those he created, but he cannot be near them or walk with them or talk to them.

So Jesus speaks to God on our behalf, 24 hours a day 365 days a year, he never slumbers or sleeps, gets bored or tired.

He keeps bringing our needs and things before God.

We read in the Old Testament if someone sinned there needed for blood to be spilt.

There was a price to pay which generally involved the sacrifice of a pure animal.

The Israelites had a list of the Laws and all the sacrifices that had to be made for sin, also sacrifices for: purity, vows, anointing priests and many more together with rites and rules concerning festivals and Holy days. If you read Leviticus, you'll get far more information.

Animals for sacrifice included goats, rams, lambs, doves: Israelite families lived in an agricultural world they were used to seeing animals and seeing them being slaughtered. Unlike in our modern world where it is generally kept away from the public.

It may seem barbaric in our 20th century world but there are still communities that publicly slaughter animals without the care we now show.

When the Old Testament was written, there were tribes that practiced Human sacrifice, Moloch one of the Canaanite gods required the sacrifice of children. This led to some of the Israelite nation starting to practice child sacrifice. How abhorrent to us. Man has practiced inhuman treatments of other men, all through history and sadly it's still happening in our world today.

If it is abhorrent to us how much more would it be abhorrent to the God who created (mankind) us in his own image.

Throughout history we read that violent Kings and Leaders practiced all types of evil towards men.

Go to Ephesus and see the arena where the Christians were fed to the lions. Consider the gladiatorial fights that were common place in Roman time. Explore the Aztecs or the Nazi's holocaust.

We have seen in more recent conflicts the genocide in:

Rwanda

Darfur

Bosnia and Herzegovina

Cambodia

Sadly, there have been many more. I have had the privilege to meet and spend time with a victim of the Yazidi Genocide who had lost so many of their family to the evil plans of man. I have never before seen anyone more harrowed, in my life and I have met and worked with many hundreds of victims.

The Israelites in Egypt did not have all the modern methods of communication, their faith was handed down from father to son, mother to daughter. If your parent practiced sacrificing children to Moloch and you survived, the probability was you would grow-up believing child sacrifice was right, you were spared, you were not 'chosen' therefore you must 'honour the god Moloch' when you became a parent.

There was no way to check it out, there was not a vocal

press to highlight the bad thinking. No-one to discuss it with, for 99% of the population there weren't even books or scrolls to study and for sure no YouTube or internet to search.

There was not an established set of church buildings to attend, if you were very lucky you may see the wandering Priest / Prophet and he may tell you it is wrong and explain why:

The people of Israel's relationship with God was often tenuous and at times a bit vague, because it relied on faith and hand downs from one generation to another.

For the few it was a passionate relationship, but it appears that they all (Israelites) called out to God: They prayed. God heard their prayer.

The Israelites lived before Jesus, even so they called out to God the Father and He answered.

When we find ourselves in a place of captivity our first thought should be to cry out to God. Indeed we should be praying to him all the time. We should not just pray in times of crisis because even those who do not love God or his son Jesus do that.

Indeed, it is said 'that there are no atheists in foxholes'

That in a time of war men in battle call out to God to save them whatever their faith or belief structure was before they went to war.

Now we should as Paul says 'pray without ceasing',[27] the more we are in communion (relationship with) with God, the more we will hear what he is saying to us and the more confidence we will have that when we approach him in prayer he won't say I don't know you.

27 1 Thessalonians 5:17

A listening God is not a passive God, rather He is a God who is on the lookout for his people to talk to him, for this is what prayer is, us talking to God.

He wants to hear from us, to talk with us. He wants to walk along next to us and know what is happening in our lives.

You may argue that is he is omnipresent (everywhere all the time) he does not need for us to tell him we are having problems; we have become captives.

God does know what is happening to us but he does need us to tell him.

We are responsible for our actions and thoughts and we need to invite him into our lives. He chose to give us free will, to make our own choices and allows us to think for ourselves. We are not robots, God gave us freedom of thought and will.

He could have made a people that did everything he said, but he gave us free choice: so for us to hear from him or have fellowship with him we need to contact him. To start the process, to show we are interested in him, he won't impose His wishes on you.

So pray. Start the time by talking to him, he will reply to you. Tell him what you think of Him, tell him you love Him and see him as your God. Thank him for all he has done, for your breath, the world we live in, the beauty of creation, our families, loved ones, friends, His provision for us, we can do all this before we lay on him all our trouble.

We need to tell Him where we are, what's going on, how we got there, what choices we had and how He can help us. So we can say with the writer of the song, 'All my troubles Lord, soon be over'.

God created man in his own image, we have been given free will to live our lives as we wish. We have already seen how some people deny God, He will not impose himself on anyone as he has given us free will.

Free will comes with a choice and a price, the choice is hard but when we make the wrong choice the price often is that we miss out from God not that we get punishment but rather there is a consequence: we are unable to avail ourselves of what God has for us.

It is out of our free will that God wants us to call out to him, not because we are in a crisis, not because we have a duty, not because we are told to but rather as a child tells its father what is going on and then says, Love you Daddy, please Daddy, pretty Please .

CHAPTER 4

Moses 'I did it my way'?

Moses grew up in the Palace, he would have had a good life compared to his contemporaries. Moses contemporaries were children of slaves who were being punished and mistreated.

Moses would have had the best food, clothing and education that was available in Egypt. He lived in the court of the Pharaoh the best of everything would have been there for him, possibly even slaves to help him.

He would have probably grown strong in the royal household and been taught combat skills, how to talk properly, certainly how to speak and read Egyptian.

He would have learnt who's who, who was important, who held the power, the political leaders, the magicians and learnt about soothsayers.

Part of his learning would have been how to conduct himself in the royal household. He would have been free to roam, to come and go as he pleased, as long as he honoured Pharaoh he would have had anything he wanted. A good life.

It would seem his mum had saved him from death when she put him in the basket in the bulrushes, I doubt she expected the events to turn out as they did, his mum put him into an amazing opportunity, to be in Pharaoh's house with the daughter of Pharaoh. Actually, it was God's plan but I am sure his mum was delighted with how things turned out.

Moses would have seen the way 'his people' were treated, the brutality, lack of food and supplies, the lack of decent places to live, their depressions, pain and hopelessness but also their faith that God would intervene.

Growing up as an Egyptian child he may well have become estranged from his kith and kin. I doubt he would have had a lot of contact with them he was after all the son of Pharaohs daughter.

Moses must have had feelings about his people but knew also that he couldn't say much for fear that his own place and lifestyle would stop and he may be made to live with his own people as a slave.

This may have been going through his mind when one day Moses went for a walk and in the heat of the moment decided to sort things himself.

On his walk on this day, whilst Moses was walking in the desert he saw a Hebrew slave being badly beaten, (I wonder how many times before he had seen Hebrew slaves being beaten or even killed) checking no one was looking he killed the Egyptian guard and buried him. Moses must have felt he had helped his fellow Israelites. he had made a small stand for right!

The following day when he was out walking he saw two Hebrew slaves fighting, he went over to them to calm them down and they asked 'will you kill us as you did the guard yesterday'[28]

Moses fled.

Moses must have been surprised at how the news had travelled, he thought he had killed the guard without anyone seeing him, certainly he had felt safe enough that he had gone home that night and gone for a walk the following day.

Then his fellow Israelites accused him, 'will you kill us as you did the guard yesterday?'

---

28 Exodus 2:14

That must have hurt and surprised him that 'his people' had not understood that his killing the guard the day before had been for them 'his people'. So Moses fled!

Pharaoh was very angry when he heard about Moses killing the guard and wanted to kill Moses.

I think Moses genuinely thought he could help the slave by killing the guard, he had fixed it, he had sorted an unfair situation. What he did not consider is if a slave kills a guard, the rest of the slaves often receive worse punishment. Also something so big as killing a guard cannot be hidden.

However, Moses actions were neither guided by God or indeed instructions from God, they were just his emotional response. Was it God's plan to use Moses while he was in the royal palace, was that God's original plan, but Moses attacking the Egyptian guard meant the plan had to be delayed?

It was a good thing he didn't just walk by and let the slave be beaten up, he didn't close his eyes and ears to the pain and suffering of others, however in his emotional response he may have put the slave(s) in greater danger.

He certainly set himself up for a major fall. He didn't it appears, seek God first, he just reacted. He lashed out.

It was possible that at best he put God's plans to save his people on hold, or at worse stopped them. Whatever they were for sure were delayed.

It is right as Christians to speak out for those who have no voices, to do all we can to assist the poor, needy, hungry and abused. However, in doing that we must not make their condition worse.

We say when we help people in crisis don't turn their problem into a crisis, if what you do will not improve their situation or make it worse, don't help them. Don't do it!

There are many examples in the history of conflict where

one person from a village has opposed the enemy and the whole village has been killed.

We cannot mitigate against evil men, however with Gods guidance and help our efforts can succeed against the strong man.

Moses when God called him, did what God said and Pharaoh set the people free.

There are many instances in the Bible where God has appointed a person to lead the people, if we are faced with a situation where we see someone being abused we cannot be silent, however we must move cautiously and prayerfully so the person being abused is not damaged further before help can be generated.

I wonder what would have happened if Moses had spoken to the guard, would the guard have held back because of who Moses was? Would the guard have changed his behaviour?

Could Moses have persuaded his Egyptian mother (Pharaohs daughter) to talk to Pharaoh and ease the situation for the Israelites?

We know that Pharaoh wanted to get rid of the Israelites, maybe Pharaoh would have been better disposed to set the people free if Moses had prayed first and then spoken to Pharaoh about freeing the slaves, rather than killing the guard and stirring up Pharaohs anger against him too.

Moses ran to the desert to hide from Pharaohs wrath, forty years were to follow, more Hebrews would be battered, beaten and die in a foreign land before they would be set free.

A whole army of Egyptians would be slain, and the people of Egypt suffer some horrible plagues and suffering.

It is conceivable that it would have been more straight forward if when Moses saw the guard beating a Hebrew slave, he had gone to God and allowed God to intervene in Pharaohs need to reduce the number of Israelites.

We don't know what would have happened if anything and speculation will not solve the issue, but as Christians we must first commit our plans to the Lord.[29] Give him the chance to sort things.

If we pray for his intervention, then let's let him intervene before we try: where invariably it will go wrong.

Moses didn't ask God, didn't speak to God, he just killed the guard, he did it his way and it nearly did for him.

As Christians we need to allow God to direct our paths, not take knee jerk reactions, we need to commit our ways to the Lord.

When we see someone suffering abuse, we may be distressed by what we see, we wouldn't or shouldn't go off and kill the perpetrator out of an emotional response. OK, it happens in films, in fiction, its good box office but not real life.

How often is our response based on feelings rather than on a well thought out measured response?

So Moses ran away, he had by a rash action given up a comfortable life, a life he would have expected to keep until he died. Forty years he had lived in the Palace of the Pharaoh. Pharaoh must have seen him up close and personal, now he was a fugitive, on the run from one of the most powerful men in the known world: running frightened for his own safety: Oops! That wasn't in the days plan!!

Pharaoh had put out a death threat on him and Moses didn't hang around to see if it would happen, he knew he was in the wrong, he knew that he had one chance, that was to run.

29 Proverbs 16:3 *'Commit your works to the LORD And your plans will be established'.*

So he ran and ran and ran, the Bible does not give us the miles he ran, however many experts estimate it was in excess of 600 miles. In a car today it is a day's journey, on foot in the desert would have taken him months. He would have had a long time to reflect and seek God.

To have killed a man (even an Egyptian guard beating a slave) is wrong:

To have interfered in God's plans is very wrong so it's curtains for Moses.

But Moses story does not end there thankfully, he marries the daughter of a Midian priest, becomes a father and shepherd. Then is called by God to go and set God's people free!

Now it is at this point we could say all's well that ends well Moses is now safe, married and all is ok.

However, the Israelites are still suffering as slaves under a brutal regime. There has been no let up and no one to set them free, but they keep on praying and in Exodus 2 [30] we read God heard their 'groanings.'

When circumstances for us Christians are dire, stretching us to our limits and beyond, we must continue to call out to the Lord to come to our aid. We can be encouraged by Jesus words 'seek and you will find, knock and it shall be opened'.

Most translators of this text say that Jesus is saying not just knock but 'keep on knocking… it will be opened', 'keep on seeking you will find' what you are looking for. To keep knocking, keep banging on the door, keep knocking and banging…' it will be opened'.[31]

Sometimes our circumstances overwhelm us and disempower us, they appear like a cloud over us. Without

30 Exodus 2:24
31 Matthew 7:7

quite understanding how and why we find ourselves alone, suffering and with no hope. All we can see is the pain and darkness of despair, like a fog that is so encompassing we can't see our own hand in front of our faces.

We take no action because we can see none to take, we have no hope because we can see none.

It seems to me that when Moses was running in the desert he must just have seen miles upon mile of endless sand, no greenery, no sea, nothing except sun and sand: with nothing to look forward too, enemies behind him wanting to kill him he must have despaired of ever finding safety, let alone a wife.

But God is always there for us when we call out to him in times of trouble he replies. He will never leave us or forsake us.

When we turn to Christ our names are written in the palm of his hand, he can't forget us even if he wanted to, which he does not!

There are many scriptures that encourage us to call out to God in times of trouble. I find the following psalm focuses back on God:

Psalm 121 [32] a psalm of Ascent says:

> *I will lift up my eyes to the mountains:*
> *From where shall my help come?*
> *My help comes from the Lord,*
> *Who made heaven and earth.*

We should look up to heaven and see God, he alone will help us, he alone can and will restore us, he alone will answer our call for help.

---

32 NASB

CHAPTER 5

Set my people free

Moses was still Gods man: it was just going to take longer to set the people free!

The Bible says *'for the gifts and the calling of God are irrevocable'.*[33]

God restores Moses and he lives a life in Midian that appears relatively untroubled, as a shepherd caring for his father-in-law's sheep. Probably a huge contrast to his former life in Egypt.

A role pretty far away from Pharaoh and probably in Moses eyes safe from God as well.

For a further forty years he just cared for the sheep and was a 'happy 'family man, like everyone else in the area he was a shepherd, a lonely but a good sound job. For Moses had, without probably realising it, been trained by God; forty years he had lived in Pharaoh's house, he knew all about Egyptians ways and etiquette and language.

Then he spends forty years as a shepherd learning how to find water and survive in the desert and lead unwieldy animals.

He was now ready to spend the last forty years of his life in serving God in the greatest call ever. Leading the Exodus.

One day after forty years God speaks to Moses, simple, go back to Egypt and set my people free! Sorted!

Moses must had wished he hadn't taken the sheep out that day to Horeb, the holy mountain, generally regarded as

---

33 Rom: 11:29 (ESV)

the mountain of God. But he did and God who had heard the cry from his people who are captives in Egypt, looks down and says, 'it's Moses time'!

Time for Moses to do what I had prepared him for, time for him to lead my people out of Egypt. God had always planned for Moses to lead the people out of Egypt, God had not forgotten:

Moses calling was not reversible, it was irrevocable.

Moses saw a burning bush!

Weird, frightening, tempting, intriguing scary, amazing.

I once saw a tree that was on fire in the middle: the top was not on fire the bottom was not on fire, the middle was a raging fire! I was on a night exercise (with three other guys) in the forest: as I was walking I became aware away to my left of a tree that was partially on fire!

I could see flames so I led the guys slowly and cautiously to walk towards flames as I got closer I could see it was a burning tree, but it was weird that only the middle third was on fire. What was even more weird was that as we got closer there appeared to be human beings dancing around the fire.

As we got close I started to feel anxious and drew my sheaf knife.

I knew then that we had to get away particularly as there were people dancing and chanting at the foot of the tree.

They were well hidden in the middle of the forest and they appeared to be not keen on being seen, there was a presence of evil, fear was rampant, we all ran very quickly and very quietly not as far as Moses but put a long distance between us.

It took ages to recover from the experience. I had felt in very real danger.

Moses knew it was different, but it must have 'woken him

up' and as they say put the fear of God in him. However, Moses heard God's voice and responded to that.

Moses knew God's voice when he heard it,[34] he wasn't shocked to hear God's voice from within a burning bush. Yet there is no record of him hearing God's voice before.

He got it right away God was speaking to him.

How do we know God is speaking to us?

Would we assume if we saw a burning bush that God is speaking to us from within a burning bush or would we think it's maybe just a quirk of nature. Or even something evil?

Or even another one of those crazy TV programs like *Candid Camera,* where people are set up and filmed to see their response to strange, challenging or difficult situations:

At the end of the 60's there were no mobile phones, and I remember one day some friends and I had an old telephone which we affixed to the front fence of a house, took a cable from it and planted it into the ground. We set up in the bushes a tape recorder and pretended to be having conversations with people.

At the time it was a good gag, people believed it, they thought we really did have a telephone on the fence. Even though in those days a telephone could not be used outdoors unless it was the military or the Post Office engineer was plugged into the telephone cable cabinet. (*Candid Camera* and these type of programmes had not been invented in 1968.)

In some ways 21st century man is too clever by half, we think we have all the answers.

We think we can do all things through modern technology, we see in modern films, men and women with amazing powers, animals that can talk, rationalize, objects that can hold

34 Exodus 3: 4-6

a conversation, artificial intelligent machines that can think for themselves and perform without humans.

We watch films about avatars,[35] we can make pieces of very special equipment using 3D printing. For example, a gun.

Just a simple music DVD uses so much technology to bring it to the point of sale.

When Moses was in the desert people worshiped gods in a pretty primitive way, including sacrifice of animals and people wearing strange garb, dancing ritualistically, chanting as they worshipped their gods. In some cases, taking substances and eating hallucinogenic plants to enhance the worship of their God.

Whilst we do have hallucinogenic substances to heighten our experience today, they are generally not used in worship.

Today in 20th century church our challenges are different: it can be so complicated, do we have the right software for musicians, preachers or for the overhead projectors.

Is the band big enough should we have, bass and drums?

Do we have a screen for the drums, fold-back speakers, stands for iPads?

Or are our levels set properly?

Have we agreed a key for each song?

Can /are we transposing?

How long for the worship time?

Do we have good stage lights?

Are we filming the service, just the worship, just the preacher?

35 Merriam-Webster Online Dictionary copyright © 2015 by Merriam-Webster, Incorporated. An electronic image that represents and is manipulated by a computer user in a virtual space (as in a computer game or an online shopping site) and that interacts with other objects in the space. Often a representation of a Human being.

Do we all agree with the song words?

Two guitars or two keyboards or both

Why is there feedback, a hum from the speaker? Feedback?

Who has been touching the sound desk?

Can/ does the worship leader have to be an ordained member of the church, or from the priesthood of all believers, does he or she have to be able to play an instrument or sing.

Do we play hymns or contemporary Christian songs, or a mixture of both?

Are the words theologically sound?

Does it matter?

Who is playing lead guitar? do we have a lead guitarist?

How big should the song list be, 80, 20, 5, 1050 songs?

How long do we need for worship?

What order should the songs be in?

How long do we need for preaching?

How frequently should we break bread.

Should we use wafers or bread, wine or squash?

Loads and loads of questions: without considering where, when, how we should meet.

Or questions on which version of the Bible we should use, should we have flag waving, when do the children go out? Should they stay in?

Tea or coffee before the service or after or both?

How do we deal with people with special diets, special needs?

Have we got in place safeguarding policies?

Is someone qualified for food hygiene?

And the questions just keep coming, partly due to the laws of the land, the rules and precepts of the denominations we follow or social mores?

Who is going to teach the children?

What will we teach the children?

What will we do with the collection?

Do we have a collection?

Should we tithe?

Questions! Questions! Questions!

The list continues but you and I will give up the will to live if we look at any more. But we have to keep on top of all the issues.

You notice in the list there does not seem to be a name check or place for God!

Maybe he should have been first?

Some churches have tried closing down to see if God is really there? AJ Tozer wrote, 'Without God the implication is will the church will continue to operate just like a club?'

Off we go on another set of questions, we have got too clever, we need to be like little children, Jesus said unless you become like little children you will not enter the kingdom of Heaven.[36]

Our focus needs to be on getting close to God, when Moses saw the burning bush he did not run away, he did not work out whether it was scientifically possible for the bush to burn. Nor, did he question the probability factor of him being there exactly at the moment that the bush burnt.

Rather he said to himself I will go over and look at it see what this is.

36 Matthew 18:3 (NIV)

It may be argued (I think in error) that Moses was by the bush coincidently, even if this was so, however he put himself in a place where God could speak to him when he went closer to the bush.

There are Christians today who are asking 'what is God saying'?

Where is God?

Yet they are not attending church or prayer meetings or putting themselves in a place where they might hear God's voice.

We are told not to ignore meeting with others in God's house yet the pressure and temptations not to attend church is immense.

Figures show a decline in church attendance, there are fewer people attending church today than there were fifty years ago.

It may be those who go now are more devout, it may be there are more temptations now but what is irrefutable there are less Christians attending church and less Christians running the risk of an encounter with God.

Recently I read a report that showed the number of church leaders that had had a quiet time or read the Bible was reducing, what hope is there for the church if the leadership is not focusing on the word of God, and are not spending time in prayer and meditation with God?

If 'faith comes by hearing[37] and by hearing the word of Christ', how will our faith grow, how will getting closer to God happen if we don't meet together as Christians, or even read Gods word?

---

37 Romans 10:17

We need to be like Moses: he had got it wrong but at the first chance he put himself in a place where he could hear from God, he went to the Holy Mountain, in the whole of the desert the best place to hear from God was probably on the Holy Mountain.

Now is the time for Moses to follow God's Plan: he was to be God's chosen messenger to Pharaoh. So God spoke to Moses and told him he wanted him to go to Pharaoh to get him to set the Israelites free. I'm pretty sure Moses wondered if the death threat against him was still valid if he went to Egypt.

Firstly, the old Pharaoh had died and there was a new King, who probably would not have been that bothered about what Moses did to the guard forty years before.

So God gives Moses instructions, but Moses argues with God, he makes God angry, you would have thought Moses might have remembered he was talking to God: surely not the best person to anger. But sometimes our strengths are also weaknesses. It could well be argued that Moses probably didn't get to talk to God that often and probably felt a bit surreal, he was obviously frightened for himself.

However, Moses did not understand that there was no choice.

God said 'I am sending you' but Moses says who am I? Why me?

What would we do in this situation?

What would you have done if you had been in this situation where God gives you an instruction?

When God says do this, what is our response?

Do we do it joyfully?

I remember when I first had people telephoning me for pastoral support prayer or ministry, they always seemed to phone just at the most important part of a TV programme and in those days there wasn't video, or a Sky box to record the end of the programme on, nor were there repeats. It was gone finished.

Oh no when the phone went you missed out on that programme.

The times my wife and I went out to help or support someone and found that we had missed the ending of a programme or worse the last programme in the series.

We had to rely on friends to tell us what happened!

But Moses either wasn't listening properly, or he had selective hearing (what some husbands are accused of by their wives).

It seems strange that Moses wasn't concentrating on listening to God, as he knew he was in the presence of God. Had he lost touch with the God of his Forefathers. Maybe his view of God was out of shape.

Did he not realise that when God talks we need to listen, answer and act on what he says? Generally, it's not for debate, God doesn't seek or need our advice, but how often do we consider Him to be the one who needs help.

Was Moses just slow in processing what had just happened to him?

There he was minding his own business walking his sheep towards the Mountain of God maybe dreaming about his supper or about his wife, maybe even about God being on the mountain then suddenly a bush near him is on fire and God speaks from within the burning bush.

I guess a bush burning had happened before in the desert, but I'm sure God had not spoken to Moses before in such a dramatic way.

God called Moses[38]and he drew closer and took off his sandals because:

38 Exodus 3: 1-11

a) He was told to

b) It was Holy Ground

Moses saw the bush on fire, maybe not unusual, what was special was the bush was on fire but didn't burn up, that gets your attention.[39]

A bush on fire that was not being burnt up it was sudden, dramatic and an effective attention getter.

Moses says, according to the Bible, 'I will go over and see this strange sight'.

You either run away or you get closer, you don't ignore it.

In the midst of the burning bush, there an Angel of the

39 **Moses and the Burning Bush**

'Now Moses was tending the flock of Jethro his father-in-law, the priest of Midian, and he led the flock to the far side of the wilderness and came to Horeb, the mountain of God. There the angel of the Lord appeared to him in flames of fire from within a bush. Moses saw that though the bush was on fire it did not burn up. So Moses thought, 'I will go over and see this strange sight – why the bush does not burn up.'

When the Lord saw that he had gone over to look, God called to him from within the bush, 'Moses! Moses!'

And Moses said, 'Here I am.' 'Do not come any closer,' God said. 'Take off your sandals, for the place where you are standing is holy ground.' Then he said, 'I am the God of your father, the God of Abraham, the God of Isaac and the God of Jacob.' At this, Moses hid his face, because he was afraid to look at God.

The Lord said, 'I have indeed seen the misery of my people in Egypt. I have heard them crying out because of their slave drivers, and I am concerned about their suffering. So I have come down to rescue them from the hand of the Egyptians and to bring them up out of that land into a good and spacious land, a land flowing with milk and honey – the home of the Canaanites, Hittites, Amorites, Perizzites, Hivites and Jebusites. And now the cry of the Israelites has reached me, and I have seen the way the Egyptians are oppressing them. So now, go. I am sending you to Pharaoh to bring my people the Israelites out of Egypt.'

But Moses said to God, 'Who am I that I should go to Pharaoh and bring the Israelites out of Egypt?'

Lord appeared to him! Wow! That must have been scary.

At the birth of Jesus, when the Angel appeared to the shepherds, the shepherds were terrified. Seems a reasonable response.

The angel said 'don't be afraid'.

For Moses this experience in the middle of the desert must have generated lots of emotions. Then as Moses starts to go to the bush, God calls out to him "Moses, Moses".

Then the Bible says 'God's voice in the fire says: don't come too close and take your sandals off its holy ground'.

A voice in the fire speaks to you, that is dramatic, that is mind changing,

When you know it is God the creator of the universe speaking to you: wow, that must have been an amazing moment for Moses, and the first of many times he would talk with God.

In Genesis 33:18 we read that man cannot look on the face of God and live, God did not want Moses to get burnt by the fire, or by looking at him directly, so he gets Moses to keep a safe distance away.

Then God introduces himself to Moses 'I am the God of your Father, the God of Abraham'.

Moses knew it was God in the bush and he also believed that God could appear to him in a bush. Moses was open to hear from God, even in such a strange place as a bush. Would we be open to hear from God in a bush, in the wilderness or as we walked along the beach?

The scripture says that at this point Moses hid his face, he might have suspected it was God before God spoke but now our Hero was certain, and he hid his face.

There are many reasons why Moses hid his face.

1. He would have known through his youth and teaching at his mother's breast that you can't look upon God and live
2. He would have been in Awe
3. He may well have probably thought if I hide God can't see me

But I think the key reason he covered his face is he would have felt dirty, guilty, unclean not wanting God to look upon what he had become.

God then tells Moses why he was speaking to him; I have heard the cry of my people the Israelites and I have come down to rescue them and I am sending you to Egypt, to Pharaoh to get my people out!

Up to where God says 'I am sending you to Pharaoh', Moses would have been ok with God's plan, at that point I think his world just imploded.

You could imagine as God says I am going to set my people free, Moses saying that's great God your gonna set my people free, they have suffered for a long time, why are you telling me about it in the midst of the desert? I'm no longer in Egypt. I don't plan on going back to Egypt 'cause Pharaoh wants to kill me.

Then God says 'I am sending you to Egypt, to Pharaoh, to get my people out'.

Moses must have had a melt-down, all the old fears he had had as he was running away from Egypt would have returned, he was no longer the man that had killed the slave drivers, probably forgotten the Egyptian language, probably also thought I am an old man, I am 80 years old.

He probably thought that he had a wife a new family, he had been living as a shepherd for 40 years, he had become stable, secure, safe he had a plan for life, it worked: he understood how to live life, he had probably almost forgotten his time in Egypt, living in Pharaoh's house.

He was comfortable and settled now, happy family man, good shepherd, then God says, 'I am sending you to Pharaoh'. Oh, what a time bomb. How was he 'gonna tell the misses'?

'Hi my lovely wife, God is sending me to Pharaoh, I may get killed, I may be captured and never come home, I may have to live in Egypt'.

'You and the boys may have to come with me and live as nomads in the desert'!

'You may never see your family again. We may all starve or die'.

Not a great message to take home after being out shepherding the sheep.

What would Moses wife say, why me? Or how will we cope what about food or shelter?

No way is this gonna happen!

Not a good plan!

I think the response God hoped for from Moses and expected was 'ok, I will go'.

That's how leaders, prophets and all of us should respond to God:

I will go. Moses of course had not read Isaiah 6:8 *'And I heard the voice of the Lord saying, 'Whom shall I send, and who will go for us?' Then I said, 'Here I am! Send me.'.*

When God says jump the response should be how High? Not why me?

What can I do? I am not worthy?

Trapp in his commentary on James 1:5 tells the story 'That Alexander the Great once gave a poor man a city, and when he modestly refused it as too great for him. Alexander replied, *Non quaero quid te accipere deceat, sed quid me dare.* 'The business is not what thou art fit to receive but what it becometh me to give.'[40]

It is easy to get into a sense of false humility but if the giver gives you a gift or a task the response is thank you. However, Moses speaks, possibly before getting his brain into gear.

Moses challenges God. Who am I that I should go to Pharaoh and bring the Israelites out of Egypt?

Would we question Gods instructions, no you cry, of course we would say I'll go!

Yet we live lives that challenge Gods way, seldom do we respond to Gods call upon our lives as: here I am I will go.

More often we look at the issues, problems and challenges and say why me?

Why now? Or maybe we can go later? Or maybe there is someone better than me?

Moses replied, Why me? Why should I do this task.

He might have added I tried before to get the Israelites free and look at what happened they turned on me and I had to hide and escape.

However, God did not want a debate with Moses, God did not say 'hey Moses, I'm thinking of getting the Israelites out of Egypt, what do you think'? Perhaps I should send in the special forces? Do you fancy going leading them for me?

When we have that burning bush experience with God we need to say as the writer of Isaiah said

40 John Trapp, Trapp, *A Commentary on the Old and New Testaments, Volume Five* (Eureka, California: Tanski Publications, 1997) Quoted in Enduring Word commentaries enduringword.com/bible-commentary/james-1

'Here I am Lord send me'[41]

Forty years before the burning bush encounter God was going to set the Israelites free, the probability is that God would have used Moses then, as Moses was in the house of Pharaoh,

But then Moses killed the Egyptian guard and fled. God puts His plans on hold.

Now 40 years later God is getting the plans back on track. Moses is better equipped. Moses is going back to Egypt with Gods providence to see Pharaoh and pass on Gods message.

'LET MY PEOPLE GO'.

41 Isaiah 6:8

CHAPTER 6

Strangers in a foreign land

As a Christian how can we be informed by the Israelites behaviour?

To answer the question about the behaviour of the Israelites we need to know more about them and work out the answers to some questions:

- How the Israelites come to be in Egypt?
- Why they were still in Egypt
- Had they tried to leave before?
- What happened to them in Egypt
- What would be the consequences if God didn't get them out?

How the Israelites came to be in Egypt?

We need to look to the book of Genesis chapter 37 and explore the story of Joseph, you may have read about Joseph the boy with the coat of many colours.

We find that the story of Joseph and a famine are the keys to Israel ending up as captives in Egypt.

Joseph, favourite son of Israel has a dream. He has a dream about sheaves of wheat and his rising over those of his brothers. When he tells the dream to his brothers they become jealous. So jealous that they scheme together, trick him then they sell him to slave traders. Joseph was taken as a slave to Egypt, where he was sold to a high ranking Egyptian, Potiphar.

Josephs brothers go home job done, they just tell their dad a lie and after a time it's all ok and they carry on with their lives, not expecting to ever see Joseph again.

How wrong can you be on so many counts?

Joseph was a very good slave and successful and Potiphar made him head of his household, because God was with Joseph.

Later, Potiphar's wife tried to seduce Joseph but he refused her attentions so she accused Joseph of trying to take advantage of her, Potiphar was angry and had Joseph put in prison. Satan (who Christians understand to be a fallen angel, who turned against God and who wages war against God and his people and who was defeated by Jesus at the cross) was trying to stop Joseph in what would become an amazing service of God and an immense move of God's power.

But God has a plan for Joseph, after many trials including being in prison he becomes a very important official in Egypt.

God had his hand on Joseph whilst he was in Prison, Joseph interprets a dream that Pharaohs cup bearer (who was in prison with him) has and it comes true. Joseph is in prison two more years and then this time Pharaoh[42] has a dream and

42 *'When two full years had passed, Pharaoh had a dream: He was standing by the Nile, when out of the river there came up seven cows, sleek and fat, and they grazed among the reeds. After them, seven other cows, ugly and gaunt, came up out of the Nile and stood beside those on the riverbank. And the cows that were ugly and gaunt ate up the seven sleek, fat cows. Then Pharaoh woke up.*

He fell asleep again and had a second dream: Seven heads of grain, healthy and good, were growing on a single stalk. After them, seven other heads of grain sprouted – thin and scorched by the east wind. The thin heads of grain swallowed up the seven healthy, full heads. Then Pharaoh woke up: it had been a dream.

In the morning his mind was troubled, so he sent for all the magicians and wise men of Egypt. Pharaoh told them his dreams, but no one could interpret them for him.

Then the chief cupbearer said to Pharaoh, 'Today I am reminded of my shortcomings. Pharaoh was once angry with his servants, and he imprisoned me and the chief baker in the house of the captain of the guard. Each of us had a dream the same night, and each dream had a meaning of its own. Now a young Hebrew was there with us, a servant of the captain of the guard. We told him our dreams, and he interpreted them for us, giving each man the interpretation of his dream. And things turned out exactly as he interpreted them to us: I was restored to my position, and the other man was impaled.'

So Pharaoh sent for Joseph, and he was quickly brought from the dungeon. When he had shaved and changed his clothes, he came before Pharaoh.

no-one can interpret it for him, but Joseph (Genesis 41).

We read Joseph was thirty years old when he started his time of God guided work. Is it a coincidence that Jesus was thirty when he started his ministry?

Pharaoh said to Joseph, 'I had a dream, and no one can interpret it. But I have heard it said of you that when you hear a dream you can interpret it.' 'I cannot do it,' Joseph replied to Pharaoh, 'but God will give Pharaoh the answer he desires.'

Then Pharaoh said to Joseph, 'In my dream I was standing on the bank of the Nile, when out of the river there came up seven cows, fat and sleek, and they grazed among the reeds. After them, seven other cows came up – scrawny and very ugly and lean. I had never seen such ugly cows in all the land of Egypt. The lean, ugly cows ate up the seven fat cows that came up first. But even after they ate them, no one could tell that they had done so: they looked just as ugly as before. Then I woke up.

'In my dream I saw seven heads of grain, full and good, growing on a single stalk. After them, seven other heads sprouted – withered and thin and scorched by the east wind. The thin heads of grain swallowed up the seven good heads. I told this to the magicians, but none of them could explain it to me.'

Then Joseph said to Pharaoh, 'The dreams of Pharaoh are one and the same. God has revealed to Pharaoh what he is about to do. The seven good cows are seven years, and the seven good heads of grain are seven years: it is one and the same dream. The seven lean, ugly cows that came up afterward are seven years, and so are the seven worthless heads of grain scorched by the east wind: They are seven years of famine.

'It is just as I said to Pharaoh: God has shown Pharaoh what he is about to do. Seven years of great abundance are coming throughout the land of Egypt, but seven years of famine will follow them. Then all the abundance in Egypt will be forgotten, and the famine will ravage the land. The abundance in the land will not be remembered, because the famine that follows it will be so severe. The reason the dream was given to Pharaoh in two forms is that the matter has been firmly decided by God, and God will do it soon.

'And now let Pharaoh look for a discerning and wise man and put him in charge of the land of Egypt. Let Pharaoh appoint commissioners over the land to take a fifth of the harvest of Egypt during the seven years of abundance. They should collect all the food of these good years that are coming and store up the grain under the authority of Pharaoh, to be kept in the cities for food. This food should be held in reserve for the country, to be used during the seven years of famine that will come upon Egypt, so that the country may not be ruined by the famine.' Genisis 41. (NIV).

All of Pharaoh's wise men and magicians, his noblemen all try to interpret the dream but are unable to interpret this dream: then the cup bearer remembers Joseph who interpreted his dream so he tells Pharaoh about Joseph.

Pharaoh tells Joseph his dream and Joseph interprets the dream for Pharaoh. The Interpretation is that God says there will be seven years of plenty and seven years of famine, that in the years of plenty they are to store up grain and oil so that they can survive in the seven years of famine.

Pharaoh believes Joseph's interpretation of the dream, none of the hundreds of his wise men had been able to interpret the dream.

So Pharaoh appoints Joseph as his number two in charge of the Kingdom,

Joseph was a slave, imprisoned falsely.

One day he is in the pit in prison wondering how did I get here?

The next he is riding in the second chariot next to Pharaoh. What a transformation in his life.

God is really on Joseph's side. Pharaoh tells Joseph to be wise and ensure the Egyptian people have enough grain in the years of famine to come. What a task what a responsibility! But it is God's plan and he ensures Joseph gets the job done, and much more.

In the first seven years God provides enough for the seven years of famine both for the Egyptians and also for the neighbouring peoples. (Genesis 41: 57 *'And all the world came to Egypt to buy grain from Joseph, because the famine was severe everywhere'.*)

The story of how Josephs is reconciled to his brothers and Josephs father and how all his family came to Egypt and with Pharaohs blessing settled in Goshen in Egypt. Is well worth reading but not fully part of this book.

Joseph had encouraged his family to move to Egypt and to tell Pharaoh that they were shepherds and they lived as shepherds.

The Israelites, Joseph's people became very successful and prospered, over time many of them becoming Goldsmiths.

Time passed both Joseph and the Pharaoh died and a new Pharaoh came to power. The new Pharaoh became unhappy at how successful the Israelites were and also how their numbers were growing and he made them slaves.[43]

This appears to have happened over time and the intensity of their enslavement grew year by year and with successive Pharaohs.

Men quickly forget the trouble they were in when the trouble goes away.

The potential impact of the famine on the Egypt and her people, the probability that thousands maybe even hundreds of thousands would have died in such a severe famine is soon forgotten.

The fact that God raised up Joseph and his divine inspired plans and provisions for providing food for the seven famine years in Egypt are also soon forgotten

---

43 **Pharaoh Oppresses Israel**

'Now Joseph and all his brothers and all that generation died, but the Israelites were exceedingly fruitful: they multiplied greatly, increased in numbers and became so numerous that the land was filled with them. Then a new king, to whom Joseph meant nothing, came to power in Egypt. 'Look,' he said to his people, 'the Israelites have become far too numerous for us. Come, we must deal shrewdly with them or they will become even more numerous and, if war breaks out, will join our enemies, fight against us and leave the country.'

So they put slave masters over them to oppress them with forced labor, and they built Pithom and Rameses as store cities for Pharaoh. But the more they were oppressed, the more they multiplied and spread: so the Egyptians came to dread the Israelites and worked them ruthlessly. They made their lives bitter with harsh labor in brick and mortar and with all kinds of work in the fields: in all their harsh labor the Egyptians worked them ruthlessly.' (NIV Exodus 1:6-14)

Pharaoh and the Egyptians had sufficient through the famine, so they just carried on. Except now they had a group of Israelite people that were flourishing in their land. They were growing in number and prosperity. Pharaoh needed a plan to curtail them and their growth.

Simple make them slaves, the Idi Amin or dictatorial response.

Remember too, the Pharaoh who was reigning at this time was possibly Thutmose 111 it was over 400 years since the famine and, God's deliverance and the role of Joseph and Israelites. From his perspective it was probably a story passed down, but over time had lost its importance to Pharaoh and the Egyptian people

Today it's often hard to remember what happened twenty years ago let alone 400!

The Egyptians initially were reasonable slave masters: it would have been strange situation for them: suddenly your neighbours are you slaves. Even though they were slaves the Israelites continued to grow in number and be prosperous?

However, over time and under different Pharaohs the people of Egypt were told to be hard on the Israelites, and became very aggressive and violent to them.

Pharaoh even telling midwives to kill any male babies born to the Israelites.

The Israelites were held captive in Egypt. This was told to Abram in a dream long before it happened Genesis 15: 13 God says to Abram: *'the Lord said to Abram, 'Know for certain that your offspring will be sojourners in a land that is not theirs and will be servants there, and they will be afflicted for four hundred years'.* in verse 16 *'But I will bring judgment on the nation that they serve, and afterward they shall come out with great possessions'.*

So the Israelites originally arrived in Egypt in real need,

there was a famine, in their land, they had no food, there was no obvious answer, there was no food bank, no Social Services. So they went as refugees to a foreign land. However, God already had a plan because Joseph his servant was there and in control.

God tells the Israelites to go to Egypt to buy food, where there was food for them, and Pharaoh gives them a new land where they could live.

A great plan, for the short term, i.e. the time of the famine? However, they become settled in Egypt. It was a big land with plenty of room. Settling down that's not necessarily a problem but the Israelite people start looking to the local culture and adopting the beliefs of the Egyptians that God says are un-Godly.

The Israelite people start getting into the Egyptian way of life and culture, following the gods and practices of Egypt and stop following their God.

The Israelites are prosperous, they multiplied, their presence must have been more visible to Pharaoh in his palace. It would seem that everywhere he looked there were Israelite people prospering and maybe his people the Egyptians were the poor ones?

The new Pharaoh who never saw what good Joseph did or how he saved Egypt: the famine had happened 400 years ago, the world was different, Pharaoh was only aware that everywhere he looked there was an Israelite, who seemed to be very prosperous, overrunning his country: doing better in many cases than his people: he didn't like that so he became concerned, then when things did not change even though he gave instructions, then he became angry: an angry Pharaoh is not what you want when you are an exile living in his country. Even worse and really bad news is when his anger is directed toward you.

In life we sometimes go to do something for the right reasons, it's well thought out and then it seems to go wrong and we end up in trouble or with egg on our faces.

Somewhere along the way we end up losing the vision or getting sidetracked, then things go wrong and we get into trouble.

This can happen on our own, as a family or as a group, or nation.

Churches appear to have a vision and be moving forward towards that vision when all of a sudden they find themselves slaves to fortune, or culture, no longer on the path to complete the vision, unsure of how to move forward, often with very sad consequences for the congregation and its leaders.

Joseph was sold into slavery by his brothers: God was going to use Joseph that is clear, however did God need his brothers to sell him to the slave traders and them be sold to Potiphar?

That scenario relies too heavily on chance, on coincidence, God does not build on chance or coincidence, true he allows us to use our wisdom, skills, knowledge and experience in his service but he does not rely on chance. Miracles are just that: they are not chance.

When Jesus and his disciples arrived at Capernaum, they were asked if Jesus would pay the Temple tax, it is probable that they could have argued that Jesus was a teacher, Rabbi, and he didn't have to pay. But Jesus says in Matt 17:27 '*However, so that we do not offend them, go to the sea and throw in a hook, and take the first fish that comes up: and when you open its mouth, you will find a shekel. Take that and give it to them for you and Me.*'

Jesus tells his disciples to throw their hook into the sea and the first fish that they catch, not at some time they will catch a fish, rather the first fish that comes out of the sea.

I recently watched a celebrity on a fishing tour, he did very well, but he could not guarantee that when he put his hook into the water he would catch a fish, equally when he did catch a fish he could not guarantee it was the right type, size, etc.

Even in our modern world fishing is an inexact science.

Jesus is specific, the first fish you catch, open its mouth. Not if and when you catch a fish, or when you catch a fish the coin will be in its belly, no opening up of the fish, needed.

These were fishermen they were used to handling fish, they would not have expected to find the coin in the fish's mouth.

They probably would not have expected it to be in the first fish too, nevertheless they obeyed Jesus and as promised there was the coin.

That must have made them think. How did that happen, did they really believe that God would have prepared the first fish with a coin in its mouth?

It was too far-fetched to be a coincidence

If it was not a coincidence, was it a miracle?

The disciples were given an instruction, they followed it they saw the miracle.

It obviously impacted them so much it was passed on to those around.

To see miracles today we need to do what God says and be where he wants us to be.

The Israelites had become comfortable in Egypt, many of them had become so comfortable that they had given up their belief in God and had embraced the Egyptian gods, they worshipped the golden calves and followed the practices of that religion. They were not going to see God do miracles.

Equally they had become captives and slaves to the indigenous Egyptian people.

They were a threat, unwanted, so they were bullied, made to work as slaves.

To be a slave in Egypt nearly 3500 years ago was a terrible brutal experience, many would have died, many were tortured.

Their lives were threatened, food was rationed they would have just got the bare minimum, they would have been whipped, beaten, beaten as they worked, starved, probably the women and children used as sex slaves, their sufferings would have been appalling all without the proper basics of life.

Moses saw a Hebrew slave being beaten and went to help.

Today many of us are strangers in a foreign land we were brought up outside the church, for some the land we were in was fun, for others the land was one of pain.

When we come to Christ we turn our back on our former lives, we move into God's land and his economy. Romans 8:16-17 says *'The Spirit Himself testifies with our spirit that we are children of God and if children, heirs also, heirs of God and fellow heirs with Christ'*. As his children we have a whole wealth of life to come, but we also have to leave behind all those years where we lived a life that was not of God.

If we were fortunate to grow up in a land and family that had possessions and wealth our experiences may well have made us proud, expectant of good things perhaps even expecting others to serve us, to provide for us. It is probable we will have grown up in a place where whatever we needed we got, but even more worrying it would be if whatever we wanted we got.

Even worse is the situation where, whatever we wanted we got but whatever we needed we did not get.

Much has been written about children of the wealthy or privileged that have all the possessions they want, not what they need. They never see their parents, they never experience the love, or cuddles, or even time with their mum and dad.

Let me give you an example.

A very wealthy man has children, he has a multi-million-pound house in the best part of town, many cars, boats, maybe even his own plane.

His children choose the décor for the bedrooms only they don't just have bedrooms they have a suite of rooms. Nothing but the best.

They have their own shower, gym, lounge, outdoor pool and terrace.

Lovely.

They also have the latest technology personalized for them and their apartment. Nothing they could want is missing from the list.

There is a professional chef to cater for them and their bodyguards are there to take them wherever they want to go.

Therein lies the first problem, their body guards or nanny, become their parents, they don't get the cuddle from Dad, because he is away making money so his children can have everything. His children should have all the things he didn't have as a child. They don't get the cuddle from mum, because she is out prettying herself or following her career.

The parents are unable to give their children the very thing they want, to have time together.

You might argue that this is an extreme case, it is but it is in some areas becoming the norm; a world where families are breaking down and children are living in families where they are with children from two or three other marriages and maybe even living with step parents.

Today there are many men who spend less than I hour a day with their children and also mothers who spend less than one hour per day'. A report in 2015 highlighted the reality.

'Fathers spend seven times more with their children than in the 1970s. While the time focused on their offspring still comes in at a fairly low average of 35 minutes a day for working fathers, it is far higher than the five minutes registered in 1974. Mothers' quality time with their kids has also risen over the same period, from 15 minutes a day to an hour.'[44]

It is getting better, but thirty-five minutes a day is such a small amount of time for a parent to spend with their child.

I do not wish to judge people who are working to provide for their families, however, in my role as a Chaplain I do frequently see people who are damaged because of a lack of time spent with their parent when they were growing up. There are many examples we can think of where people appear to have amazing amounts of wealth yet are emotionally scarred, who are broken people, the wealth appears to make matters worse.

Living in a land or world of plenty does not always provide for our needs it may provide for some but for many people it proves inadequate. We are people who need provision for mind body and spirit and for emotional provision. We need to be loved and to love.

Being a slave to sin, we are in a foreign land: obviously it is not the place we want to be, but you might argue there are very few examples of slavery in our modern world, for example if we are addicted to a behaviour we are a slave of that behaviour. We need to understand what we become slaves too.

People can be captured by all manner of things and become slaves to them.

Many have all watched the alcoholic, sometimes even laughed at their antics as they try to walk a steady, straight path.

44 *Parents and parenting*, The Observer, June 15 2014, © 2015 Guardian News and Media Limited

We may even have experienced some of their problems when we have had too much to drink.

But when you become bound by alcohol, when you are a slave to its powers it is no longer funny, it tears you apart, it destroys you physically, emotionally financially.

To be the child, husband, wife, parent of such a person is a great burden to bear, they suck dry those around them, they often emotionally batter them and in some cases physically batter them too.

There are many instances where the family of someone who has an addictive behaviour, warped belief structure or some anti-social pattern has been damaged or destroyed by their loved ones.

In our modern world how awful it must be for the families of children who have been brainwashed into responding to the call of the terrorist cult or group, that are planning terrible atrocities.

To whom we are born, where we live, how we live, what possessions we have, the beliefs our parents hold, the practices associated with them are outside of our control. We cannot take responsibility for what has been done to us, we can only take responsibility for how we have responded.

We can and must accept responsibility for our choices and the experiences of our lives good and bad. We must not take responsibility for the wrongs that were done to us.

If we were beaten by our parents as a child we must ask ourselves several questions.

Was it within what was regarded as normal parental response when we were children? Was it done for 'our benefit' or was there something else going on, i.e. was our parent drunk? Just a bully? Was it part of a ritual?

If our parent thought it was for our benefit was it a slap or a beating with an item?

Did we feel 'better' after. Was it a one off``?

Did we do something seriously wrong to deserve such a level of punishment?

Was it just a tap on the hand? Was that justified?

There is no justification for someone to beat you.

When I was at school I held the unofficial school record for being caned the most times in one week. Six! All by the same teacher!

All over the same piece of homework allegedly not done.

My home situation was not conducive to doing homework. Many evenings were spent cleaning rusty bikes or similar items so that they could be sold, so homework, which in truth I never understood the reason for, was not a priority in the home: so was generally not done or done in 'playtime'. Or if I was lucky in other lessons.

With this particular subject I was interested in it but the teacher was a real stickler for the rules. On the week in question:

I arrived at school on the Monday,

Day one, arrived at the lesson with no homework done. Caned

Day two. No homework done… caned

Day three. I had done the homework… it was not good enough… caned

Day four. Re-did homework Still not good enough… Caned

Day five am, Re-did homework again. according to the teacher it was work of poor standard… Caned

Day five pm Was told to see teacher at end of school'. Teacher informed me that for wasting teachers time and not producing homework of a sufficient quality, or when required – caned again

I guess it was a bonus!

I don't think I learnt anything from that teacher after that week!

Moving on:

The Israelites under Josephs leadership had bought positive things to Egypt.

The Egyptians had been spared the consequences of a seven-year famine.

Yet the new Pharaoh decided to take advantage of them and abuse them because of his issues.

Sometimes we are abused or taken advantage of by the very people we have helped or by the people who would be expected to care for us, protect us, provide for us, nourish us, love us and lead us safely.

How disturbing it is to see in the news about those in special positions who have abused their staff, pupils, patients, parishioners; those they are supposed to nurture and develop. I have felt bullied and abused because of my age and other reasons, due mainly to the insecurity or controlling nature of the other person. Just so sad.

As a Chaplain I have met many people who are no longer in the church because of the way they have been treated by their church leader. I know too that some people need / demand extra help and care, but it must sadden God's heart to see those he has called to ministry, hurt those they are supposed to serve?

We need to understand the action and motivation of the person that took advantage of us, in order that we may move on. As well as receiving care and support as we process all that we have endured. That we may escape from Egypt and move into the promised land. God does not want us to remain captives.

God says in Jeremiah 29: 11-13.

> *'For I know the plans I have for you,' declares the Lord, 'plans to prosper you and not to harm you, plans to give you hope and a future. Then you will call on me and come and pray to me, and I will listen to you. You will seek me and find me when you seek me with all your heart'.*

Many people feel after they have had an Egypt type experience that they are Guilty, that they are in some way diminished as a person.

When someone takes advantage of you, of your kindness, your vulnerability, age, gender, sexuality, misfortune culture, creed, disability, faith or any other discriminating factor, it is wrong, it is not defendable it is wrong!

You are not guilty they are!

Invariably the perpetrator will try and make you feel guilty, 'you need this', 'you are bad so I'm gonna make you good'. They may say 'I wouldn't have beat you but you are bad and I'm going to knock it out of you'.

They make it seem like your fault.

It sounds logical.

But we must not believe their lies or wrong statements.

No-one has the right to abuse you or take advantage over you.

Even God who the Bible says created us gives us free choice.

You are not diminished as a person, you are still you, sadly though you are different, no longer as innocent of the world as perhaps you were, no longer feeling as clean as you did before you were abused

But the you is still there: needing to be healed, rebuilt, restored, cleansed, vindicated, set free from the captivity that abuse brings, set free from the chains it places around you, set free from all the damaging memories, that transcend the passage of time. You need a Moses to come forward and set you free.

Jesus promises us, whoever believes in him will not perish. He heals all our sicknesses and infirmities: he sets the captive free. He loosens the chains of the prisoner.

He can heal all the damage we have suffered: he asks only that we respond to his call. Revelation 3:20

> *'Behold, I stand at the door and knock. If anyone hears My voice and opens the door, I will come in and dine with him and he with Me'.*

I was four when my mother took me by bus and put me into a children's home and left me.

However, over 60 years later I can still vividly remember the day, the pain, desertion, fear, loneliness, remember her outfits, but they have no hold or power over me now. Just a sadness for her.

Thankfully on that day I didn't know the abuse that would follow, I didn't understand that as a child you are vulnerable to male and female adults that want to hurt you, you learn quickly though.

As a child I was abused both in the orphanage and in the foster care home.

It was wrong, I knew that at the time, I was unable to change it, I would have been punished for speaking out.

But I couldn't have voiced it, I would have been punished.

It was wrong. I had to deal with it, I had to cope with it, I knew that at age four I had to deal with it on my own, 'no other bugger was gonna help me'.

It was wrong: Wrong is wrong! yet the victims are often made to feel guilty by the perpetrator as well as society. I was told it was all my fault?

Whenever people abuse you or leaders abuse their authority or job, or roll.

It is wrong.

No way to justify it, it is wrong.

Wrong is wrong.

The Israelites who had entered Egypt because they were without food and had had a good relationship with the Pharaoh, suddenly found themselves being abused by the new Pharaoh, and his minions.

The Israelites who in many cases had forgotten their God: the God who had led them from famine to a place where there was food, and had arranged that someone from their nation was running the food programme.

These same Israelites ignored their God and turned to other gods and practices that were abhorrent to their God. After years of slavery finally they called out to their God to save them and he did.

For some reading this book today it will evoke painful memories, some that you do not wish to revisit, and if you have received some support over time, be it Christian ministry, secular counseling or any other support that has set you free, then I would encourage you to skip the next few pages and not stir up that which is at peace.

However, if the memories and the events have not been addressed until now and that perhaps have become dim, or are still very sharp, I would encourage you to seek support from the many organizations that are available today: or if you have a relationship with a church or faith group meet with one of their counsellors, if they are trained.

God loves us and he doesn't want us to carry the burden of captivity and all it means around with us: he wants to set us free.

This book is not designed to be a self-help book to help people who have been abused be free: rather it is designed to help us understand how we can change from being captives to an old life that was a problem for us, and how we can move into a new life.

Additionally, remember you are not the guilty one. If you are part of a church talk to the leaders, they will support and help you.

If you suffered at the hands of a group or person that should have been helping you, i.e. Youth leader, teacher, church leader, then try talking to another professional person. Talk to your GP, senior church leader, or Chaplains, if you are part of a caring organization that has trained people talk to them.

At the back of the book there is a list of contacts for you.

If you have been abused or suffered at the hands of another person or group, I would encourage you to look for help, groups like the Samaritans, Mind, Survivors Trust are a few of the many, groups that are well equipped to support you in your time of need. I would encourage you to also seek your local church there are many caring churches out there who would want to support you too.

Jesus promised us he is here for us he said '*Come to me all who are weary and heavy laden and I will give you rest/peace.*' Matt 11:28

If you are a person that has been one of the 'Egyptian guards', you too may be carrying a burden but one of a different type.

What you did happened, it is not possible to deny what you did or were part of.

For the Egyptians the evidence of the captivity of the Israelites was ever present, it was before their eyes day and night. They couldn't run from it, the cries of the slaves must have haunted them.

Throughout history there have been numerous times when men and women who are perfectly normal citizens have abused those of a different, creed gender, culture.

We only have to look at the treatment of the Jews in the last great war, the Conquistadors, troubles in Northern Ireland, Kosovo, the bloody conflict between the Tutsis and Hutus and many more: thousands killed in the name of Religion, or of political power or some other political idea.

Unbelievable atrocities carried out by men and women, who look and act exactly the same as us.

Whatever their justification the pain they caused and the suffering they ignored will be Judged by God on the final day.

I would encourage you if you have been a slave driver or an Egyptian guard to own up, there are many ways that you can address these issues in your life.

The guilt will eventually destroy you, the only answer is to face what you have done and whilst you will probably not be able to make amends, you can probably walk in truth. The Bible says if we truly repent God will forgive us; 1 John 1:9 *'If we confess our sins, He is faithful and just to forgive us our sins and to cleanse us from all unrighteousness'.*

Society will have more difficulty forgiving you and indeed society demands that if you have committed a crime you should pay the price.

If you have broken the law as a 'Guard' or 'Ruler' in 'Egypt' you will expect to receive the due process of law. There was no excuse for the German soldier at the concentration camp who said 'I was only doing my duty', but a certain amount of sympathy.

We need to challenge the rules and rulers that would cause us to break the law. We live in a democracy and there are ways for us to challenge wrong laws.

The Israelites were captives, they did not elect to be

captives, did not volunteer they were taken forcibly, their possession taken from them and they were abused and tortured.

They had no choice but they believed in a God who heals and sets people free.

They were slaves to one of the most powerful kings on earth, if not the most powerful man and country and Kingdom on earth at that time.

Pharaoh led Egypt, Egypt and Pharaoh were to be feared.

But when the Israelites finally called out to God: God showed he was stronger: more powerful, more compassionate, more attentive to them than Pharaoh and he set them free.

Sometimes we make a decision that backfires on us and lands us in the smelly stuff.

God can and will get us out of whatever we land in if we seek him. If we own him as God,

There is hope, whatever has happened in your lives there is hope, God can and will set you free from captivity and slavery however you ended up there, cause being in captivity that's just not his plan for you.

The Israelites had become comfortable in Egypt: we can learn to endure the most horrible experiences.

The *Stockholm Syndrome*[45] or the process of bonding to

45 *Stockholm syndrome* is a condition that causes hostages to develop a psychological alliance with their captors as a survival strategy during captivity. These alliances, resulting from a bond formed between captor and captives during intimate time spent together, are generally considered irrational in light of the danger or risk endured by the victims. The FBI's Hostage Barricade Database System and Law Enforcement Bulletin shows that roughly 8% of victims show evidence of Stockholm syndrome.

https://en.wikipedia.org/w/index.php?title=Stockholm_syndrome&oldid=862493037

one's captor could have played a part in the way the Israelite nation lived their lives as slaves.

They had lived in the land of the Egyptians during the time of famine and would have developed some level of friendship and relationships with their Egyptian neighbours, some even intermarried. The Israelites lived for some generations in Egypt before they were enslaved. They had become part of the furniture.

However, when the Egyptians were told to treat them as slaves it is quite conceivable that the Israelites would have known their guards and would have either had a relationship with them or because of the years they had shared the same land, food and in some cases religion they may well have formed a bonding with their slave master.

It's possible that they justified the guard's treatment of them in a sympathetic manor, maybe making excuses for the guards behaviour.

Maybe arguing that the guards were only doing what they were told to do, knowing if the guards did not punish the Israelites as they were instructed too, the guards themselves would be punished and made slaves.

It is estimated that 8–10 % of captives respond in a manner of bonding with their captors. Justifying the abuse, some even believing that by forming a relationship with their captor they can change their captors behaviour. It is difficult to get a percentage figure of the number of Israelites that would have needed to support the captors for the majority of the group to follow.

Some say as little as 3%.

The Israelites were fully integrated in the culture, it was wrong to be made slaves but the Israelites knew the pressure the slave drivers were under and many would probably have had a great sympathy for the slave drivers.

Philosophers may argue that it was not bonding rather the Zeitgeist or as Hegel puts it 'Spirit of the times'.

The sense that one has changed from captive to fellow traveler of the oppressor is a very powerful sense that may override that natural instinct to feel wronged or abused and supersede the natural desire to escape or harm the abuser.[46]

Throughout the ages there have sadly been children that have been sexually `groomed and abused' by a teacher, older friend, church or youth group leader or other professional leader or parent.

Although initially the things done to them are abhorrent to them, they know they are wrong, yet in time they can become peaceful 'lovers' of the perpetrator.

They then take on a different role in the relationship. The relationship becomes 'special' to them, it changes and appears good, the victim would even defend to the death the right of their abusers to have done what they have done. That is until the abusers finds another 'victim'. Or the victim is truly set free.

You cannot be a fellow traveler with someone who took you captive, and or abused you even if they have said sorry: the basis of the relationship is wrong. They need to demonstrate contrition and be willing to subject themselves to the law to be punished for what they have done.

The abused person needs to know peace and freedom that only the Lord Jesus Christ can give.

Free mind

So often people bring into relationships the baggage from a previous relationship, it is always there as the Elephant in the room no matter how hard they try to ignore it.

---

46 https://en.wikipedia.org/wiki/Lectures_on_the_Philosophy_of_Historyhttps://en.wikipedia.org/wiki/Lectures_on_the_Philosophy_of_History

It may be sitting quiet but every so often something of the previous relationship slips out, the room is not big enough for all three, the stampede is just nearby.

If you have been anyway involved in capturing or harming an 'Israelite prisoner', now is the time to deal with it, for you to own it, the Bible says to repent and turn from your ways. To make amends to the person you have harmed.

A friend, after coming to faith in Jesus had to face up to their past and deal with the situation to the point of being imprisoned.

They had to trust Jesus: over time God has changed them and they are a reliable tool in God's hand.

I pray God will help you to do what you need to do and that you will be set free to be who God wants you to be.

If you have been a 'prisoner in 'Egypt' my prayer is that you will be set free. That the Lord of Heaven and Earth Himself will set you free and heal you.

May you know his peace and that in the fullness of time you will be able to forgive.

That you will live a full and fruitful life. Remembering, nothing is impossible for God (Luke 1:37) his love lasts forever (Psalm 136).

God bless you.

In the Appendix there is a list of charities that will provide help and support. Alternatively contact your GP or church or faith group.

CHAPTER 7

Moses and the slave driver

Genesis 47:27 *'Now the Israelites settled in Egypt in the region of Goshen. They acquired property there and were fruitful and increased greatly in number'.*

There is some debate how long the Israelites were in Egypt, God said they would be in Egypt 400 years.[47]

For the years of famine Joseph had looked after them as he did the Egyptians to ensure they all had food through the time of famine.

During the first years the Israelites settled in Egypt, gaining houses flocks and wealth. This continued till Joseph's death some 70 years later.

These were plentiful years where they enjoyed life, the Israelites were a free people living in the land of Egypt. They had land property and possessions and the Bible says they prospered and grew in numbers.

Sadly, things changed, external circumstances started to have an impact on them. Pharaohs died and were succeeded, their views changed, till finally the Pharaoh did not like the Israelites in his land.

It's not clear how devout the Israelites remained after the death of Jacob Josephs father, or of Joseph, but there came a point where the new Pharaoh certainly did not like the Israelites. He was not happy with the number of good things they had, their prosperity and their growing population.

---

47 *'Then the Lord said to Abram, 'Know for certain that your offspring will be sojourners in a land that is not theirs and will be servants there, and they will be afflicted for 400 years.'* (Genesis 15:13)

Pharaoh saw the Israelites as a threat.

Initially he decided to take them as slaves and make them work for their land and possessions.

Then when it was reported to him that the work the Israelites were doing was insufficient he resorted to punishment which his slave drivers became very brutal at.

Did the Israelites get too comfortable in the foreign land?

Did they forget their own God Yahweh?

Whatever happened the Israelites were slaves for several generations, possibly 14 generations or approximately 430 years.

The experience of Israelite slaves in Egypt was grim: we read that one day Moses was walking along and saw a Hebrew slave being beaten by an Egyptian slave master, so Moses intervened and stopped the person doing the beating, but in so doing he killed the Egyptian. I'm sure this was not Moses plan, maybe the slave master hit back at Moses but I guess Moses had not planned to kill anyone that day, if he had I'm sure we would have read about it.

Moses who had grown up in Pharaohs house in the Royal household would have been used to slaves and slave masters and how treat them. There would have been slaves in Pharaohs palace and Moses would have used them.

Maybe the slaves in the Royal palace were not beaten?

He must have seen his people being beaten and have been fully versed in the life of a slave. But on this one day, he saw a slave being beaten in a way that caused him to react, and react violently.

He saw the harsh treatment being meted out to his people and reacted in a like manner, he showed he could beat someone. Was that what he wanted, did he just want to stop the slave being beaten or did he want to cause harm to the slave driver?

Even so, the result could not have been what he wanted, nor even envisioned. I guess he thought his people the Israelites would see him as a Hero, it didn't happen: even his own people were frightened of him and wanted him to leave them alone.

So Moses fled before Pharaohs guards could capture him.

There were consequences of Moses killing an Egyptian slave driver. Moses he had to flee, to stay would have been death for him because Pharaoh was angry and wanted him dead.

Moses had to walk to find somewhere safe, he couldn't go in a caravan, (long group of camels and people that travelled together for safety).

He walked the desert, he would not have been able to pop home and stock up, he went as he was, possibly bare footed and travelled some say between. 100 – 300 km to Midian.

There is no real accurate location of Midian in Moses time, but it was through the desert: he probably travelled for up to 30 days.

The consequence for the Israelites of Moses killing the guard and running away, is they had to wait for another generation to pass before they would be released.

I wonder how different it would have been if Moses have not killed the Egyptian guard and had just gone to Pharaoh and said look the way my people are being treated is wrong?

Would Pharaoh have listened? Would Pharaoh have been more responsive to God.

However, Moses knew he had got it wrong, knew too that Pharaoh would send his best troops after him to capture him and kill him.

So he ran away to another land because what he had done was wrong? or because of his fears for his own life?

I think the latter?

However, the Israelite people did call out to God and seek his help to set them free.

The Israelite people saw their fortunes change from times of plenty to deep enslavement and bondage. The place of hope, food, succor, and plenty had become a place of pain, sorrow and death.

For many people today events happen to them in their lives that appear on the surface to be good for them, places that initially seem to provide for all their needs. Places and situations where there is much rejoicing, it seems that in all they do, they prosper.

Other people make decisions about them, that again initially that appear to be good, then one day for both groups, it all changes, that which they thought was safe, becomes a house of horror or a land of slavery and torture.

I have worked with many young people and adults who have started to use cannabis or experimented with drugs. They have liked the feelings and the experiences they get with the drug, they have had a measured usage, not spent too much money or taken too many puffs, and then suddenly it all goes horribly wrong.

It seems a sudden change, one minute their drug use is well under control, the next minute chaos.

They become addicted to the drug needing more and more and spending more and more. Their bodies start to react, they can't get the day going without their drug of choice, they borrow and borrow more and more money or steal to pay for their new Master.

Before long they have lost their house, family and in some cases they have lost their lives. How did it go so wrong? They were just 'experimenting?!

I have worked too with people who have been in a loving relationship. The person of their dreams suddenly becomes a monster. Their life has changed and they are abused by the person they trusted and their world has collapsed. How did it go so wrong?

Sometimes disaster creeps up on us we have done nothing wrong or indeed we have not in any way contributed to the disaster that has befallen us. How did it go so wrong?

The Israelites find themselves as captive slaves, how did it go so wrong?

We can at that time only do what the Israelites did and call out to God to save us.

The disciples of Jesus from a different point of view must have asked that question, after Jesus died on the cross. 'How did it all go so wrong?

Praise God that Jesus rose from the dead and is alive today, we can call out to him and he hears us and he will save us.

The Israelites had probably tried to persuade Pharaoh that they were being treated unfairly, and were unhappy. But pharaoh was not prepared to listen, the Israelites needed a more direct approach. When we find ourselves in the 'land of Egypt' or we are slaves we need to do as the Israelites did and pray the Lord will set us free.

We need to pray; God release me from my oppressor.

God will respond to our cry, he sent Moses to set the captives free from the Egyptians, today we call out to Jesus Son of God to set us free and he will do just that.

Like he said on day he went into the temple and read the scripture out load as recorded in Luke 4:18-19;

'The spirit of the lord is upon me, because he anointed me to preach the gospel to the poor. he has sent me to proclaim release to the captives, and recovery of sight to the blind, to set free those who are oppressed, to proclaim the favorable year of the Lord.' [48]

48 http://biblehub.com/luke/4-19.htm

If as you read this, you realise you are a captive pray to Jesus and he will set you free. Sometimes the journey to freedom is long, painful, convoluted, sometimes it is rugged but you will be free.

I recently had the privilege of working with Christian refugees that had travelled from places like Iran, Iraq and Syria where they had been the victims of terrible crimes against them and their families, they had lost loved ones, experienced horrendous torture, seen family members executed before their eyes, and all their possessions taken, but somehow they had escaped.

The journey for many was long arduous and dangerous, some dying on the way, but they died free people, and those who made it to the west had the opportunity of new lives, not perfect, not necessarily flowing with milk and honey, but for sure, safe, with the basic needs provided for and people working to support them and help them adjust to the new world they now are in. They all were praising God for his grace and for setting them free, for being with them on their journey: for giving them a new hope: a new life.

But Pharaoh was not listening.

Pharaoh was a stubborn man, he believed he could argue against the God of creation, because of his stubbornness millions would die. He was so stubborn that even after letting the Israelites go free he chased after them and that led to his death and those who were with him.

Pharaoh had turned against the Israelites, it might be argued that he had inherited 'the problem', he had not seen the famine, nor had he understood the help the Israelites were to his nation. Whatever, he had become their enemy not their friend.

Pharaoh was concerned that the Israelites would take over his Kingdom, that they consumed too much and that they were multiplying, meaning the problem could only get worse. He was after all the King of his Kingdom and he wanted it to thrive.

He would fight against any threat real or imagined.

We don't have numbers of Israelites and Egyptians but at the time of the Exodus it is estimated the Israelite nation numbered between 1.5 and 2.5 million people. That's a huge body of people to have in your land. Further estimates say there were approximately 3-4 million Egyptians in the land at the time.

So the Israelites may have been a body the size of 50% of the population.

I wonder how modern-day leaders would feel at such an 'invasion'.

We know how Hitler responded to the Jewish population.[49]

According to 1933 census there were 505,000 Jews in Germany out of a total population of 67 million.

Or 0.75 percent.

Pharaoh had far more people in his land, maybe we can understand his concerns, fears and anxieties not his response.

The Israelite's leaders tried to talk to Pharaoh and get him to ease their burden to make life better for them, but he would not listen. However, God in his heaven heard their cry and decided to answer their call for help, he was going to set them free.

Gods ways are not our ways: generally, he will not do things the way we plan to do them. However, when we look back and see what God does, invariably we say WOW, how

49 United States Holocaust Memorial Museum.

good was that. It is often the case that people seek God for help and then try and sort things themselves, it really is not a good way to go about things.

Moses had grown up in the Royal place in a very privileged position, he was adopted by Pharaohs daughter, he would have had the best food, education, training, clothes and servants to help him. It would have been a very good place to live your life all the while the Pharaoh and his daughter were alive.

Moses would have been able to wander anywhere in the kingdom that he wanted, the fact that he was walking on his own suggest that he had not done anything to upset any of the Egyptian royal family so he was free to do what he wanted, when he wanted.

We read in Exodus 2 that when he had grown up Moses 'went out to where his people were and watched them at hard labour, he was interested, maybe there was a deep-seated understanding of his roots:

Maybe he was checking on his roots, maybe he had heard in the palace that the Israelite were complaining.

Whatever the cause Moses goes out and sees a Hebrew slave being beaten by an Egyptian guard. We don't know if this was the first time he had seen a Hebrew slave being beaten.

His response was not totally a crime of passion, or heat of the moment, because we read he looked about to check no one was around and then he killed the Egyptian guard and buried his body in the sand.

The following day two Hebrew slaves were fighting and Moses was out and about so he went to them and tells them to stop fighting, their response shocked Moses, 'or what they say, will you kill us as you killed the Egyptian guard'?

Moses then became afraid and fled. He knew that if Pharaoh heard he had killed a guard, he would have been either dead or forced to work as a slave and he would have been brutalized by the other guards.

When Pharaoh heard what Moses had done he sent people to kill Moses but Moses by then had fled from Egypt.

We can understand that Moses was trying to sort the problem of the slaves being beaten, he may have had some success if he had talked to Pharaoh, he may have had success if he had prayed, maybe God would have used Moses then.

Maybe all the deaths and suffering of slaves would have ceased?

Saved 40 years in the wilderness?

But Moses tries to sort the problem himself and it backfires, his life is at risk, he loses his home, place and position and becomes a fugitive, an asylum seeker in a foreign country.

God is able to answer our prayers to undertake for us in every situation, true it seems sometimes his timescale is not the same as ours, however we should give him the chance to answer the prayers first.

Then having prayed we need to be in faith that God will provide the answer because many millions can testify that he does. A friend used to say God is always late, if we start our prayers from that standpoint we will invariably pray not with the 'grain of mustard seed' faith but with unreality; we pray expecting for God to miss our point or time of need: therefore, we will then start planning how too sort things if God doesn't show up. At that point God will leave it to us.

Recently I needed new tyres and brakes for my car and also to pay a bill for a course I was going on.

On the Thursday I prayed – 'Lord I need money for the tyres and brakes'. Of course, I had no savings but a credit card.

I knew God did not want me to use the card, but the bills had to be paid.

So I prayed and told him that if I did not receive some money, I would not be able to pay the bills unless I put them on the credit card, which I believed God did not want me to do.

The following Monday a cheque arrived in the post (unexpected source) that covered the cost of the bills.

Praise the Lord. He is faithful.

If you are aware of someone you love that is not free but being held captive, seek the Lord for them, Jesus says he 'came to set the captives free,' they or you or together you must ask him: then watch what He will do.

Just to clarify, captives can mean someone with an addiction, someone being held in in an inappropriate relationship, someone being still affected by abuse they suffered as a child: someone who is maimed or someone suffering a chronic illness. It may also include victims of crime. We can become captives to so many things.

To be a captive is to be held by greater power against your will, when we look at ourselves we often wonder why do I do that? We can be disappointed with our responses to situations, but God wants to intervene and set you free.

Now if a friend of yours or you are someone who is in prison for a crime you or they have committed, then I would suggest that the consequences of the crime namely the prison time will still need to be completed.

God will heal you and set you free from all the spiritual and social issues, but sometimes there are consequences of our actions that will need to be worked through.

I would suggest the problems for the Israelites started because they spent longer in Egypt than they should have.

They went there because there was a famine, because

Egypt by Gods providence was a place where they would survive.

God had taken Joseph from being a slave to being the most important person in the land. God gave Joseph the interpretation of Pharaoh's dream.

Pharaoh gave Joseph total responsibility to ensure that all the people were fed during the famine. The answer to the dream told Pharaoh and the Egyptian people that they would be fine if they followed Joseph, that in the years of famine they would all be fed, and so it was.

The Israelites continued to live in Egypt after the famine, they settled, they intermarried they became craftsmen at working gold. They stayed in the land until Joseph died. Did they miss signs from God?

Were they supposed to return to their land? We don't know, but we know when they cried out to God he answered their prayer.

When we follow what God wants we will be fine, however if we try and do things our way or change the way God has planned things to happen, then our troubles start.

The more you seek God and follow his plan the more you will see him work.

If you are going to enter a time of famine, he will ensure that there is sufficient food for you and your family.

We read in 1 Kings 17:7-16, that the brook has dried up because there has been no rain in the land and Elijah the Prophet is told by God to go to a village to a widow who will feed him. Elijah does as God directs and when he meets the widow he asks her to feed him.

Her reply is that I was about to 'cook a last meal for my son and I, we will then die as there are no crops'.

Elijah tells her first to feed him then to feed her son and

herself, and that God promises her that the jars of oil and flour will not run out until the rain comes again,

That is what happened as she obeyed God she and her son survived, did not starve nor did they die because of the famine.

It is vitally important that we try and hear Gods voice and do what he says, then all will be well for us and those we love.

In our 21st century we have the knowledge that Jesus, Son of God, Messiah, came that he died and rose again for us, we know that if we commit our lives to him we have a hope and a promise that will never fade or fail.

Jesus died and rose again that we might live and have eternal life, that we can be free from all the chains that bind us.

That one day he will come and take us to His Father's house in heaven where he tells us there are many mansions and a place is prepared for us.

So, how can we live in a land and not conform to the views that oppose our belief?

The Israelites knew this problem, the line from Psalm 137 gives us some idea of the challenge. The Psalm was written about the Israelite captivity in Babylon, a much shorter period than when they were captive in Egypt.

The Psalm is often attributed to the prophet Jeremiah. (Psalm 137:4 *'How shall we sing the LORD's song in a foreign land?'*)

Daniel, who was a good example of how to live in a foreign land and still serve God, was held in high esteem by King Nebuchadnezzar, He had interpreted dreams for the King, no one else could. He had proven that by observing the food laws the Jewish people observed he was healthier than the people who followed the Kings plan.

One day the King had made a Golden statue of himself and said that everyone had to bow down to it or face a terrible death. Daniels friends, Shadrach, Meshach and Abednego were seen ignoring this command, so they were cast into a furnace for ignoring the Kings rules.[50]

The story tells us that the King was so angry he had the furnace made seven times hotter than normal. That the guards who pushed the young men into the furnace were killed by the heat from the furnace.

Yet the King observes four people in the furnace, because their God was with them.

When they come out, there is not even the smell of burning on their clothes!

The king honours them and their God, the God of creation God the Father, one with the Son and Holy Spirit. One God three in one.

It is possible we may have to sing our song in a strange land. When I was young Great Britain was called a Christian land; so much has changed; at present the influences in this land have changed, in many areas we have moved away from Christian public worship in schools.

The established church has watered down much of its biblical foundations: it has started on paths that are not in keeping with the Bible.

Some will argue this is the way to honour God in a 'foreign land', to water down your values, to decry your holy scriptures. To try and be all things to all men.

However, if Daniel and his friends are to be an example we need to remain strong to our beliefs, to our holy book the Bible: to seek God for Him to answer and help us.

---

50 Daniel 3.

CHAPTER 8

One God?

One God who can do all things: One God who does not slumber.

Depending on where you live, what culture you grew up in your views of God will be influenced by your culture.

It can be hard to understand what is right and what is wrong: even if there is a God?

Who is God?

Where does he come from?

How do I find him?

In some countries your life is at threat if you do not follow certain belief structures. Irrespective of whether you agree with them or not.

Yet in other countries if you don't follow the 'national religion' you are at best ostracised.

In some other countries you become aware there are as many different gods as there are temples in their honour. Some religions have millions of gods or deities.

In the western world it may be argued some churches promote their denomination rather than their God. People often refer to themselves for example as Anglican, Baptist, or Catholic rather than as Christians. No wonder many non-believers are confused.

There are many gods in the eastern world, for example for the Hindu there are over 30 million deities or gods. We live in a world where it always has been that each tribe or nation or people group appears to have their own belief structure and gods.

For the Judeo-Christian believers there is One God, the Jews believe in Yahweh.

To the Christian, it is one God in Three Persons. Known as:

God the Father, God the Son and God the Holy Spirit. The Triune God.

As Christians we believe that Jesus is God the Son. This same God is also the God of the Jews; he was their God before the Christians were adopted into his family. He is God of the Jews.

That same God brought the children of Israel out of Egypt and put them in the promised land. We as Christians are adopted into his family.

Now the Bible says the God of Israel and the God of the Gentile (those not born a Jew) is the same God, he was there before the beginning of time, he created the world.

He is an amazing creator God, able to make the earth and the heavens the seas and all that live therein.

Right at the very beginning of the Bible[51] we can see there is more to GOD, than just creator, which in itself is not a bad CV. In verse 2 of Genesis 1, we read now that the spirit of the Lord was hovering over the water.

God was not alone, he says 'let us' make mankind in our own image, God wanted to create a being that had aspects of the Godhead in them.

51 Genesis 1 *'In the beginning God created the heavens and the earth. Now the earth was formless and empty, darkness was over the surface of the deep, and the Spirit of God was hovering over the waters.'*

The Bible says God the Father created man in his own image, again the words we read in Genesis 1 suggest Mankind was created in the likeness of God therefore it is natural that there is a spiritual aspect to man. (*'And the Spirit of God was hovering over the waters.'*). [52]

Right at the beginning of time the Spirit of God was there, God is spirit and if man is made in his own image man will be spiritual.

Jesus before his crucifixion when he went to be with his Father, said that he would leave the 'Comforter' with us on earth, the Comforter also known as the Holy Spirit, the same Spirit of God that was there in the beginning as told in Genesis. In John 1:1 in the opening verses we read:

> *'In the beginning was the Word, and the Word was with God, and the Word was God. He was with God in the beginning. Through him all things were made: without him nothing was made that has been made. In him was life, and that life was the light of all mankind. The light shines in the darkness, and the darkness has not overcome it'.*

I love this part of John: the confirmation of the Bible story that God with Jesus and the Holy spirit was there in the beginning, that through him all things were made.

I think that David Guzik in his Enduring Word Bible commentary explores this opening to the book of John so well.

'And the Word was with God, and the Word was God:

With this brilliant statement, John 1:1 sets forth one of the most basic foundations of our faith – the Trinity. We can follow John's logic:

52 V.26 *'Let us make mankind in our image, in our likeness'*

- *There is a Being known as the Word.*
- *This Being is God, because He is eternal (In the beginning).*
- *This Being is God, because He is plainly called God (the Word was God).*
- *At the same time, this Being does not encompass all that God is. God the Father is a distinct Person from the Word (the Word was with God).*
- *So, the Father and the Son (the Son is known here as the Word) are equally God, yet distinct in their Person. The Father is not the Son, and the Son is not the Father. Yet they are equally God, with God the Holy Spirit making one God in three Persons'.*[53]

The God of the Bible is far more than people understand and this same God loves us! Jesus when he walked on the earth knew we needed some help, Jesus had to die so we could be saved and have the comfort and power of God the Holy Spirit in our lives.

However, spirituality as given by God is something special. The gift of the Holy Spirit is unique, special, amazing. It is totally different from our 'spiritual' ideas. The Holy Spirit is a person: being part of the Holy Trinity.

Whereas in our 21st Century post-modernist relativism, spirituality has become to mean anything that makes you feel good, anything ethereal, anything that we can't immediately explain.

For many Spirituality bears little resemblance to the aspect shown by the Holy Spirit in the Godhead. Many drug users talk about the experience of taking an illegal substance as spiritual. This is not what God intended.

Jesus said when he met with the disciples after his resurrection. I will send the Comforter, The Helper, the Holy Spirit.[54]

---

53 ©2018 David Guzik – enduringword.com
54 John 16:7-8

God is more than just a Loving Father, he sends his Spirit to assist us to do his will, he also endues us with his spirit.[55]

The meaning of endue is to invest in, to empower to clothe. God invests in us so that we can be his people and do his will.

Our God investing in us!

How special God is. He empowers us through the Holy Spirit, the Bible says he clothes us with robes of righteousness, *'I will rejoice greatly in the LORD, my soul will exult in my God: For He has clothed me with garments of salvation, He has wrapped me with a robe of righteousness'*, (Isaiah 61:10).[56]

Through the shed blood of the lamb[57] through the power of the Holy Spirit.

Right from the moment we come to know Jesus if we are willing we experience a Creation miracle where we are made new, where the old is past, as we repent and follow Jesus, he changes us by the power of his Holy Spirit and we are made new.

Then we are baptised and filled with his spirit and go on being filled through our daily lives as we walk with Jesus. Paul writes to the Corinthian church we are baptised by one spirit.[58]

In Egypt the Israelites had not received the Baptism in the Holy Spirit because Christ had not yet come into the world nor yet risen from the dead. The Israelites had Holy priests who acted for them. God instructed the Israelites how to worship him, who to appoint as priests and what they were to do.

55 1 Corinthians 4:13

56 Isaiah 61:10

57 Revelation 12:11

58 *'For by one Spirit we were all baptized into one body, whether Jews or Greeks, whether slaves or free, and we were all made to drink of one Spirit'.* 1 Corinthians 12:13

However, sadly, many turned from God and followed the gods of the people of Egypt.

Those who remained faithful to the God of Israel, the God who created the world and saved the nation from famine: they all prayed and complained to God about their suffering, they called out to him and he heard them.

Now God was naturally unhappy that people did not normally respond to him, only calling out when they were in trouble. That the people he created and the nation he chose to be his people were more interested in making gods out of gold, as the Egyptians did, also they worshipped many gods including those based on animals and planets.

God (Yahweh) the God of creation was not happy about the Israelites worshiping other gods and not following him, having said that, God was also not happy about their suffering and not happy about the way the Egyptians were beating and abusing the Israelites. God has shown that he will save a remnant, so he heard their cry and set a time to speak to Moses to tell him (Moses) that he would be God's tool to lead the Israelite people out of Egypt.

God does more than one thing at a time. So why Limit God?

God heard their cry is a simple statement, yet for many people today their god's are not awake, do not hear them. These gods are in truth just pieces of wood or metal statues.

In some cultures, when you get to the temple of your god, there is a bell, this needs to be sounded to wake up the god. The God of the Christian neither slumbers or sleeps,[59] he has no need of sleep he is a tireless God who watches over the earth 24 hours a day 365 days per year.

59 Psalm 121:4

Yet sometimes it seems as though God does not answer our prayers, more often than not this is when God is using someone (a human being not an angel) to answer that prayer and the person fails.

Having said that God is outside time he is not limited by our time scales or timeframes. Whilst he sometimes chooses to answer our prayer through human beings, he is not bound by time.

God created time, there have been debates by theologians over the years as to whether God is bound by time or whether for God it is as the Apostle Peter says 'one day is like a thousand years'.

I believe that God is outside of time that he is not limited by our concept and experience of time but that he operates within our time frames because that is how we work.

I have seen God heal immediately, answer a prayer in the moment and at other times there has been a delay in the answer and yet, in hindsight everything makes sense.

If he is God, then he has the power to do what he wants when he wants in the time that he wants. The gods of the Egyptians were man made and therefore limited by man: And of themselves had no power only the power that man gave them. God in scripture challenges and at times mocks the gods of man,

Deuteronomy 4:28 (ESV) *'and there you will serve gods of wood and stone, the work of human hands, that neither see, nor hear, nor eat, nor smell'.*

God is reminding his people he is a living, breathing creative God, why would you give up on him for a piece of wood?

So God heard the Israelites prayer and in the same instance prepared Moses to be his tool for the task.

However, Moses doesn't just say OK God lets go, he prevaricates, God was patient with Moses even though he makes God angry, nevertheless God has his way and Moses starts on the most momentous journey of all time.

At the time he sends Moses on his way he has already got his brother making his way to meet Moses.

Now communication then was poor, they had no satellite navigation only the stars, no mobile phones or any of the methods of communication we take as natural today, email, text, phone, Twitter, Facebook, etc.

Yet they would meet in the wilderness, we don't know if either of them waited for the other but we do know they met. Today it can be a nightmare meeting a friend in the middle of a city, yet they met in the middle of the desert!

God said to Aaron go into the wilderness and meet your brother, in order that he might accompany Moses as God's messenger on his journey to Egypt.

Whilst preparing Moses and Aaron God is also preparing the Israelites and also speaking to Pharaoh.

Now I don't know what you think, but 'go into the desert and meet Moses' is a bit of a vague statement? God is sending Aaron on a mission, it is a very special mission, there appears to be a lack of detail in the instruction, there is no GPS, no map, just go into the desert. It's a big place, maybe Aaron says that to God, or even, where in the desert? Talk about needing a divine appointment.[60]

God is able to multi task to be outside time, he works in

60 Divine appointment. An apparently coincidental encounter or event that has actually been caused by God for some specific purpose. This purpose may be obvious during the encounter, or the purpose may become apparent only some time later. www.dictionaryofchristianese.com/divine-appointment

each aspect of every situation you invite him into, he is not merely spinning plates to keep things going he is able to do immeasurably more than we can imagine,[61] he will bring anything that he starts to a conclusion, he prefers to work through his people, where they don't work with him he will complete the task himself.

Many of us have an idea, a need, a situation that we can't handle and so we pray *Lord help!* It is often said there were no Atheists in the trenches, men in war zones call out to God.

Lord help! is the shortest prayer and is a great prayer, God's response is yes and amen, however, at this point many people take the problem back from God.

Almost like saying 'hey God I need help here',

Gods response is ok, trust me

We say 'You will help that's amazing Thanks'

Then: We say well perhaps I'll start to sort it.

We take the problem back ourselves, the *'me do it' syndrome*. Why ask God if we are not going to let him into our situation. My children used to say when anything needed doing 'me do it'

Toddlers want to do far more than they are able to do so they often fall over.

I can do it, oops I've fallen over, but they will keep on trying and trying, and falling and trying till they master it.

Sometimes it is better to let someone else more / better equipped than us do the task.

That's why we go to God because he is far more able than us.

Why then having asked God to help us, do we take back the task, we already know we can't do?

61 Ephesians 3:20

We are putting ourselves in a place where we can't cope.

In business there are sayings about promoting people to the level of their own inability, for example 'In a hierarchy, every employee tends to rise to his level of incompetence.' Laurence J. Peter, The Peter Principle.

When we seek God to solve a problem that we have already decided is beyond us, taking it back is the same as promoting ourselves to a level of our own inability, it will fail it will not be a surprise: we had already realized we couldn't cope, it would end in failure, that's why we prayed: we can't do it alone. it won't work. We need to let go and let God.

In those places and countries where you need to ring a bell to wake a god, I can understand people taking back the problem, but Jesus taught us to cast all our cares on Him. He and his Father are well able to deal with each of our problems at the same time.

As he never slumbers or sleeps he can answer our prayer whenever it is made, if he created all things and made man in his image, he can 'handle' all that troubles us.

Jesus walked on the earth as man and understands the many trials, challenges, temptations and good things that crowd into our lives.

Nothing we face, will face, or experience will be new to God.

So when you pray and ask God to help: let him do it! He will, he's got your back, he wants to go with you.

The Israelites prayed to the Lord, help!

God heard their prayer and prepared Moses and Aaron to see Pharaoh, so that the people could be set free from slavery and abuse.

God prepared Moses and Aaron, at the same time he prepared the Israelites to receive Moses

Thankfully God is not limited by time or any other constraint we face.

He is eternal, He was in the beginning and He is now. He is not temporal: the Bible says God is Spirit. John 4:24. ESV. *'God is spirit, and those who worship him must worship in spirit and truth.'*

God is also not bound by only doing single tasks as man is so often accused of being.

We read in Exodus 4 that while talking to Moses God starts Aaron off on his journey to meet Moses and God opens the door for them to have an audience with Pharaoh.

Moses had been afraid to go back to Egypt in case Pharaoh and those who were close to Pharaoh when Moses killed the guard, were still wanting to kill Moses for killing their guard.

But God knowing all things says to Moses 'its ok to go back to Egypt those who wanted to kill you are all dead', so Moses was safe to return to Egypt.

Moses is reassured. Probably!

Moses and Aaron met together in the wilderness, I'm not sure how easy it would be today with satnav to meet someone in the wilderness, imagine what it was like several thousand years ago with no help. It had to be a divine meeting.

So Moses and Aaron travelled to Egypt and met with the Israelite leaders.[62] Simple!

However, it was not just Moses and Aaron that travelled to Egypt. We read Moses took his wife and sons: there is no clear text about Aaron but one would believe he did not travel alone either.

62 Exodus 3:29. *'Moses and Aaron brought together all the elders of the Israelites, and Aaron told them everything the Lord had said to Moses. He also performed the signs before the people, and they believed. And when they heard that the Lord was concerned about them and had seen their misery, they bowed down and worshipped'.*

Did they take food for the journey?

How did they navigate?

Were they safe walking through the desert with a donkey to carry their kit?

They only had to walk for a couple of hundred miles through a desert, with their families and their possessions, pitch tent each night.

In those days it has been estimated that a man would travel twenty miles in a day. So 200 miles about a 10-day walk. However, Moses and Aaron had their families with them. I wonder what reasonable pace they could they walk at?

Even though they were used to walking in that type of environment I would have been surprised if they had travelled more than 12-15 miles per day. I think it would have taken weeks to get to Egypt. They would have had to carry food, tents, clothes and all that they needed. Would they have taken sheep for food? That would have slowed them down.

Moses has done this before the other way, but not with his family, it would be a good training to prepare them for the future. For the Exodus.

The future? They didn't know the future, Moses and Aaron and their families didn't know that they would spend 40 years in the wilderness!

God knew but didn't tell Moses it would have been too much for him to handle.

Moses, Aaron, and their families knew God was sending Moses to Egypt, to speak to Pharaoh and tell him that God wanted Pharaoh to set the Israelites free.

They had an idea it was going to be a challenge, God told Moses 'I will harden Pharaoh's heart' (Exodus 4:3). It didn't sound as though it would be easy.

In life it is best not to know the future, good or bad.

We can over prepare and then freeze when we have a challenge to face, or become over confident and respond wrongly.

God wanted Moses to trust him, it was his plan and God wanted a servant (Moses) who would do things God's way and not try and sort it alone.

Moses and Aaron and their families set out on a long trek through a very tough desert, we don't know what they thought would happen.

We can imagine the discussion at night after they have made camp, cooked their meal and put the children to bed.

How will we get to see Pharaoh and why didn't God just speak to him?

How's your Egyptian?

We will talk with Pharaoh: how do you think he will receive us? Will the palace be the same?

Gods says he is gonna 'harden Pharaohs heart 'what will that mean? Pharaoh is not gonna be in a good mood. When he is angry he can be very violent.

Eventually though Pharaoh will let the people go, and then God will show us where to lead them: then in a few months we will be able to go home.

Or the children saying 'are you going to fight with Pharaoh Daddy'? 'Will you kill him Dad'!

Little did they know they would be in the desert for forty years, that they would probably not see 'home 'again. The dessert would become their new home!

God had said go to Egypt, they went trusting that God would provide for all their needs, they made it to Egypt.

Amazingly they made it to Egypt or is it? They were following God's plan. He had sent them, He (God) would ensure they got to Egypt.

CHAPTER 9

Sins of Moses?

Other than killing the guard, Moses appears not to have had any sins?

When we come to Christ we confess our sins and the Bible says *'if we confess our sins, he is faithful and Just to forgive us our sins'* (1 John 1:9)

God forgives what we have done wrong, however generally we continue to do wrong which is why as Christians we need to daily confess our sins to God, and pray for his forgiveness for the things we do in the here and now.

It says in 1 John 2:1 *'But if anyone does sin, we have an advocate with the Father, Jesus Christ the righteous'*. For me it seems that it would be better if it said *when* we sin not *if!*

However, for many of us there are areas of sin that we hold back from God for many reasons, including,

- Fear of being found out,
- Fear of public shame:
- Loss of position,
- Sense of self disgust,
- The sin happened when we were not Christians and we forgot it
- We haven't seen it as a sin
- We don't want to lose the pleasure of the behaviour
- We have made friendships/relationships and we will have to break them?

Moses was in that place as he started out to meet Aaron and Go to Egypt.

Moses had not circumcised his son as God required, it was a custom among the Jewish people. (For those unfamiliar with circumcision[63] WebMD had a good article I have enclosed some key points in the footnote.)

Moses had not done what God expected and had therefore disobeyed God.

This was a serious matter to God, if Moses had met with the leaders of Israel and it became known his son had not been circumcised, they would not have spoken to Moses, nor would they have believed he was from God. Not a great start!

We read in Exodus 4: *'At a lodging place on the way, the Lord met Moses and was about to kill him'*. This gives you an idea of how important to God keeping his laws were and are. In those days a new male baby was circumcised on the eighth day. This was the instruction given by God to Abraham. (Genesis 17:10-14).

Circumcision was a sign that the Jewish people were

63 When is circumcision done? Circumcision is usually performed on the first or second day after birth. (Among the Jewish population, circumcision is performed on the eighth day.) The procedure becomes more complicated and riskier in older babies, children, and men. How is circumcision done? During a circumcision, the foreskin is freed from the head of the penis, and the excess foreskin is clipped off. If done in the newborn period, the procedure takes about five to 10 minutes. Adult circumcision takes about one hour. The circumcision generally heals in five to seven days.

Is circumcision necessary? The use of circumcision for medical or health reasons is an issue that continues to be debated. The American Academy of Pediatrics (AAP) found that the health benefits of newborn male circumcision outweigh the risks, but the benefits are not great enough to recommend universal newborn circumcision. The procedure may be recommended in older boys and men to treat phimosis (the inability to retract the foreskin) or to treat an infection of the penis. ©2005-2015 WebMD, LLC.

committed to the covenant made between God and the Patriarch Abraham and his people.

God kept his side of the contract, sadly the Jewish nation often went astray.

However, for Moses by not circumcising his son, Moses was dishonouring the covenant agreement and therefore he would not then be someone the Israelites would respect as a leader.

God had set Moses on a journey and Moses had started, but he still had not circumcised his son. This was a flagrant disregard of both God's law and also the Jewish culture.

Moses would have known the covenant God made with Moses's forefather Abraham. *'any uncircumcised male, who has not been circumcised in the flesh, will be cut off from his people: he has broken my covenant'*. (Gen 17:14).

For God a covenant can never be broken.

A covenant is made with blood: with man a covenant is for the life of the people involved. When God is involved there is only one time frame it is forever.

Moses was in a desperate situation. He had failed to obey God. In those days even if the person Moses had angered was an ordinary leader his position was precarious, he would be lucky to survive. But Moses had angered God, no-one did that and got away with it.

Remember too that when God told Moses to 'go and set his people free' Moses argued with God, pointing out to God that Moses was not able to be the person to undertake the task.

If you remember God initially was patient with Moses and then the scripture states 'Gods anger burned'.

Moses was skating on very very thin ice.

In Jewish law if you as a parent especially a father, failed to ensure your son was circumcised, the leaders could and would punish you. They would enforce the law that you be 'cut off'. No longer regarded as part of the family, or the nation. How could Moses then go and say 'God has sent me'?

To be 'cut –off' in those day was serious, very serious, at the very least one would expect to be expelled from the community and life expectancy on your own in the desert lands would not be good.

How much more vulnerable and a more dangerous situation was Moses in?

He was not answering to humans but to God: the same God who had sent him on a mission to rescue the Israelites to save them from a violent a cruel slave master, namely Pharaoh. The same God who had shewn Moses his power in the desert with the burning bush and then the signs and wonders with the staff.

God could not allow his ambassador to be anything other than pure and correct, and fully compliant with all the covenant laws that existed at the time.

God wanted Moses to show to Pharaoh signs that God was with Moses:

Yet God cannot align himself with sin, disobedience or anything that is not pure.

Pharaoh would have known this and exploited the weakness in Moses.

God's ambassador has to be pure and clean.

Today this is just as true, it doesn't mean we don't sin, but we need to be careful that in our lives we are not doing the opposite to what the Bible says. That we are not living a lie.

Each of us must consider before we start on a path, our behaviour or lifestyle choice.

Asking ourselves, is this in keeping with the scripture? What does the Bible say about my planned actions?

In our 21st Century world there are many temptations before us, society says do what you feel is right. The Bible says, do what is right before God, do not do what he, God has condemned.

The question we must individually answer before God is: if God says in the scripture do not do something or he abhors a practice and we chose to do it, will his anger burn against us?

If we do what God has said is wrong, what will the consequences be?

When David (the King) went with Bathsheba and then arranged for her husband to be at the front of the fighting and be killed: God was very displeased and David paid a heavy price for his sin, there were big consequences for David and Bathsheba.

If dear reader, you are engaged in or planning a course of action or lifestyle that you know God says is wrong, please think afresh and seek God for a way forward that will not leave you vulnerable to God's anger. Don't seek man's confirmation or wisdom, but rather seek what God says on the matter.

The Leaders and Priests of the Hebrew slaves would have been keenly aware of the covenant God had made with Abraham and would neither have listened to someone claiming to come from their God who did not live by the same covenant laws they did. Nor would they have respected Moses or even followed him into the unknown. They would not have allowed him access to their people.

This was a crucial issue for Moses, how could he have found himself in that situation?

Moses may have had a time when he planned to circumcise his son. Or he may have felt living in Midian as a Shepherd it was not so important.

The requirement was set by God that eight days after birth the male child was to be circumcised, this did not apply to female children.

But Moses had not circumcised his son. It appears it wasn't on his mind either.

I am not convinced God wanted to kill Moses as the scripture said, God had just told Moses to go in his name to Egypt. I think God wanted Moses to know that he had sent Moses on such a vital mission. To God and the Israelite nation Moses mission was such an important task that nothing could be wrong in Moses or his family, they could not be spiritually unclean.

As head of the family it was his duty to ensure his family followed the covenant agreed between God and Abraham for all future generations. It is estimated that there were 250 years between the death of Abraham and the birth of Moses, still new enough for the Jewish people all to be aware of the covenant.

There is much debate amongst theologians about this part of the narrative,

Did God appear to Moses?

How did God appear to Moses?

If God was unhappy with Moses why didn't he mention it at the burning bush?

Did God appear to Moses with a sword in his hand?

Did he send an angel?

I think that the commentators that say Moses was very sick near unto death is the more likely scenario: God could have appeared with a sword or sent an Angel, but I don't think that is what happened. I think Moses became so ill it was thought he would die. I understand that some people who have faced a life-threatening illness or a near to death experience often seek God at that time or experience a divine revelation that is life changing for them.

This whole issue is huge: I think this subject could very well be the main theme for another book, so many questions so many possible answers, however I sense God wants me to explore one aspect of this passage.

Moses did not have a Jewish wife he was married to a Medianite woman. He had fled Egypt, so the chance of him finding an Israelite woman to marry, were nil. So he is given as a wife, Zipporah, the daughter Jethro a priest of Midian.

Moses was a stranger in a foreign land: he is given a wife by a (priest) leader of the people.

Moses had grown up in the Royal Household of Pharaoh, I'm not sure how much freedom he would have had to explore and practice his Jewish faith.

Then he marries a woman from a different faith:

I wonder whether Moses and Zipporah discussed circumcising their son., whether Zipporah was against the circumcision?

I would guess Moses was not overly forceful to ensure his son was circumcised, equally I would imagine his wife would not want Moses to cut her new baby. Infant mortality in those days was very high, and circumcising a new baby would probably have seemed barbaric to Zipporah. Especially if it was her first baby and she did not understand the significance of the covenant between God and Moses forefathers.

I suggest Moses and Zipporah had discussed circumcising their son, but Moses had been persuaded by Zipporah to delay doing it. Maybe Moses had agreed not to do it or had said he would leave it till the child was older?

This I believe is an example where 'Egypt' was still in Moses.

He had not paid sufficient attention to his duties as a Hebrew father: it was his responsibility to ensure that his children were brought up in a right way, for a Hebrew boy it was a right that they be circumcised as a baby. Moses had failed.

Moses had grown up in Pharaohs palace, so he would be used to assimilating the beliefs of a strange culture. Moses would have been taught by his mother, the Hebrew ways: but his daily experience would have been that of a young Egyptian boy.

In Midian, Moses was living in a foreign land and probably did little to threaten the stability of his life and marriage especially as his father in law was the high priest.

Insisting that his religious views were adhered to. May have brought him into conflict with Zipporah's dad, maybe the other leaders too.

It might be argued on behalf of Moses that he probably did not expect to return to Egypt or indeed see his people again: that as a shepherd it probably seemed less important to him to be pious.

If Moses had known, he was going to meet God and go on a mission for God it is conceivable Moses may well have changed his behaviour.

We tend to live our lives with little thought given to that day when we will meet God face to face, we get involved in our daily routines, in the minutiae of living. If we lived our lives believing that today would be our last day and that we would come face to face with God, I'm sure most of us would do things differently.

When I was a parent with young children and a sick wife, I had less time for thinking spiritually although I tried, what took most of my time, was how I could keep working to pay the bills, arrange for daily care for my wife, ensure that there was baby-sitting in place for my daughter when I could not be around, (because my wife was in hospital in another town and I was her carer). Additionally, trying to ensure that my son who was older but with different needs was not neglected or ignored.

I wanted to spend time reading the Bible, attending church, spending more time with God, but sometimes it was all I could do to pray as I drove daily to and from London and near the coast.

It's interesting that when God threatens Moses with death whether this was 'just' a serious illness leading to death or whether God appeared to Moses again with a sword in his hand. That it's Moses wife Zipporah who saves the day.

God does not do things by half, if God says you are going to die because you have done something wrong, you are going to die, the only hope is that he will have mercy: God does not make idle threats, he is not given to emotional tantrums., emotional blackmail, no this was serious stuff for Moses and Zipporah.

Thankfully Zipporah appears to understand the nature of the threat from God and the need to respond immediately to 'save' Moses and I would guess she thought she was at risk as was her son.

History shows that wives would feel vulnerable when a threat was issued against the husband it seems that it was normal in those days that if you killed the father invariably you killed the whole family so they didn't become a threat to you in later years. Or the wife was taken as a slave or worse.

Zipporah, reacts quickly, she gets it, if their son is not circumcised then it is probably the end for them all.

Zipporah carries out the circumcision, interestingly she knew what to do.

Very many doctors today would not know how to circumcise a child? Even less mums today would know how to circumcise a child.

Not that it would be allowable in most countries, unless it was conducted by a doctor.

Zipporah's actions certainly save Moses and probably herself and their son.

As Christians today we live under the blood of the new covenant, we are made righteous and acceptable to God through the death and resurrection of Jesus Christ. There is no other way to God. [64] (John 14:6).

We do not live under a covenant of law as Moses did, we are not required to physically circumcise our children, but we are required to love the Lord our God with all our hearts and minds.[65]

In Romans 2 Paul mentions circumcision of the heart, ensuring our heart is completely submitted to God and he is our only god. Willing to sacrifice everything for him: circumcision of the heart, that is the way for the follower of Jesus Christ today.

When God shows us an area in our lives where we have not done what he wants we must respond in the way that Zipporah did, with alacrity. (speed and eagerness). When God convicts us we should take every opportunity to seek the answer and to embrace the learning that we need to undertake.

We do not want to be in that place where God gets angry with us.

We are all called to love God, to obey the great commission,[66]

64 John, 14:6. *'Jesus said to him, 'I am the way, and the truth, and the life: no one comes to the Father but through Me''.*

65 Mark 12:30

66 Matt 28 16-20

making disciples of all nations. 'To be the salt of the earth'.[67]

As Christians, the Bible teaches us about worthwhile lifestyle choices; including visiting the sick, feeding the hungry, loving others as God loves us, and many more.

However, God gives some a special calling to perhaps lead a church, a denomination or a nation.

If God calls us to such a role, then we must prepare for the role ensuring that there is nothing in our lives or behaviour that is incongruent with the calling. Moses was called by God for a special role: it's conceivable that if God had not called Moses to set the Israelites free, God may have allowed Moses son to continue through life without being circumcised.

However, God did meet Moses and give him a special call, vital for the future and well-being of the Israelites, Moses was to be Gods hands and feet to set the Hebrew slaves free.

Therefore, a higher level of purity and commitment and adherence to the covenant relationship was expected of Moses.

Perhaps you will feel the call of God on your life, maybe as the next 'Moses', you will then need to examine all you do very carefully to ensure that you are not knowingly disobeying God.

God called Moses

Moses was going to be meeting Pharaoh on Gods behalf: also as God's spokesman to the Leaders of the Jewish people, he was going to tell them what God was saying, what God was going to do and then he, Moses was going to lead the Jewish nation to freedom.

How wrong would it have been if when doing all these things it had been found out that Moses family was not following the covenant? He would have lost his credibility

67 Matt 5:13

with the leaders of the church and his authority over the people: Moses wife Zipporah acting quickly, saved the mission and the call on Moses life.

What would history have read like if Moses had died on the way to Egypt?

Equally when there is sin in our lives, because that is what disobeying God is, we are no longer effective for God. Or at best our effectiveness s diminished.

We human beings are so easily distracted, when we have major issues in our lives we tend to focus on them finding it more difficult to be 'spiritual'. If you haven't eaten all day and have worked hard, your primary need is for sustenance, not spiritual food.

I have found that if before a prayer meeting I watch something on TV that is dynamic, maybe a motor race, or a dramatic news item, when I close my eyes to pray in the meeting all I seem to see is what I had just seen on TV!

That's a problem, how much more of a problem it would be if what you watch is unsavory, or is ungodly?

Whilst it was vital Moses in his private life obeyed the Abrahamic covenant, I would suggest this whole issue was not about the covenant, but whether Moses was willing to totally obey God and serve him. When he got before Pharaoh would Moses put his own story to Pharaoh or use the words God said.

God wanted Moses to go to Pharaoh and speak his words to Pharaoh, God required Moses to have no 'skeletons in his closet'. In order that he was not constantly distracted or looking over his shoulder, wondering if someone would find out his son was not circumcised.

When Zipporah circumcised their son she fulfilled the covenant law, but additionally she also showed that she was aware of the covenant and that she too was willing to do all that was required under the covenant.

It was important that although Zipporah was a Medianite by birth she was now of the tribe of Israel and as the wife of the soon to be leader of the people of Israel she had to know and obey the covenant law that existed between the people of Israel and God.

In Jewish tradition and culture when a person joined their community as a slave or as guest they were required to keep the rules of the Jewish faith. A male servant was circumcised, any male captured or entering the Israelite nation, would be circumcised.

For the new Christian this is an important lesson to understand.

When we become Christians it is vital that we learn all that we can about what being a Christian means, how to live the life; we learn what the Bible says and what does God require of us. As men, when we come to Christ, we are not required to be circumcised, thankfully, the need for that covenant rule was removed when Jesus went to the cross.

Rather new Christian men and women need to learn and practise as we circumcise our hearts. To repent, dedicate our lives to Jesus, to sacrifice (give up) the things that we previously did that were wrong and turn away from them and be free.

It is a lifetime journey, sometimes it will seem a battle, sometimes be brilliant, but whatever we have the promise as did Moses, that we will not be alone on the journey; for God has said, *'Never will I leave you or forsake you.'* [68]

68 Hebrews 13:5

We may not see a cloud or pillar of fire but God will lead us and guide lovingly by Holy Spirit.

God will never leave us or forsake us, that is an amazing promise first given to the people of Abraham and now repeated to us Christians who have been grafted into God's family through Jesus Christ our Lord and Saviour, redeemer and brother!

CHAPTER 10

Moses' journey and the meeting with Pharaoh

So Moses is on his way to see Pharaoh.

A man on a mission, a mission he did not volunteer for, however, he was called and appointed and obviously Mrs. Moses is going with him, it appears willingly because as we read she saves the day in circumcising their son.

But I wonder what their discussions were about on the journey over?

One, how would they find Aaron?

Will their son be ok?

How will they cope?

When can they go home to Zipporah's family.

What would Pharaoh do to Moses?

Would Moses see anyone from his past?

What a great movie opportunity. Moses to have flashbacks, to thinking about being a child in Pharaohs household.

Picture the scene in the desert:

Moses and family walking along, maybe the odd strong desert wind blowing, clothes being blown around, sand everywhere. It's noisy from the wind, it's hot and very sandy, no respite. In the background the orchestra is playing with big string section and brass to emphasise the wind.

So they stop for a cuppa (or whatever the drink of the day was).

Cue Moses laying down on a rock and gradually fade into Moses as a boy, playing in Pharaohs palace, maybe hide and seek, (I guess it wouldn't have been cowboys and Indians) or practising with a wooden sword.

We see the young Moses, a young handsome boy, clean, in best clothes, maybe adorned with gold jewellery, we see those around him, women dressed like Cleopatra, and men in extravagant pharaoh like costumes. Before a large opulently dressed man in purple and gold robes, all with heavily made up faces.

We see him at banquets, maybe he remembers his step mum?

Maybe we see Moses as he remembers the day he killed the slaves?

And then Mrs Moses starts asking Moses questions about Pharaoh, his palace, what should she wear?

The dream ends and he returns to mile after endless mile walking in the desert, day after day, on and on and on. 'Till one day you see the beginnings of civilisation: skyscrapers, airport?

What would have been a sign of civilisation in those days, I guess there would have been some sign of cultivation, slaves working.

It's been an arduous journey that will have prepared them for the wilderness that is to come although they don't know that at the time.

A few miracles have occurred from the start, the burning bush, Moses staff turning into a snake, (scary) finding Aaron, Zipporah saving the day and circumcising their son.

They arrive in Egypt, ready for the call.

It would have been fascinating to have been on the Journey. Or to have been in the palace and seen Moses before Pharaoh as God's messenger, to have witnessed the way the magicians appeared to be able to equal what God has given

Moses to do. Until Moses snake eats all the others!

To see the meetings, to see the stubbornness of Pharaoh, that he would allow his people to suffer the way the Egyptian people did, because of his decisions.

There is much we can learn about leadership through this whole story.

As Christians, we can see that when you are a slave and the thing or person that has entrapped you is powerful, crafty, manipulative, all-consuming, vicious, violent, or uncaring our ability and chance to get free on our own is nil to extremely small.

We need a powerful warrior on our side. Moses alone could not have persuaded Pharaoh to 'Let the people go'.

He would have been lucky to have kept his own freedom. He could only pass on God's words to Pharaoh, and then he needs God to be all powerful.

For us when we were slaves to sin, trapped in our own lives we needed a mighty warrior to make a way out for us. God has a plan for us just as he had a plan for the Israelite people.

His plan for us was at a vastly higher cost to himself:

John 3:16 says, *'For God so loved the world, that he gave his only Son, that whoever believes in him should not perish but have eternal life'.*

God knew that man had fallen a long way from him, that we had embraced the things of the world, we had followed false gods, we were abusing our bodies, children, vulnerable adults.

We had signed up for things that were of Satan. That did not honour God.

God knows what each of us has done, that does not please

him and one day everyone he has created will meet with him face to face.[69] We shall all give account to him about the way we have led our lives and the deeds we have done, good and bad.

In Egyptian times some of the Israelite people followed the god moloch, that required sacrificing their children in the most awful ways.

God needed a huge warrior, someone who could live in the world and be sinless, to defend the people he created from the power of Satan, the only answer was for him to send his Son, to allow him to die in our place for the wrongs we have done and to defeat forever the power of Satan.

We have the promise in several places in scripture of a new heaven and a new earth[70] and that when we die, those who are in Christ will go to be with him in heaven.

---

69 *'For we must all appear before the judgment seat of Christ, that each one may receive the things done in the body, according to what he has done, whether good or bad.'* 2 Corinthians 5:10.

70 *'Then I saw a new heaven and a new earth. The first heaven and the first earth disappeared, and the sea vanished. And I saw the Holy City, the new Jerusalem, coming down out of heaven from God, prepared and ready, like a bride dressed to meet her husband. I heard a loud voice speaking from the throne: 'Now God's home is with human beings! He will live with them, and they shall be his people. God himself will be with them, and he will be their God. He will wipe away all tears from their eyes. There will be no more death, no more grief or crying or pain. The old things have disappeared.' Then the one who sits on the throne said, 'And now I make all things new!' He also said to me, 'Write this, because these words are true and can be trusted.' And he said, 'It is done! I am the first and the last, the beginning and the end. To anyone who is thirsty I will give the right to drink from the spring of the water of life without paying for it. Those who win the victory will receive this from me: I will be their God, and they will be my children. But cowards, traitors, perverts, murderers, the immoral, those who practise magic, those who worship idols, and all liars – the place for them is the lake burning with fire and sulphur, which is the second death.'*

We Christians are adopted into the family of Christ but we needed his sacrifice for us at Calvary, it needed for Jesus to suffer and die, and then for God the Father to miraculously raise him up. Wow.

For this book we don't need to look at each of the plagues nor yet the story of the escape, other than to realise it had to be done God's way.

If we want freedom from our old lives it has to be done God's way.

There is no other, there is no short cut, it is his way that works.

I don't feel that we should spend chapters on the journey but maybe pick a couple of points we can learn from the time Moses spent on the journey.

So then, what can we learn from Moses journey?

For him it was a time of preparation, a time to understand and remember what life in the desert as a nomadic tribe would be like. A time to get closer to God, to remember his Jewish heritage, maybe even remember scriptures his mum had taught him.

When God calls us on a journey, we need time to prepare, time to get close to him so we can hear what he wants to say to us.

We need to use that time to understand the place where he is leading us:

Franklyn Graham in his excellent book *Through My Father's Eyes,* says that when his father went out on to a mission field, he took time before he started his mission to learn the place, to understand the people and culture and that today Franklyn does the same when he goes on mission.

We should know that God wants us to understand the pace, culture and people where he has placed us or where he is sending us.[71]

We need to use the time to ensure that all our practices are right in God's sight, that he will be able to use us and no-one will be able to stop him.

The time of the journey often is a time to build up our strength for the new calling.

I would encourage you all who have journeyed with me this far to read the account of the plagues and the Israelites leaving Egypt.

We are not going to study the time in Pharaohs palace, although I was tempted to explore what happened, imaging the whole floor covered in frogs?

I remember one day my wife and I coming home and on entering the house we found the whole of the lounge door and surrounds covered in ants.

There were hundreds maybe even thousands, they were spreading up the wall, under the carpet, along the skirting board, onto the lounge curtains.

They were everywhere and my wife was most distressed. I didn't blame her I was not happy. Imagine if that had been frogs?

There are however a couple of key points to consider from the process of setting the Israelites free.

1. The messenger had to be faithful

He had to hold onto his belief in God, constantly be doing and saying only what God wanted him to say and do.

71 *Through My Fathers eyes,* Thomas Nelson: Special edition. 14 Jun. 2018. ISBN-13: 978-0718021801

Jesus was faithful to the end, in Luke 22:42 we read *'Father, if You are willing, remove this cup from Me: yet not My will, but Yours be done.'* Jesus wasn't willing to take a short cut; he knew the reason for his Father's plan, a plan he wanted to be part of. He said *'I only say what the Father has commanded me to say'* John 12:49.

We have a great High Priest, Jesus Christ the Righteous and he has proved faithful even unto death, even death on the cross, His father The Lord Almighty was faithful to raise Jesus up from the dead and give him new life.

So if you believe in Jesus, he will not let you down: he, Jesus, like his Father in heaven is a faithful God. As Christians we serve a faithful Father, Son and Holy Spirit.

2. God showed his power

Egypt at the time of the exodus was a great power, probably the greatest power in the known world: when Moses appeared before Pharaoh and passed on God's message 'to let my people go', the people in pharaohs entourage and roundabout were more inclined to believe that Pharaoh was all powerful.

He was King, he was the one who they believed held their life or death in his hands. When they saw the plagues and experienced the horrible nature of them they realised there was another power, but still stubbornly followed Pharaohs lead. He thought he was stronger than God.

When his magicians threw their staffs on the floor and they became snakes as Moses staff had Pharaoh and his magicians must have felt all powerful, until Moses 'snake ate all their snakes!

This battle continued: who to believe? It continued right until the point of the red sea crossing, when God showed without any possible doubt or debate forever, that he was the all-powerful one.

I am not sure that God wanted to kill Pharaoh and his troops, but God gave Pharaoh many opportunities to let his people go, finally God acted to stop the threat to his people by a cruel Pharaoh and his troops. If you go head to head with God, there is only one outcome, God will win: You and all your supporters will perish.

3. The Israelites had to hold on to their beliefs

Some Israelites intermarried and took on the beliefs of the Egyptians. Several of the beliefs of the Egyptians were against God and his values. Gradually the situation changed and the Israelites became slaves, then over time they became abused slaves, to a point where their suffering was immense.

Those who remembered the God of their forefathers started to call out to God, set us free. Perhaps those same people who were still believing in the God of their forefathers were ostracised or teased or bullied by their fellow Israelites who were following moloch or one of the many other Egyptian gods rather than following 'an ancient God'.

However, those who held onto the God of creation, the God of their forefathers, the God of Abraham, their faith was rewarded God set them free.

4. The people had to obey Gods plan

When we read (see below) the story of the Passover,[72] we may

72 Exodus 12: 1-13. *'The Lord said to Moses and Aaron in Egypt, 'This month is to be for you the first month, the first month of your year. Tell the whole community of Israel that on the tenth day of this month each man is to take a lamb for his family, one for each household. If any household is too small for a whole lamb, they must share one with their nearest neighbour, having taken into account the number of people there are. You are to determine the amount of lamb needed in accordance with what each person will eat. The animals you choose must be year-old males without defect, and you may take them from the sheep or the goats. Take care of them until the fourteenth day of the month, when all the members of the community of Israel must slaughter them at twilight. Then they are to take some of the blood and put it on the sides and tops of the doorframes of the houses where they eat the lambs. That same night they are to eat the meat roasted over*

not understand the relevance of God's instructions but the people of Israel understood. God gave Moses very specific instructions to follow.

- Time, Month (first of their year)
- Set day (10th day)
- Time of day (twilight)
- Lamb (year old)
- Care for the lamb (until the 14th day)
- Lamb (without blemish)
- Blood (take some and put it on sides and top of doorframes)
- Eat the Lamb (roasted, not boiled or raw, eat it that night with herbs)
- Eat bread (without yeast)
- Don't leave lamb till morning, (any left must be burnt)
- Dress: (your cloak tucked in, your sandals on your feet, your staff in your hand).
- Eat it in haste.

God was specific, he needed his people to follow his instructions to the letter, he was going to set them free, and so they needed them to do all he said.

Recently my children had an adventure afternoon.

---

the fire, along with bitter herbs, and bread made without yeast. Do not eat the meat raw or boiled in water, but roast it over a fire – with the head, legs and internal organs. Do not leave any of it till morning: if some is left till morning, you must burn it. This is how you are to eat it: with your cloak tucked into your belt, your sandals on your feet and your staff in your hand. Eat it in haste: it is the Lord's Passover. 'On that same night I will pass through Egypt and strike down every firstborn of both people and animals, and I will bring judgment on all the gods of Egypt. I am the Lord. The blood will be a sign for you on the houses where you are, and when I see the blood, I will pass over you. No destructive plague will touch you when I strike Egypt.'

It was a code breaking afternoon. They were locked into a room and could not get out until they found several different hidden clues and decoded the associated codes. Then they could begin to unlock the door and get free. There were no shortcuts and if you didn't do as instructed you didn't get out.

The only thing that was at stake for them on that day was their pride, if they got it wrong someone would have to let them out. For the Israelites their very lives and the lives of their firstborn was at stake. So they had to do it God's way.

As Christians we need to live our lives understanding that our lives may be forfeit if we don't follow God's plan.

God gives us instructions: we are not under law as Christians but rather God's desires for us should be written in our hearts. Jesus tells us that the commandments we should live by[73] are to love God with all our heart souls and mind, and to love our neighbour as ourselves. That upon these two commandments hang all the law and the prophets.

Our lives should be governed by the commandments not legalistically, but rather as Christ lived his life, to serve those God calls us to serve and to love as Christ loved sacrificially, not counting the cost. Being an example to those around us, allowing the presence of God to flow through us into situations and the people around us.

5. The Israelites had to watch for God's sign.

God gave them many things to do to be ready for God to Passover, he told them that the blood over the doorframes would be a sign for the people of Israel that God would

73 Jesus replied: *"Love the Lord your God with all your heart and with all your soul and with all your mind.' This is the first and greatest commandment. And the second is like it: 'Love your neighbour as yourself.' All the Law and the Prophets hang on these two commandments.'* Matthew 22: 37-40 (NIV)

'Passover' them, they would not be harmed.

As Christians we must be on the lookout for Gods signs to us today, to learn how to hear his voice and respond to his call to us.

6. The Israelites had to obey the leader God gave them

The people did not know Moses until he appeared out of the desert and now he was telling their leaders what to do 'what God said'. This was a huge issue of trust and obedience.

Consider today in our modern world if a new man suddenly, with no known background walked out of the desert and appeared before our Prime minister or before the American President and told them God was saying this... and that the Prime minister or President should lead their nation in a strange / different way. Would they listen? Would the people listen? Would we judge their motives? Would we ignore the person? or even the Prime Minister, or President?

7. If you fight God you can't win even Satan found that out [74]

Human beings often think they are the most superior beings, throughout history we learn of many men and women who thought they either had a divine call or they were divine.

---

74 Revelation 12:7-9 *'Then war broke out in heaven. Michael and his angels fought against the dragon, and the dragon and his angels fought back. But he was not strong enough, and they lost their place in heaven. The great dragon was hurled down – that ancient serpent called the devil, or Satan, who leads the whole world astray. He was hurled to the earth, and his angels with him.'*

Isaiah 14:12-16 *'How you have fallen from heaven, morning star, son of the dawn! You have been cast down to the earth, you who once laid low the nations! You said in your heart, 'I will ascend to the heavens: I will raise my throne above the stars of God: I will sit enthroned on the mount of assembly, on the utmost heights of Mount Zaphon. I will ascend above the tops of the clouds: I will make myself like the Most High.' But you are brought down to the realm of the dead, to the depths of the pit. Those who see you stare at you, they ponder your fate: 'Is this the man who shook the earth and made kingdoms tremble.'* *(continued over)*

History teaches us that they all failed and generally ended up dead.

The Bible says that God created the earth, seas and skies and all that therein is. He is the creator God. The Alpha and the Omega, the beginning and the end. There is no greater God; look for example at the following scriptures:

Deuteronomy 10:17, *'For the Lord your God is God of gods and Lord of lords, the great, the mighty, and the awesome God, who is not partial and takes no bribe'.*

Revelation 1:8 *'I am the Alpha and the Omega' says the Lord God.*

Hebrews 1:3 *'The Son radiates God's own glory and expresses the very character of God, and he sustains everything by the mighty power of his command.'*

Jeremiah 10:12-13 *'But God made the earth by his power, and he preserves it by his wisdom. With his own understanding, he stretched out the heavens. When he speaks in the thunder, the heavens roar with rain. He causes the clouds to rise over the earth. He sends the lightning with the rain and releases the wind from his storehouses.'*

Romans 13:1 *'Everyone must submit to governing authorities. For all authority comes from God, and those in positions of authority have been placed there by God.'*

After God has passed over the Israelites all the first born of the Egyptians are struck down: Pharaoh calls Moses and Aaron to his palace, where he and his household are suffering and tells them to take the Israelite people out of his nation for them to go and worship their God as they had wanted.

What an amazing Moment for Moses and all the people of Israel, yet a terribly sad time for the people of Egypt. Because

2 Peter 2:4 *'For if God did not spare angels when they sinned, but sent them to hell, putting them in chains of darkness to be held for judgment.'*

Pharaoh had refused to hear God's voice he and the Egyptian people suffered great loss. The Bible says they were up all night.

What pain and suffering they must have gone through. All was avoidable.

God had prevailed, Pharaoh now said take the people! Was this the time to party and celebrate, they were being set free?

Actually there was no time for partying, the Israelite people had to be ready to move. God said the Passover meal was to be eaten with cloak tucked in, sandals on feet and sword in their hand. Go!

They were told by God and Pharaoh had agreed that they should ask their masters for supplies and gold and silver, and they were given as they requested.

You may argue the gold and silver belonged to the Israelite nation anyway, when they became slaves it was taken from them.

Whether so or not it was a major thing for the people that had held them captive for so long to give them valuables from what the Egyptians would have regarded as 'their own wealth'.

The people of Israel had to leave: to leave immediately. The Egyptians now wanted them out urgently, we read in Exodus 12:3 The Egyptians urged the people to hurry and leave the country. 'For otherwise' they said, 'we will all die!

The scripture goes onto say that now the Egyptian people looked favourably upon the Israelites.

It is often said by God and man that the Jewish nation is a stubborn stiff-necked people. It would appear from this account that the Egyptian people were also were a stubborn people. So the Israelites left Egypt.

CHAPTER 11

Preparing for the Exodus Journey

This journey to the promised land that should have taken a few months was gonna take them over 40 years!

It sounds so simple to say the Israelites left Egypt.

In our modern world we get the people to meet at a prearranged spot, book a couple of coaches, or book a flight, load the people in and be on our way in a few hours. Simple!

Ok so they didn't have coaches or airplanes so this was gonna be a slow march / walk through the desert. They were used to the heat and the sand the Israelite people had lived in Egypt as a people for over 400 years.

But the task for Moses and Aaron was mammoth. Moses was to lead the people.

There were probably over two million people and herds of sheep!

Moses may have wondered why his Father in Law taught him how to be a shepherd in the desert, but he was about to lead the largest group of people and animals ever gathered on a trek through the desert. Maybe now he understood his last 40 years of training.

Moses was approximately 80 years old when he led the Exodus. Forty years of his life living in Egypt had now been proved valid as he had communicated with Pharaoh. Now the hard part, to use his knowledge of the desert, his management skills and his gifting from God to lead over two million people and animals through the desert. An amazing feat that has never since happened in our world.

It is difficult to be sure how many Israelite people there were that left Egypt: Exodus 12: 37-38 tells us *'Then the children of Israel journeyed from Rameses to Succoth, about six hundred thousand men on foot, besides children. A mixed multitude went up with them also, and flocks and herds – a great deal of livestock'.* NIV

If there were 600,000 men, there would probably have been at least the same number of women plus children, it also says a 'mixed multitude went up with the also' these were probably other slaves, or prisoners of Pharaoh or people who were malcontent with life in Egypt and they saw the power of God.

When you study Jewish scholars, theologians, historians, the estimates for the total number of people who left Egypt is between 1.5 million people and four million people.

We will never know for sure and to an extent it's not too important for our journey here. For me I think there were around two million people that left Egypt that night.

Imagine gathering two million people, telling them we are leaving and to follow me.

Have you ever watched a carnival procession? It moves at its own pace, the person leading tries to set a sensible speed, but in the procession there are people of different ages, abilities, differing skills, methods of transport.

You have bands, dancers, people walking, people in trucks, lorries, cars, some on bicycles. People in costume, the procession meanders along at its own pace and eventually gets to the meeting point. When I was younger I used to marshal on carnival processions, great fun, we had 4x4 vehicles, two-way radios, spotters, breakdown vehicles, replacement vehicles, first aid vehicles yet to keep everything moving at the same pace was an immense challenge.

When governments have tried to evacuate people because

of an impending disaster it has been fraught with difficulty. Invariably it hasn't worked, queues form and people begin to get very distressed.

In Athens in 2018 when there was a terrible fire, many people lost their lives.

There was a lot of accusation that the police did not guide those people fleeing fires and therefore some people were trapped in their cars, stuck in traffic and sadly died in their cars. Whenever there is a disaster people are blamed sometimes unfairly, first responders, emergency service staff and men and women do the best they can in circumstances that take them completely by surprise.

Moving two million people plus herds of sheep and assorted animals in the desert and in a place where there weren't made up roads, must have been a logistical nightmare.

How do you get the message from the start of the procession to the end of the procession?

How do you get them all to stay together?

How do you pass messages from one to another?

What does a gathering of two million plus people look like?

What would 2000 plus sheep and other animals as well look like.

How wide an area would this procession cover?

How long would the procession be?

The questions and challenges facing `Moses and Aaron were incalculable It's bad enough if there are just people, two million people, it's almost impossible to envisage what that would look like.

Help! They could cry out to the Lord. It could only work if God was in it.

How many of you have been on a dog walk and another dog appears? The peaceful calm walk is over as the other dog disturbs the dog you are with or your dog chases the other dog.

The stress mounts, the dogs get excited, the adults get tense, then finally the other owner arrives and generally it all begins to settle.

How do you make your sheep follow you when everyone else's sheep are running around? You need great shepherding skills.

How many sheep were there on the Exodus?

Why were there sheep on the Exodus?

(Well some of them, would be for food).

If each man had 1 sheep there would be 600,000 sheep, if he had 10 sheep = 6 million sheep!

And people say herding cats is tough:

I would suggest leading two million people plus animals in the desert for forty years could only be done under divine guidance.

Moses, the leaders of Israel, the people all had to be open to follow Gods instructions, to make the exodus, to stay together, to survive 40 years and to enter the land promised to the Patriarch Abraham.

Moses led the people of Israel out of Egypt, he led them by the slow route: natural thinking would be let's go by the quickest route to get the people to safety as quickly as possible. But God led Moses by the slowest route.

Moses got all the glory for the exodus, but he knew God guided him to go the slow longer route to avoid going through the land of the Philistines and probably having to fight for their lives.

If the nation of Israel had gone the shorter way and had to fight with the Philistines to survive, then they would have moaned! I would suggest too that many of them would have been killed by the Philistines.

When we read the account of the Exodus it appears leaving Egypt takes no time at all.

The Israelites were all prepared, they had been told to eat the Passover meal ready to move. The messengers would have been sent from Moses to all the places where the Israelites were camped. Then the Israelites would have had to speak to their masters to ask for provisions for the journey and gold and silver, then pack all that up, then they could go.

Getting two million people and animals out in 12 hours seems improbable

To get two million people and animals out of Egypt in 24 hours is not even I would suggest conceivable: however, to get them out of Rameses in that timeframe is. They were ready, they just needed to collect the gifts the Egyptian people gave them and then go!

These were provisions for their journey, items that the Israelite nation would need to set up in a new land.

When we turn to Christ, we don't take gifts from our old life, we shouldn't take the 'gold and silver' of our old worship practices, the special items, icons and pictures of the gods we used to serve.

For the addict we leave behind the paraphernalia of substance abuse. For the criminal the tools of the trade.

But more importantly we leave behind the old mind-set that told us what we did was ok, that our bad behaviour was acceptable and we needn't worry.

Before we were Christians we put ourselves first second and third, when we believe on Jesus Christ as our saviour we put him first, we turn away from our old ways and beliefs; and we embrace the ways of God.

To love God with all our heart, all our mind and all our souls and to love our neighbour as ourselves.

Some might say well, I wasn't an addict, a thug, criminal, a thief before I met Jesus what then do I need to leave behind.

We need to renew our minds, we need to put Jesus first in all we do, we need to learn how to hear the voice of God and do all things in accordance with his will. Paul writes in Romans 12:2 *'Do not conform to the pattern of this world, but be transformed by the renewing of your mind. Then you will be able to test and approve what God's will is – his good, pleasing and perfect will'.*

From our birth we are encouraged, pressured and maybe deceived into believing all that we hear from the world and people within it, that their view of the world is right. Invariably the people we hear do not follow God so we change from being someone who wants to love God into a person that just drifts along, being swayed by the latest fad or invention.

Without a care in the world, not seeing the suffering and abuse that is around us. Not worrying that in practice we are often supporting people and businesses that are working against the will of God.

If we look around us at our local community and ask ourselves the question, is this behaviour or practice something that God would approve of?

A simple example. Do shops near you open on Sunday? The Bible says in the book of Exodus *'six days shall you labour but the seventh is hallowed and you should do no manner of work'.* In the UK, Sunday was generally regarded as the day of rest. Shops were closed and the main events were attending church.

But over time parliament has waved the laws and now you can do pretty much anything on a Sunday: the reason it was said to take a day of rest was that God knew we needed to rest to break from our works, we also needed to spend time with God. An article in WebMD addressed this issue.[75]

More and more research is indicating something that several Christians have believed for a long time: Namely, that attending church and taking part in an act of worship is good for you and leads to many benefits not least an extended life.

During my research into my first degree I learnt that prayer and meditation increases the levels of dopamine in the brain, this is one of the chemicals in the brain associated with senses of well-being and happiness.

When we turn to Christ and start focusing on him and his ways and spend time in prayer and meditation and worship, we will be transformed, no longer a victim of fear, no longer letting the things that trouble us take control of our lives, no longer filled with self-doubt.

But we become a new man /woman able to be all that God created us to be.

The best place to be is where God wants you to be.

The best relationship to be in is the one that God ordained for you

The best job to have is the one God prepared You for.

---

75 **Go to Church, Live Longer**

Among the most recent findings in this area: People who attend religious services at least once a week are less likely to die in a given period of time than people who attend services less often. These results - published in the August 1999 issue of the Journal of Gerontology: Medical Sciences - came out of a study examining almost 4,000 North Carolina residents aged 64 to 101. People who attended religious services at least once a week were 46 percent less likely to die during the six-year study, says lead author Harold G. Koenig, M.D., of Duke University Medical Center in Durham, North Carolina. 'When we controlled for such things as age, race, how sick they were and other health and social factors, there was still a 28 percent reduction in mortality,' he says. www.webmd.com/balance/features/spirituality-may

The best of everything is to listen to God's plan and follow that.

God knows what is best for us, he made us, he knows how we are wired: after we have been Christians for a while and been through some challenges and some great times, we know that the sensible thing for us is to submit our ways to the Lord. 'And he shall direct our paths' Prov. 3:5-6

God does not want to harm us: he wants us to prosper. He wants us to be all that he created us to be, he wants us to be a blessing to those around us.

God made us a people in his image: to be a people after his own heart.

So when we get free from our past we need to leave it alone, it has happened let's move on. For some of us we will need a bit of extra support, that's ok too whether that comes from a Pastor, the body of Christ or from a Christian Counsellor God will set you free and heal your wounds.

So the Israelites escaped from Rameses and moved toward the Red Sea.

The distance according to the experts is only twenty-five miles.

I hour at the most in the car. 6-7 hours walking at a military walking pace.

No problem, simple.

Some say it would have taken the two million plus people and their animals two days. Walking at about 1 mile per hour for twelve hours.

For me I think they would have needed more time than that, I have led walks and rambles, people are not always easy to lead, a group that size even wanting to escape the Egyptians would have been unwieldy, making herding cats seem easy!

However, the time the Israelites left Egypt was also a time

of great mourning, in Egypt: every Egyptian family had been affected, they had all lost their first born child. Egyptian culture at that time decreed a 72-day period of mourning.

At the start of the Exodus Pharaoh and his people just wanted the Israelites out of their sight, they were not thinking of revenge or of recapturing the slaves.

They were happy to be shot of them and to mourn.

Then one day Pharaoh says to his advisers 'What have we done'[76]

Notice it's not what have I done, he made the decision. But now it is a collective decision so he shares the blame with his advisors. Pharaoh now realises he and his people have lost all the slaves.

Pharaoh doesn't say let us get some more slaves, or maybe let us learn how to live without slaves?

No, his response is immediate, he gathers six hundred of his best chariots and his other chariots together with his army. Estimates are that Pharaoh took an army of 250,000 men.

That would have taken time too for them to get ready and to start on the journey.

In recent history when Argentina invaded the Falkland Island it took three days for the UK to prepare to send the task force.

76 Exodus 14: *'When the king of Egypt was told that the people had fled, Pharaoh and his officials changed their minds about them and said, 'What have we done? We have let the Israelites go and have lost their services!' So he had his chariot made ready and took his army with him. He took six hundred of the best chariots, along with all the other chariots of Egypt, with officers over all of them. The Lord hardened the heart of Pharaoh king of Egypt, so that he pursued the Israelites, who were marching out boldly. The Egyptians – all Pharaoh's horses and chariots, horsemen and troops – pursued the Israelites and overtook them as they camped by the sea near Pi Hahiroth, opposite Baal Zephon'.*

When your troops are ready you can achieve much, we don't know how long Pharaoh and his troops took to start their pursuit but we know they caught up with the Israelites as they were camped near the sea.

God knew the heart of his people, they had been captives for generations, they were not a fighting force.

They were probably scared, maybe even terrified about what would happen to them. They weren't a trained fighting force, not even sure if any of them had weapons. So to lead the Israelites the short way to safety, where they may have had to fight the Philistines was a non-starter.

God knew this but to lead them on a journey that included crossing water as big as the Red Sea made no sense either.

There is much debating amongst Theologians Historians and Archaeologists, from did the exodus happen to did the Israelites cross the Red Sea, to where did they cross the sea, to how long did it take and also did God intervene.

I don't think it is part of this book to do an in-depth study of the archaeology and history, however, it is worth noting in passing that there is evidence of remains of human bones and chariots in the Gulf of Aqaba the name used for this part of the Red Sea today. Additionally, that there is a column by the side of the sea where it is believed the Israelites crossed over (that has been restored) that dates back 3,000 years and universally is believed to be of Hebrew design.

When the Israelites had crossed the Red Sea they built a column of stones to remind them of what God had done in getting them across the sea.

When we turn from our old lives and respond to the call of God: God will lead us out, he will by his Holy Spirit guide us and protect us. We have to totally believe in him, we have to trust him. We have to do what he says and we have to take the path he chooses.

What would have happened if the Israelites had decided to take the other route via the Philistine land. There would have been no Red Sea to save them from the might of the Egyptian army, nor would they have been able to stand against the might of the Philistines.

The Red Sea at the point of crossing is said to be half a mile wide, it would have appeared to be an immense body of water to people who lived in the desert. As a guide for those who are familiar with the River Thames it is approximately half the width of the Red Sea crossing. The River Seine is only about half the width of the Thames. It would have seemed impossible to cross over that amount of water, even with modern vehicles: additionally, how do you get thousands of sheep and animals across such a vast river?

The Israelites were frightened, they really were between a rock and a hard place.

The Israelites were camped at Migdol, in front of them the Red Sea, behind them the armies of Pharaoh. The old King James translation of the Bible says 'they were sore afraid'. In front of them an uncertain and terrifying future. Behind them, to return as slaves to Egypt with a terrifying and uncertain future.

Uncertain, they were supposed to be going to the promised land but what did that really mean. What would it look like, how could they survive? At least in Egypt they understood their place in the world and had got used to settling for the punishment and privation.

Whilst behind them was an angry Pharaoh with his army, some of them were going to be killed, and those that went back as slaves were really going to be beaten and abused. So they were sore afraid. The Egyptians were really hurting from their suffering at the hands of the God of the Israelites, they would probably not have seen Pharaohs decisions as wrong.

When we turn to Christ and give our lives to him, we don't know what the future holds, we just don't know.

Will we manage to keep going with God?

Will we be able to please God?

Will we be wealthy, happy, fulfilled, safe, complete, healthy, likeable?

Will our friends still like us?

Will we become like some Christians seem to be, bigoted and holier than thou?

So we can become very nervous. But, like the Israelites God will take us and lead us through the Sea into the promised land, if we just put our hand in His hand and hear His voice say I Love you my child. We tell him, I love you Lord, I will serve and obey you.

Then we will crossover through the waters of baptism into the promised land.

God knew his people, he knew their strengths and frailties. So He took the people of Israel the long way, He knew the heart of this people and their capabilities, their fears and anxieties. The people had been slaves for over 400 years, the latter part of those 400 years they had been very badly treated, abused and beaten. For God to have got Moses to lead them via the Philistine lands would have been very risky for them and a disaster. They weren't warriors, they were not trained for battle, they were not even confident or bold. They had been brow beaten and downtrodden for generations.

They were a people used to kowtowing to others, a people who expected to be slaves, a people untrained in battle or warfare: additionally, they were a people with all their families and possessions, their sheep and the valuables they had been given by the Egyptians.

This would not be a good state to come up against a trained Philistine army.

They would have been ripe for destruction and plundering.

So God took them the long way even though when they were camped at Migdol it must have looked pretty bleak, but God knew the outcome. He would ensure they crossed the Red Sea safely.

When we give up our old lives and follow Jesus, sometimes the journey seems long, we may not face an armed Philistine warrior or a troop of chariots, but we will face great temptations. We will have to battle old habits that are bad for us. In addition, the Bible says that Satan is on the prowl looking for opportunity to bring us down. 1 Peter 5:8. *'Be alert and of sober mind. Your enemy the devil prowls around like a roaring lion looking for someone to devour'.* NIV

As we journey on in our new life as Christians God through the Holy Spirit will guide us how to live; learning to do the things we should do and how to resist things it is best not to do. However, as the Holy Spirit guides us he does not enforce his or God's way on us, we have free will to choose the path we want to follow.

At this point we would all say I will only do what God wants, sadly that can be easier said than done.

Our old lives and way of living are very strong pulls; our old clothes are more comfortable, when we get up in the morning we tend to put on comfortable clothes, invariably the old ones feel more natural.

If we go on diet say giving up coffee for a month, generally every time we reach for a drink we make coffee, if we are out and someone says what would you like to drink we say coffee: then we realise we no longer are drinking coffee and have to find an alternative drink.

It's true for our new lives as Christians we know how we would normally react to a situation, we know what we would normally do and its comfortable, but now we have that thought 'but, is it OK'?

Is this a behaviour that works for me as a Christian? Is my language ok, you may be someone that always swears as part of your general speech, now you pause and think is that ok? Is that what Jesus would do?

There are occasions when you have reacted without thinking and then you feel convicted that maybe you could have responded better, God will not condemn you it's not his way. He will convict you, that sense of knowing what is right and wrong, you will feel convicted, you will learn from the experience, but you will not feel condemned. Our Teacher the Holy Spirit is gentle like a dove. If we feel condemned it is from Satan or our own self condemnation. This may be a thing from our past where we always put ourselves down even when we do well and so when we get it wrong we are very hard on ourselves, telling ourselves we are failures, a walking disaster. We continue to condemn ourselves. Satan has very little to do but will claim the victory.

God does not condemn us, he tells us when we do wrong, the Bible says 'God is slow to anger'. When we are trying to live a life pleasing to him and we make a mistake, he forgives us and helps us to not repeat out mistake.

God will tell you when you have done well, to hear him say 'Well done my child' is very special.

God wants you to succeed, to be all that you can be, to have a good life, to have good fellowship with him, to be his servant: being a blessing to those around you and showing God's love to all those people he brings you in contact with.

The Israelites left Egypt with all their possessions

including sheep, cattle and gold and silver given them by the Egyptians. Loads and loads of baggage of every type, size, colour and texture.

Baggage!

When God sets us free from our old lives we are free but we have all our old baggage with us. Our behaviours, possessions, prejudices, likes dislikes, lusts, habits, wealth or poverty. Loads of baggage, some we don't even know we have. We have them all and they can be a drag on us just like leading thousands of sheep they can slow us down, take us the wrong way, take our eyes off God.

For some it's as though the old life wasn't there: but for others it is a battle to sort out those things from the past we are to keep and those things that need to change. If we are open to allow the Holy Spirit to guide us we will know the things that we need to change and the things we can keep and the right timing when we will be ready to address each of these things. When we move house we have to consider all we are taking with us to the new house and often we reject certain items because they won't fit in the new house.

Coming to Christ is similar in that our bodies now become living temples where God by his Holy spirit dwells in us, therefore we want to ensure that all we do, think and say is in keeping with God's Holy ways. It's not legalistic it is our free choice to be more like God and be the person he called us to be. Imagine when a super luxury car is designed it is designed to give a perfect travel experience, if someone takes such a car and adds items to it, wheels, tyres, roof rack, it may no longer be able to perform in the way it was designed to do.

When we are born we have within us the possibility to become the person God created us to be, but throughout our lives we change, follow different views, values and beliefs, when we come to Christ we often need to unlearn or take off all the after-market additions.

God's desire for us to change our lifestyle is not because he is grumpy and wants us to suffer, but rather the opposite he wants us to be free of the things that bind us, that cause us problems and that will stop us being all that we can be. The things that come between God and us, what the Bible calls sin: the thing that is seldom mentioned in church today, yet is important for our wellbeing and our relationship with God.

Sin separates man from God, God is without sin, he is pure, loving kind, but he hates sin. God cannot have a relationship with someone who sins, mankind sins, how can we be in a relationship with God if our actions and behaviours are those he dislikes or detests or even abhors?

Our well-being is at the forefront of God's mind, it says in Jeremiah 29:11, *'for I know the plans I have for you for you says the Lord, plans to prosper and not harm you'*. In the English Standard version translation, it reads;

'For I know the plans I have for you, declares the LORD, plans for welfare and not for evil, to give you a future and a hope'.

God's plans for us are for our welfare and to give us a future and a hope. Other translations use the word well-being or, prosper, hope, peace or an affirmation of God. We can take comfort knowing God wants the best for us and there are many other Bible verses that confirm God's desire for our well-being.

Because the Jewish nation could not live by the law, they often tried and often failed; if we read the book of Kings we read how even their Kings frequently did things that God hated, they worshipped other Gods and led the people astray.

Jesus came to the Jewish people, he was their Messiah, his coming had been foretold in the scriptures.

- Jesus was born in Bethlehem as foretold in Micah 5:2
- Jesus was born of a virgin: Isaiah 7:14
- Jesus was rejected by the Jewish people: Psalm 118: 22
- Jesus was crucified and suffered for all: Isaiah 53
- Jesus showed miracles and signs and wonders: Isaiah 35.

When he first spoke in the temple Jesus read from the book of the Prophet Isaiah chapter 61 Proclaiming *'the Spirit of the Lord was upon Him to bring Good news to the poor, to bind up the broken-hearted, to set the captive free and to proclaim the year of the Lord's favour'* and much more. But many of his own people refused to accept him as Messiah, the promised Messiah: the son of God. So he offered to everyone the chance of salvation.

When we accept Christ as our saviour we have new life we are saved from the consequence of our sins.

That which separates us from God is destroyed and instead of us facing God burdened down with our sin, we are cleansed in the sacrificial blood of the Lamb (Jesus). God sees Jesus and what he has done for us and Jesus says to his Father about us: they are mine. God says welcome. He stretches wide his arms and welcomes us into his presence.

So when we come to Jesus and become Christians; followers of Jesus Christ.

We are cleansed and set free from all our sins, but the consequences of our sins may well remain. If just before coming to faith, we rob a shop. We believe on Jesus confess our sins, we are forgiven by God: however, the law requires we go to prison for such a crime and we may well have to go to prison as the law of the land requires. There are also stories of people who have faced punishment by the law of the land for sins they did as a non-Christian and the courts being very lenient to them.

When we come to Christ not all of our ways and behaviours need to change. However, there are often behaviours and beliefs that need to change.

The process of leaving behind our old ways and habits or addictions and behaviours may take time for us to be fully free of them, yet for some of our ways it happens immediately.

When I came to faith I was a 60 a day smoker. I was a happy smoker, I was totally addicted to smoking, at the time nothing would dent my belief that smoking was ok and I was ok.

I enjoyed smoking so why should I give it up because I now believed and had accepted Jesus as my saviour?

Then over time I heard the arguments against smoking but didn't really consider them:

Things like 'it costs a lot of money' true but I was coping well if having debts and an ever increasing overdraft were coping. 'It was bad for my health', that was only partially true in the winter I had a bad cough.

'It was harmful for my son who had very bad asthma'.

So I went and chatted to his paediatrician who said 'as long as I smoked outside the house it was ok'? A view or comment that would today be wrong.

So I carried on smoking for about 4 years. Usually 60 cigarettes a day, day in day out, some days at parties or work events it was even higher. It directed my day, thinking timeframe, even the act of worship was interrupted to pop out for a ciggie break!

Then one day my son's asthma was bad and we called for a friend who had a healing ministry to come and pray for my son.

He did pray, sadly my son's asthma only improved marginally, however the friend suggested while he was there he could pray about my smoking. I was ambivalent, wasn't sure I wanted to be prayed for. However, my wife thought it a great idea, the thought of no smelly curtains and smoke stained paint appealed to her, also not least the lack of expenditure each week.

So I consented. My friend said I had a spirit of addiction, he prayed set me free.

Simple so I said what do I do now? He said don't smoke!

I had cigarettes all over house, in my briefcases, in the car, study, cupboards even the first aid kit! I never wanted to be without a cigarette and find the shops were closed! But I wasn't addicted!

For the next three days I never thought about smoking as though I had never smoked, then from day four I realised I could choose, whether to smoke or not, I chose not to smoke. That was over thirty-seven years ago!

There have been flashbacks, temptations, battles, there have been days when I have wanted to smoke, but God set me free and has given me the grace to be smoke free since then! I would hate to work out what I would have spent if I had continued smoking!

God has done similar things for millions of believers and will do for you, what will help you be all you can be.

CHAPTER 12

Pharaoh's response

When we leave our old lives behind there is often no time to celebrate: nor to look back, else if we do we could end up like lots wife.

Lot and his family as they started to escape were told don't look back, but as they ran away from Sodom and Gomorrah, Lot's wife looked back, and she became a pillar of salt. (Genesis 19:26)

When we become new Christians, it's a time to look forward with intent and anticipation of what God will do in us, through us and for us. Looking back may stop us from getting all that God has for us.

Moses was appointed by God to lead God's people out of captivity, he was God's appointed spokesman. Moses did what God wanted and when Pharaoh said take the people, they were ready.

Moses had told the leaders and the people to be ready for the final sign, the last thing that God would do to Pharaoh, for his refusing to let the people go.

When Moses says go, they leave the land of their captivity, two million people and their animals going to the Red Sea.

Now they had to travel 25 miles to get to the Red Sea. As previously discussed, as their caravan was so unwieldly and slow: probably they did not travel more than a mile a day.

More than likely it took 25 days to travel to the coast a time of adjusting, learning and beginning to come to terms with all that had happened to them. A time of learning to live in the desert.

In those days in Egypt the official period of mourning was 72 days, Pharaoh and his court and people mourned.

The people of Israel made their escape and processed to the Red Sea. I wonder how the Israelites felt when they arrived at the Red Sea?

Then God told the people to set up camp.

They were still a long way from safety and yet God says set up camp. I wonder how many of the 'up and at them' brigade wanted to press ahead in getting across the sea?

Whilst the Israelites are setting up camp or maybe a bit before, Pharaoh in the midst of his grief, suddenly realises that all the Hebrew slaves of his nation have gone together with many other slaves from different nationalities.

Pharaoh realises that he has now no one to be his slaves, he needs to get them back, so he calls to his men:

Mount up prepare the 600 best chariots of war and indeed all the chariots of war and soldiers.

Imagine what that would have looked like, Egypt had a formidable army and Pharaoh is preparing the best to go after the Israelites. Hundreds and hundreds of chariots, thousands of soldiers. To the Israelites, former slaves, all those chariots and loads of the best trained soldiers coming after you must have spread terror throughout the ranks. Very Scary.

The Israelites were terrified, and cried out to God. 'Why have you brought us out into the desert to die, were there not enough graves in Egypt? They were really scared: The Israelites knew they were no match for hundreds maybe even a 1000 or more chariots and thousands of troops. It would have been slaughter, with any remnant dragged back into Egypt and torture and whatever a vengeful Pharaoh wanted.

No wonder they were terrified.

However, Moses says, *'Don't be afraid, stand firm and you will see the deliverance the Lord will bring you today. The Egyptians you see today you will never see again. The Lord will fight for you: you need only to be still'.* Exodus:14: 13-14

Bold, confident strong words. Great words from a great leader, showing his confidence in God and God's plans.

Stand still and watch, you have nothing to do only believe. God tells us that to stand still and let God sort it out. The 'let go and let God' response.

It is the best plan in any situations, *'God is able to do abundantly more that we can hope or imagine',* Ephesians 3:20. NIV

Stand still and trust, when you have been battered and beaten for years, when you are down and in a foreign land, when you are on the run from those who have tortured you, it is tough to be confident that it will all be ok.

When your aggressor is bigger, stronger, better armed, younger, quicker, highly trained it's hard to believe that a God you can't see will beat the huge bully you can.

But that is the message for the Israelites, that is the message for us today as we leave the past behind and the tentacles from the past strain to reach us.

When we step forward and Satan sees it as time to attack us, when we step forward and that bully self-doubt wades in on us.

When we enter the promised land and the first thing we see are the giants that we must overcome to enjoy the fruit of all that God has for us; we must trust in the God we can't see, who promises to be with us and lead us into the promised land. He will not let us down.

The promise to the Israelites was to be free and enter a land flowing with milk and honey. Later we will see that for many Israelites it was hard to see the good promise God had for them, rather it was easier to experience the fear of the giants in the land. Those giants may become a battle for many new Christians. But, hindsight teaches us older Christians to trust God and do it his way: always better!

Seems easy to do but it isn't because it's about Faith and as new Christians we learn to live in faith.

Additionally, many of us are 'fixers' we see a problem for us or someone else and we try and sort it because we say I'm a Mr Fixit.

But it doesn't work in God's kingdom, the best plan is to let go and let God and do it his way.

Moses is convinced God will set the Israelites free from this new terror. Moses knew God never does part of the work, he always completes what he sets out to do. Moses had faith to trust God, that He would save the people, Moses has learnt not to become a Mr Fixit. But rather a Mr Faith.

At that point all he knows is God will sort it, it is not until God tells Moses what to do he understands Gods plan.

Then it will need a real step of faith.

God was setting the Israelites free and leading them to a promised land flowing with milk and honey. A few Egyptian chariots was not gonna stop Him.

We need to see the battle /challenge from God's perspective.

David (of David and Goliath fame [77]) certainly understood this. He didn't see how big the giant was he saw how big GOD IS!

God has a plan, but God has not revealed it to the people yet. I think God wanted to give Pharaoh and his armies the chance to turn back. God had led the Israelites with a cloud and pillar of fire

77 I Samuel 17:1- 25:7

Then the Bible says, *'The Angel of the Lord came out from in front of the people and stood behind them'*. The pillar of cloud that had been leading the Israelites also stood behind them.[78]

The Angel of the Lord.

Commentators and theologians have argued who or what 'the Angel of the Lord' was.

Some simply say a divine or 'Godly' presence, while others say it is Jesus appearing before the people. Others argue it is the Archangel Michael.

When we are in dire straits and the immediate future looks terribly bad. When there is no hope it seems we can only fail maybe even die, there is no way we can save ourselves, no way we can patch it up or sort it out.

That's when we need a divine presence, when we need God to show up in whatever form he chooses, our only request is that he shows up.

I can believe it is any one of the three or more arguments. My own feeling is it more likely the Archangel Michael who appears.

When the Lord appeared to Moses in the burning bush it was clear it was God

Later we read a description of Jesus as Captain of the Lords army or Captain of the hosts of the Lord. At these

78 Ex 14. John Gill says: and the pillar of the cloud went from before their face, and stood behind them: the Targum of Jonathan adds, 'because of the Egyptians, who cast arrows and stones, and the cloud received them:' and so Jarchi: whereby the Israelites were protected and preserved from receiving any hurt by them: so Christ is the protection of his people from all their enemies, sin, Satan, and the world, that sin cannot damn them, nor Satan destroy them, nor the world overcome them: for his salvation is as walls and bulwarks to them, and he is indeed a wall of fire about them. The New John Gill Exposition of the Entire Bible". https://www.studylight.org/commentaries/geb/exodus-14.html. 1999..

meetings there was the requirement for people to remove their shoes at it was Holy ground. This happened to Moses in the presence of God in the bush fire.

Whoever it was, the Angel of the Lord had led them with the pillar of cloud and protected them.

The cloud brought light to the Israelites and darkness to the Pharaoh and his men so neither could then see the other.

So commentators and Hebrew scholars argue that the cloud also absorbed the arrows that were shot at the Israelites by the Egyptian army. With God anything is possible. We don't know if the Egyptian army was close enough to fire arrows.

At the time of the Exodus it is believed the Egyptians were using a composite bow, that in the hands of a trained archer was capable of reaching a distance of 400 yards.

It is possible that arrows could have penetrated the outer edges of the fleeing Israelites.

Crossing Over

The Israelites are in that place no one wants to be: before them an impossible task, behind them no option of return.

To return means to be defeated, to give up all your goals, your hopes, your dreams.

For the former slaves of Pharaoh, they knew they would be severely punished and abused if they were captured. I'm sure they thought many of them would be killed by the chariots and armies of Pharaoh.

The Israelites knew that Pharaoh and his men would show no mercy, they would hunt down those who ran away and tried to hide, they would kill indiscriminately, it was the way. They Egyptians would seek revenge for their loss.

But, to go forward meant that they would have to somehow cross a huge sea: they didn't have any boats and no time to make any.

If they had had boats they would have been at the mercy of the Egyptian archers and thousands would have been killed. Nor would they have had time had time to embark two million people and animals and sail across the sea. True some would have got away but many would have perished, and many retaken as slaves.

In World War Two we saw the heroism and the pain of rescuing 300,000 soldiers from Dunkirk, the distance was greater approximately 45 miles, but it took nine days.

Here we have over two million people and animals, over a distance of between 1-10 km.

It is a vast task, not achievable by man.

The situation for the Israelites is dire.

There appears to be no hope.

So they moaned to God and Moses.

They cried out, they asked 'had God brought them to the desert to die'?

I would guess they were tired, confused, terrified: they just wanted an easy life.

When we are at the point of turning to Jesus, we can also feel that sense of hopelessness, the old ways are comfortable, familiar. Maybe even safer than this new life. If we become Christians, will we be persecuted, what will our old friends think?

Will we become outcasts?

What's all this suffering for our faith thing?

Then to add to our anxieties the Bible says in 1 Peter 5:8 *'be sober-minded: be watchful. Your adversary the devil prowls around like a roaring lion, seeking someone to devour'.*

We live in a spiritual world, there are forces of evil as well as the forces good. They battle in the heavenlies even though the Bible is clear that Satan is defeated. Romans, 16:20, Revelation 17:14, Revelation 12:11, Luke 10:18.

When we leave behind us the things of this world and embrace the things of God, endeavouring to live Godly lives, Satan is not happy.

Satan's plan from the beginning is to deceive, destroy, to break down all that God has done and is doing for us.

Where God wants to bring love, Satan wants hatred, where God wants peace Satan wants chaos, fear pain.

So there is a battle but God is the victor, the Bible says in Ephesians 3:20 'Now to him who is able to do far more abundantly than all that we ask or think, according to the power at work within us'.

Our God is able to 'do far more abundantly' than we can imagine.

Our God will go with us through the journey to faith as we trust in him and let him do what is right.

As we *let go and let God.* We have to trust him, to have faith in the Creator of the universe, the King of Kings, our Saviour The Lord Jesus Christ.

The same God, who gave his son Jesus that we may be set free, was known by the Jewish people as the God of Abraham, Isaac and Jacob, needed to respond to the Israelites cry in what was a hopeless situation. It was a no-win situation.

They needed a miracle, because man couldn't solve the problem.

Even Moses: God's man on the scene couldn't sort it out, he was good but not that good. Moses needed to seek God and then to do what God said. He had the faith, he told the Israelites don't fear, don't worry, stand firm and God will sort this.

And boy did God 'sort this out'.[79]

---

79 Exodus 14. NIV. *The LORD will fight for you: you need only to be still.*

Then the LORD said to Moses, 'Why are you crying out to me? Tell the Israelites to move on.

Raise your staff and stretch out your hand over the sea to divide the water so that the Israelites can go through the sea on dry ground.

I will harden the hearts of the Egyptians so that they will go in after them. And I will gain glory through Pharaoh and all his army, through his chariots and his horsemen.

The Egyptians will know that I am the LORD when I gain glory through Pharaoh, his chariots and his horsemen.'

Then the angel of God, who had been traveling in front of Israel's army, withdrew and went behind them. The pillar of cloud also moved from in front and stood behind them, coming between the armies of Egypt and Israel. Throughout the night the cloud brought darkness to the one side and light to the other side: so neither went near the other all night long.

Then Moses stretched out his hand over the sea, and all that night the LORD drove the sea back with a strong east wind and turned it into dry land. The waters were divided, and the Israelites went through the sea on dry ground, with a wall of water on their right and on their left.

The Egyptians pursued them, and all Pharaoh's horses and chariots and horsemen followed them into the sea.

During the last watch of the night the LORD looked down from the pillar of fire and cloud at the Egyptian army and threw it into confusion.

He jammed the wheels of their chariots so that they had difficulty driving. And the Egyptians said, 'Let's get away from the Israelites! The LORD is fighting for them against Egypt.'

Then the LORD said to Moses, 'Stretch out your hand over the sea so that the waters may flow back over the Egyptians and their chariots and horsemen.'

Moses stretched out his hand over the sea, and at daybreak the sea went back to its place. The Egyptians were fleeing toward it, and the LORD swept them into the sea.

The water flowed back and covered the chariots and horsemen – the entire army of Pharaoh that had followed the Israelites into the sea. Not one of them survived.

But the Israelites went through the sea on dry ground, with a wall of water on their right and on their left.

Moses told the people God will fight for you. This is the moment you feel compassion for the enemy. God will fight for you, the battle has now become uneven in the favour of the Israelites, until that moment Pharaoh and his army held all the aces, now they had none.

God says 'tell the people to move out': to Moses he says 'raise your staff (the same one that had eaten all the serpents of Pharaohs prophets), and stretch out over the waters of the Red Sea to divide them'.

Yeh right! That takes faith. What was Moses feeling at that time? If I get this wrong I and my family will die right here. Did God really say that?

Faith is the act of doing something God tells you to do whether you believe it or not.

'Faith is the assurance of things hoped for the conviction of things not seen'. Hebrews 11:1.

What faith Moses showed.

Moses raises his staff and wow the waters of the sea divide!

There is a clear path through the sea, it says the Israelites walked through the sea, with a wall of water on their left and a wall of water on their right.

A-MA-ZING!

Have you ever walked in the middle of high snow drifts, very scary but you are careful and you're ok?

How would it be to walk between walls of water. Probably 60 metres high!

That day the LORD saved Israel from the hands of the Egyptians, and Israel saw the Egyptians lying dead on the shore.

And when the Israelites saw the mighty hand of the LORD displayed against the Egyptians, the people feared the LORD and put their trust in him and in Moses his servant.

We know there are big aquariums where you can walk and see huge sea creatures through very thick glass, you know if the glass fails, you will either drown or be attacked by the sea creatures. But we have confidence in the glass, in mans' ability to build strong exiting structures.

It would take months even years to build and prepare walls that could separate a sea.

Imagine the building work necessary, cranes, steel girders, concrete piles, huge hammer drills to drive the girders and piles into the earth. Tons and tons of steel, trucks, floating barges!

Without even thinking of the planning permission or the permits needed to do such a thing.

Yet God stops the water instantaneously. He makes the sea separate for some distance between 1-5 km: he makes it stand up like a wall, and holds it in place while two million people and their animals walk through.

AWESOME.

Wow God really is able to do more than we can hope or imagine.

He did it for the Israelite people.

He can do it for you.

Call on him in your time of need and he will answer.

However, if you call on him when you are not in need, it may just save you getting into a crisis that you need to be bailed out of.

When we respond to the call of Jesus and commit our ways to him, the Bible says 'he will direct your paths'.

Calling on Jesus is not as some say 'it's for him to spoil our lives and stop our fun', no it's to give us a hope[80] and a good

80 *For I know the plans I have for you, declares the LORD, plans for welfare and not for evil, to give you a future and a hope.* Jeremiah 29:11. ESV

future and lead us in a way that will be best for us.

God saves the Israelites is a good title for a book, it is great reading for the Jewish nation, less good for the Egyptian army and Pharaoh.

It had taken some time for Pharaoh to realise that God was serious, he was going to win and that he Pharaoh needed to let the Israelite captives go free.

Now Pharaoh realises the consequences of letting the Israelites go free, he no longer has any slaves to brutalise and use for his service.

So he decides to chase after the Israelites: he uses his best and biggest chariots and soldiers.

He was determined to get the Israelites back: there would have been extreme loss of Israelite lives. Pharaoh was going to follow them until they were his, he would have pursued them across the sea. He did actually enter the Red Sea.

The Israelites would never have been safe from his attack and from capture.

Pharaoh did not send an emissary to negotiate with Moses and the leaders of Israel, if he had Pharaoh and his armies may well have survived. But he was hell bent on revenge and capturing and destroying the Israelite people. God would not and could not allow that to happen. He had sent Moses to set his people free, He could not allow his plans to be destroyed together with his people.

When the pillar of cloud and the Angel of the Lord stood behind the Israelites, that was the time for Pharaoh to take his army home, but he didn't.

He could have done it without losing face, saying that they could not find the Israelites because there was a huge impenetrable cloud, that when they fired into it nothing came back, it was so dense. The Israelites had escaped.

Resisting God or harming his people is never a good plan, God will give you time to stop, to repent, to change your wrong doing, however, if you don't he will take action. You will not like the action he will take.

If you are on the other side of the cloud trying to get free from the past: seeking God's help, God will reply, he will answer you even though sometimes we don't understand the answer that we get. If you are like Pharaoh, then you need to seriously think of what will happen if you continue on your path.

God's heart is toward those he created and he gives us every opportunity to turn around from our ways that are wrong and follow him.

When Jesus was on the cross he was between two criminals. They deserved to die he didn't. One criminal mocked Jesus and taunted him. The other didn't, he said to Jesus have mercy on me. This was moments before he died.

Jesus says to the criminal that asked for mercy, 'today you will be with me in Paradise'.

It is the hope of many Christians with loved ones that have led a life away from God, that at that last moment they will turn to Christ and say Jesus forgive me.

Jesus ministered right to the very end of his life. The lesson from the cross at the end is: to everyone who truly repents will be given the gift of eternal life.[81]

Romans 6:23. *'For the wages of sin is death, but the free gift of God is eternal life in Christ Jesus our Lord'.*

Jesus will save you whatever you have done: Jesus came into the world to save sinners, to give everyone the opportunity to be reunited with God the father.

---

81 Jesus said to her, *'I am the resurrection and the life: he who believes in Me will live even if he dies, and everyone who lives and believes in Me will never die. Do you believe this?'* John 11: 25-26 NIV

For the new Christian God has saved you by Jesus dying on the cross, you are precious to him, go on in peace and serve the Lord, and he will direct your paths.[82]

When the people of Israel had crossed over the Red sea and seen the mighty power of God the people feared the Lord and trusted him. You might say who wouldn't after such a powerful display. Yet there can be doubters even after such an amazing act of God.

When Jesus was on earth he said to Thomas you believe because you have seen, *'blessed are those who have believed and not seen'*. True for many Christians today.

So the people are safe and they join in singing a song of praise to God. (Exodus 15.)

This is a lesson that as Christians we can learn and apply in our lives. We pray and ask God for help, we seek him for guidance, we ask him for help in our jobs, relationships, even for parking spaces, the list of things we ask God to do for us is enormous, there are myriads of things we seek him for.

There are also things that some people don't feel comfortable to ask God for but generally, the list is endless. So we pray and we beseech and we call out to God.

God responds and we go our way happy that our cry or prayer has been answered. Our supplication has been heard.

We need at that point to thank and praise God for what He has done for us, we need to acknowledge that God has answered our prayers.

Imagine if you are a parent and you do something for your child and they just receive it and get on with it, or when you do something for them they say thanks Dad, love ya loads!

82 *'Seek his will in all you do, and he will show you which path to take'.* Proverbs 3:6. NLT

Which one would you prefer?

I'm fortunate my children are great at doing the latter. Makes me feel good, I don't do something for them so I feel better, I do it because I want to love and bless them, however it's nice to have the thanks.

That's what God as our Heavenly Father wants from us, he doesn't need it but he loves us to show him that what he has done for us has meant something to us, and that we acknowledge both our thanks and also our love for him.

So the Israelites have crossed the sea, they are safe on the other side, the threat from Egypt and Pharaoh is no more.

Moses words at the beginning of the day you will see these people no more is true.

God has set them free, he has shown his love for his people and his faithfulness.

The people do a good thing, they say thank you to God.

So after the people have sung a song of praise to God they travel for three days in the new land, its desert but they are free people and also free of the risk of attack from the Egyptians! What a great place to be.

The start of a new life where they have just seen God do an amazing miracle.

But after three days they did not find water, that in the desert is bad. They came to a place but could not drink its water for it was bitter.[83] So the people grumbled against Moses.

Not a long honeymoon period for Moses.

You'd think that as Moses had arrived, been God's man to get them out of Egypt and been faithful to do what God said so the people saw miracles, they would be feeling quite warm towards Moses.

83 Exodus 15: 22-27

But they were a people that had suffered and were a people used to moaning about their suffering.

When we come to Jesus we have to leave in the past some of our behaviours that are not nice, that can be unpleasant for those around us. But it can be hard and take time, so we have to pray about these things and then thank God when he answers.

Moses role models what the people should do, they have a genuine need, there is no drinkable water, in the desert that could prove fatal.

So Moses calls out to God and God shows him a piece of wood, that when he throws into the water the water becomes drinkable. Another amazing sign yet another miracle for them to see.

When the people have drunk their fill and filled all their water containers, then God gives the Israelite people a message.

'There the Lord issued a ruling and instruction for them and put them to the test. He said, 'If you listen carefully to the Lord your God and do what is right in his eyes, if you pay attention to his commands and keep all his decrees, I will not bring on you any of the diseases I brought on the Egyptians, for I am the Lord, who heals you.' Exodus 15: 25-26 NIV

God gives the Israelites a lesson that we need to learn as Christians, a teaching that if we embrace will hold us in good stead as we start our journey of faith.

Listen to God, do what God says is right, keep all his commands in our case, all the teachings of Jesus which enhance the Old Testament laws, then God makes a promise.

Jesus says to the new Christian: Jesus answered him, *'If anyone loves me, he will keep my word, and my Father will love him, and we will come to him and make our home with him'.* John 14:23 ESV.

That is the promise we have from God the Father and God

the Son. We will never be alone because we will have our God living in us by the Power of the Holy Spirit.

After this it says the people of Israel came to Elim, a place with twelve springs, seventy palm trees and they were able to camp near the water. The word *Elim* means an oasis, a watering hole. What a great thing to find in the desert. A safe, secure place to camp and drink in the midst of the desert.

As we start our journey with Jesus he brings us to Elim, a place where we can be refreshed and we can be still. A place where we can camp safely and reflect on all that has happened to us and prepare for the future with Him.

Look for the watering holes that God provides for you on your journey, the Bible says that *'God will supply all your needs according to his riches in Glory in Christ Jesus'*. Philippians 4:19.

As we follow the story of the Exodus the whole community then left Elim and headed out and arrived at the Desert of Sin. Exodus 15:16 says it is the fifteenth day of the second month after they left Egypt. Forty-five days in the desert experiencing at first hand the power and might of God.

Now let's do a little recap.

- The Israelites were captive in Egypt and had been there for over 400 years.
- They called out to God to set them free.
- So God meets Moses and prepares him to be his messenger to Pharaoh. (Miracle 1).
- Moses meets with Pharaoh and his magicians and Gods power is greater by far. Egypt suffers from 10 plagues because Pharaoh is against God.
- Then Pharaoh says let the people go. (Miracle 2).
- So they celebrate the Passover and leave Egypt. (Miracle 3).

- Then Pharaoh changes his mind and chases after the Israelites.
- Pharaoh and his chariots and men corner the Israelites.
- God parts the Red Sea the Israelites are safe and Pharaoh and his men are no more. (Miracle 4).
- The people are thirsty and the bitter water becomes drinkable. (Miracle 5).

You may wish to argue some of these things are not miracles or I haven't included enough things that God did and called them miracles.

That's OK.

The key point is whatever you call these acts of God they were all pretty special. Have you ever wanted to cross a sea and after prayer it parted?

That's exactly what happened for the Israelites. Imagine arriving at Dover on your way to France and thinking I don't fancy the ferry, so you pray and the water parts and you drive through to France!

But the Israelites were camped on the side of the sea, with an angry Pharaoh and his troops hemming them in, so God parts the Red Sea, simple.

Bearing in mind too this is not about one or two people no, this is two million people and their animals. Wow.

However, you may argue the point, the Israelite people had seen the hand God move in power for them. Their faith must have been huge, they must have been fully trusting in God and believing God for amazing things.

But they weren't, they arrived at the Desert of Sin they had no food, maybe all the sheep had gone, maybe the sheep remaining weren't for the pot?

So the whole community grumbled against Moses and Aaron and by inference God as he was everyone's leader.

They grumbled well their argument was powerful but wrong.

Exodus 16 says *'If only we had died by the Lord's hand in Egypt! There we sat around pots of meat and ate all the food we wanted, but you have brought us out into this desert to starve this entire assembly to death.'*

They accused Moses and Aaron and God of bringing them into the desert to die!

The people were hungry, we often don't think straight then. They were traumatised.

What had happened was for their good and was amazing but, for some of them the process of being chased and the possibility of violent death at the hands of the chariots and warriors of Egypt, left them traumatised. To say nothing of losing their homes even though they were slaves. Of living in the dessert and being without water. It all took its toll. They had had enough crisis in their lives. Neither were they used to trusting God for their needs.

As new Christians we can find ourselves exited as it were on cloud nine.

Enjoying the new feelings of God in our lives, maybe experiencing pure love for the first time. We enjoy meeting with other Christians at church and in other places, the times of worship move us and give us feelings that we have not experienced before. We feel close to God, we want to be in his presence more, we want to follow his ways. We try very hard to accomplish these things: we give our best, 100%.

What is hard though is to bring things to God and trust him to move. We are conditioned to sort out our everyday needs, to work out our finances, cope with health issues: just to do the aspects of daily life, but we are not used to submitting our plans to God and letting him direct our paths.

For most new Christians that is harder to do.

Or we can as it were fall over the cliff the other way where we do nothing unless God specifically tells us too. So we choose not to eat anything or buy bread, clothes or even soft furnishings unless God gives us a specific word, we could end up very hungry or living in an empty house.

We know with the benefit of history and the texts of the Old Testament that God did not bring the Israelites out of Egypt to kill them.

He had a promised land for them to move into, but before they could go there, they needed to learn to behave and live as free people and to trust God. To be a slave was ingrained in them, they needed to learn what it was like being a free person.

Now we see the people moan against Moses and Aaron, the people say it would have been better if God had killed them in Egypt, at least they had pots of meat to eat. We can see in the text that they were abused as slaves, but in this new moment of crisis how quickly they forget their unpleasant past experiences or blot them out.

Yet after escaping from Egypt, fleeing and being threatened with death or recapture, here they are in the desert, hungry and unhappy and feeling like their gonna die anyway. They have forgotten all God has done.

But God has a plan to feed them.

Whenever you trust your life to God and ask him to intervene he will, but not always in the way you tell him to do.

So God says to Moses he has a plan that will feed the people and at the same time see if they are willing to follow Him.

God will rain down Manna (Ps. 78:24 Bread of heaven) for them. He gives instructions how to gather the Manna, how to only keep what they need for each day, but on the sixth day they are to gather extra and prepare it for the seventh day as there will be no Manna on the 7th Day.

God tells Moses to tell the people that he has heard their grumbling! 'That as they gather and eat the Manna they will know that it was God who brought you out of Egypt and feeds you with bread in the morning and meat at night'.

Moses gathers the people and tells them what God is doing, just as in the desert the people saw the Glory of the Lord appear in a cloud.

So God responds in a powerful and caring way.

When the people wake up in the morning, there is dew on the ground, as that dries up then white flakes appear and Moses tells them that is the bread to eat.

In the evening the Bible says the camp is covered in Quail.

Quail was a good choice for the Israelites, it can be boiled, fried, roasted, evidently easy to cook and good for you.

God responds to their needs, two million people at a sitting!

God can out give anyone,

God can out provide anyone,

One of the Hebrew names for God is 'Jehovah Jireh' meaning God our provider.

Quail and bread for two million people is some provision!

As a Christian we learn that God is able to provide for us, we learn to trust him and to seek him and to do what he says. We learn to make our requests known to God and he responds.

Philippians 4:6 says '*Be anxious for nothing, but in everything by prayer and supplication with thanksgiving let your requests be made known to God*'.

Moses has done what God wanted, he has led the people out of Egypt, Moses was following the pillar of cloud. Somehow (by God's grace) he has kept two million people and their animals in order following the same path. Everyone arriving at the same destination within a reasonable period of time.

He used his staff at the Red Sea and saw the water part for the Israelite nation to pass through safely, then saw Pharaoh and his army defeated.

Moses had listened to the moans of the people and told them what God's answer to their moans was, he had encouraged the people. He had a tough job, there was no management journals or management Gurus to consult. There were no self-help books on how to lead two million people and their 'pets' in the wilderness. I have a Master's Degree in Management: if God gave me the task of leading two million people et al, I'm not sure I would attempt it let alone achieve it. Hats off to Moses.

Moses had to make it up as he went along after first seeking God, finding out what God's way was and then doing it God's way.

Somewhere along the way Moses sends his wife and children home, there may be many reasons for that decision but it makes sense, especially with the threat of the Egyptian army and moaning of the people, and it was a few less mouths to feed.

In addition to leading the people out of Egypt, parting the Red Sea and interceding for the people before God, Moses also was acting as Judge for the Israelite people but it would become too much for one man.

Jethro, Moses father in law, (who was a Priest of Midian) has taken in Zipporah (Moses wife, his daughter) and her and Moses 2 sons. Jethro hears about all that God has done for Moses and the people of Israel. He decides to visit Moses and take his family back to Moses.

In Exodus 18 we read that Jethro visits Moses and brings with him Moses wife and children. We read too that Jethro sends word to Moses he is on his way and Moses goes out and meets him.

Moses then tells Jethro all God has done and Jethro (Priest of Medianites), says, *'Now I know that the Lord is greater than all other gods, for he did this to those who had treated Israel arrogantly.'*

Now Jethro, as a Priest of the Midianites was probably experienced in dealing with the issues of the people, whereas Moses was experienced in dealing the issues of sheep.

So Jethro observed all that Moses was doing and suggested to Moses that it was too much for one man and that he appoints other leaders and gives them rules to judge the people by. So Moses appoints leaders and they deal with the day to day issues of the people but the difficult things are brought to Moses to deal with.

Moses listened to Jethro and then carried out the practical process of appointing valued men into leadership and sought God for his guidance.

When we walk with the Lord He will use different people to guide us and help us, when we ask God for help in whatever situation, He answers our prayers, we have to be open to receive the answer whether it comes from the Bible, the preacher, a mature Christian friend or in a dream or vision.

God says to Moses tell the people; Exodus 19:5 *'Now if you obey me fully and keep my covenant, then out of all nations you will be my treasured possession'*. What an amazing promise God makes to the Israelite nation.

So Jethro goes home and Moses leads the people with a more ordered method of administration and judiciary as he helps the people solve their problems, disputes and issues.

CHAPTER 13

Becoming free

As the Israelites continue in the desert they come near to Mount Sinai at that point God meets with Moses and God gives Moses the ten commandments which he brought to the people on tablets of stone.

HISTORY: simple dictionary explanation of the origin of the Ten Commandments.[84]

---

84 Ex. 34:28: Deut. 10:4, marg. 'ten words' i.e., the Decalogue (q.v.), is a summary of the immutable moral law. These commandments were first given in their written form to the people of Israel when they were encamped at Sinai, about fifty days after they came out of Egypt (Ex. 19:10-25). They were written by the finger of God on two tables of stone. The first tables were broken by Moses when he brought them down from the mount (32:19), being thrown by him on the ground. At the command of God he took up into the mount two other tables, and God wrote on them 'the words that were on the first tables' (34:1). These tables were afterwards placed in the ark of the covenant (Deut. 10:5: 1 Kings 8:9). Their subsequent history is unknown. They are as a whole called 'the covenant' (Deut. 4:13), and 'the tables of the covenant' (9:9, 11: Heb. 9:4), and 'the testimony.' They are obviously 'ten' in number, but their division is not fixed, hence different methods of numbering them have been adopted. The Jews make the 'Preface' one of the commandments, and then combine the first and second. The Roman Catholics and Lutherans combine the first and second and divide the tenth into two. The Jews and Josephus divide them equally. The Lutherans and Roman Catholics refer three commandments to the first table and seven to the second. The Greek and Reformed Churches refer four to the first and six to the second table. The Samaritans add to the second that Gerizim is the mount of worship. http://dictionary.reference.com/browse/commandments--the-ten. 'commandments, the ten'. Easton's 1897 Bible Dictionary. 19 Feb. 2016. <Dictionary.com http://dictionary.reference.com/browse/commandments--the-ten>.

The Commandment were not about salvation, but rather a set of rules by which to live. Each person could measure themselves against the list and see how they measured up. Additionally, they could plan their lives to live in a way that did not go against Gods rules. They were a set of laws that were there to guide the people: in themselves they have no power however if you choose to live by them they can be a powerful help to you equally if you decide to live in opposition to them then they will make a strong judgement against you.

The apostle Paul refers to the commandments in much of his writing.

There is much discussion about the commandments being two tables and that commandments 1-4 represent man's duty to God, and commandments 5-10 represent man's duty to man.[85] For those who would like to look further into this I have

85 **Two tablets**

The arrangement of the commandments on the two tablets is interpreted in different ways in the classical Jewish tradition. Rabbi Hanina ben Gamaliel says that each tablet contained five commandments, 'but the Sages say ten on one tablet and ten on the other', that is, that the tablets were duplicates.[49] This can be compared to diplomatic treaties of Ancient Egypt, in which a copy was made for each party.[50]

According to the Talmud, the compendium of traditional Rabbinic Jewish law, tradition, and interpretation, one interpretation of the biblical verse 'the tablets were written on both their sides',[51] is that the carving went through the full thickness of the tablets, yet was miraculously legible from both sides.[52] https://en.wikipedia.org/w/index.php?title=Ten_Commandments&oldid=704564148

Traditionally the reference to 'two tables' has been understood to refer to the fact that the Decalogue falls, as we have seen, into the two sections of our duty to God and our duty to man. It has been assumed that each of these sections was given a tablet to itself. This is intrinsically unlikely because it would put asunder what God has joined, making it appear as if the commandments Godward and the commandments manward are essentially separable. We ought therefore to follow the line opened up by more recent knowledge of

included a couple of quotes in the footnotes. However, I would suggest unless you are a student of theology we will better use our time looking at and understanding the commandments than perhaps studying the method of writing.

To the Jew the commandments are the Law, to the gentile who believes in God they are for guidance, we no longer live by the law but rather by grace and the guidance and power of the Holy Spirit. There is much written about the relevance of the Old Testament and the Ten Commandments to a Christian today.

We are under Grace but the we cannot ignore the teachings of the law with the guidance of the Holy Spirit it should inform our Christian walk. I have included a couple of scriptures for you to read and examine, additionally it is worth reading Paul's letters especially the book of Romans.

'But now we have been released from the law because we have died to that in which we were held so that we might serve in newness of the spirit, and not in the oldness of the letter' (Romans 7:6). NIV

'Are we, then, abolishing law through faith? May it never be! Rather, we are establishing law' (Romans 3:31). NIV

'For sin shall not rule over you because you are not under law, but under grace' (Romans 6:14).

'All Scripture is God-breathed and is profitable for doctrine, for conviction, for correction, for instruction in righteousness: So that

---

ancient covenant forms in which the stipulations of the covenant—the laws imposed by the covenant-lord—were written in duplicate. The covenant-lord retained one copy and deposited the other in the sanctuary of the god of the people on whom he was imposing his covenant. In the case of the Decalogue, Yahweh is both Covenant-Lord and also God of Israel. He, therefore, takes both copies into his care: the whole care, continuance, and maintenance of the covenant relationship rests with him.

See more at: https://www.biblicaltraining.org/library/ten-commandments#sthash.7pS0f9dy.d

the man of God may be complete, fully equipped for every good work' (2 Timothy 3:16). NIV.

Let us briefly look at some of the commandments and see how they relate to us as Christians, in fairness the commandments deserve a book on their own and indeed many commentators and theologians have written long and in depth works on the ten laws.

Exodus 20:1-17 The Commandments[86]

---

86 1. *I am the LORD your God, who brought you out of the land of Egypt, out of the house of bondage. You shall have no other gods before Me.*

2. *You shall not make for yourself a carved image – any likeness of anything that is in heaven above, or that is in the earth beneath, or that is in the water under the earth: you shall not bow down to them nor serve them. For I, the LORD your God, am a jealous God, visiting the iniquity of the fathers upon the children to the third and fourth generations of those who hate Me, but showing mercy to thousands, to those who love Me and keep My commandments.*

3. *You shall not take the name of the LORD your God in vain, for the LORD will not hold him guiltless who takes His name in vain.*

4. *Remember the Sabbath day, to keep it holy. Six days you shall labor and do all your work, but the seventh day is the Sabbath of the LORD your God. In it you shall do no work: you, nor your son, nor your daughter, nor your male servant, nor your female servant, nor your cattle, nor your stranger who is within your gates. For in six days the LORD made the heavens and the earth, the sea, and all that is in them, and rested the seventh day. Therefore the LORD blessed the Sabbath day and hallowed it.*

5. *Honour your father and your mother, that your days may be long upon the land which the LORD your God is giving you.*

6. *You shall not murder.*

7. *You shall not commit adultery.*

8. *You shall not steal.*

9. *You shall not bear false witness against your neighbour*

10. *You shall not covet your neighbour's house: you shall not covet your neighbour's wife, nor his male servant, nor his female servant, nor his ox, nor his donkey, nor anything that is your neighbour's.*

From *Life of Hope and Truth*. https://lifehopeandtruth.com/bible/10-commandments/the-ten-commandments/10-commandments-list

1. *'I am the LORD your God, who brought you out of the land of Egypt, out of the house of bondage. You shall have no other gods before Me'.*

Quite straight forward, unequivocal. God reminds his people that he was the one who led them out of Egypt, that was the promise to the people. God got them out of Egypt and freed them from slavery and from the threat of Pharaoh.

God reminds them that he is the one they called out to in their distress and He God responded to them bigtime!

He reminds them that he is their God, 'I am the Lord your God, who brought you out of Egypt', out of the land of slavery or bondage. God reminds them in those few words what their lives were before they sought him.

The Israelites were badly abused slaves in a foreign land. When they prayed to God to save them he responded and they saw amazing miracles.

He raised up a leader for them who could go to Pharaoh, and tell Pharaoh what God wanted for his people.

The people were set free from slavery in the Egyptian land, God led them with a pillar of cloud by day and a pillar of fire by night.

Pharaohs army chased them and God protected them from Pharaohs army, he led the Israelites through the Red Sea and then they saw Pharaohs army washed away. They knew God provided for their physical needs, water, manna and quail: also that the Egyptian people gave them gifts before they went, gifts of gold and silver and things to start a new life.

So at the beginning of the commandments He, God reminds the people what he has done and therefore the first commandment is really to tell them their duty is that if God is their God then they should not be like other people in their known world and worship lots of Gods. He expected them to worship him.

The Egyptians had lots of gods and goddesses, some of the Israelites as prisoners would have been the craftsmen that had made the golden animals or icons to represent the gods.

God was telling the Israelite people that they were not Egyptian, they had asked to be set free from captivity and all the things that go with it. They had called out to God as their God and he had answered them.

It's a simple question, when we are set free from captivity and are out of Egypt why carry on with the old practices? Oh that it was easy to answer.

Why, when we have the chance of new life do we cling onto the old ways, doing things we know are wrong?

So the Israelites as free people no longer needed to do certain practices required of them under the Egyptian law.

They were free

God had always wanted to have a relationship with his people and says he is a jealous God.

This is an aspect of God we don't often hear about, yet it seems to me a reasonable point from God.

God responded to the cries from his people the Israelites because he loved them, he set them free. God created man in his own image he wants to be with us.

As a Christian we too should have only one God: however, too many people let things in their lives become gods. For example: their car, career, money, hobby, sport, football team, pop idol, holidays, their bodies, friends work mates, clothing, all these things can become more important in a person's life than anything else, even more important than God!

When we become Christians, we are set free from the old

life, we need to look afresh at our lives and see if what we do is pleasing to God.

For the Christian it's good to see how much of our life is given to God.

A friend of mine, a very Godly man felt God ask him how much time did he give to God, he replied 85% and was shocked when he felt God say it was more like 15%.

On reflection he thought God was right and decided to revisit the time he spends with God.

God says we should have 'no other gods but him'. Imagine how we would feel if our loved one spends all their time in places and with people you can't go to.

Doing things that are offensive to you,

You would quickly challenge them I'm sure.

You would want to tell them right from the start the dangers of the things they are doing, how wrong they are and how to avoid doing them.

You would also want them to know that the things they were doing were painful to you.

Right at the beginning of time God said to Adam and Eve (Genesis 2:16) *'you can eat of any tree in the garden, but from the tree of the knowledge of good and evil you shall not eat, for in the day that you eat from it you will surely die'*. That's pretty clear

Yet the Bible tells us they did still eat of the tree they were expressly told to abstain from. To abstain means to leave alone, not touch, not eat the fruit of that tree.

So God is mindful of man's weaknesses and particularly the Israelite nation, his chosen people: how they seem to be easily led to follow false gods.

God has set the Israelites free they asked him to be their God, so He then says You should only have me as God!

Seems fair: He, God, has done much for them, all he wants is them to love him!

Seems very fair he is not asking for their blood! He actually wants to bless them.

Jesus, who came to the earth approximately 1500 years after the time that God gave Moses the commandments is asked, 'which is the greatest commandment?

Jesus replies, to 'Love the Lord Your God with all your soul and all your heart and mind'.

This is what God wanted at the time of Moses, for his people to love him and have no other gods.

God's message has remained the same throughout the generations and it's the same for us today.

Jesus then says what God said through Moses over 1500 years before: 'You should have no other gods but me'. The message doesn't change its mankind that changes.

We are to love the Lord with our whole heart, with our whole soul, with our whole mind and with our whole strength. If we love him with our hearts and love him with our minds, both support the other, if we truly loved the Lord our God with all our heart mind and soul, we will have no time for any other Gods!

It would appear that to love God means concentration on him and not multi-tasking as we focus on him. So many people try and have a quiet time with the telly on in the background.

Question if we are to love the 'Lord with all our strength', is praying and jogging, or praying and gardening, or praying and playing sport correct?

You may wish to consider:

What are the gods that try and lure you away from God the Father?

What are the gods that keep you from the one true God?

Years ago when I was studying with a University, the

words 'you may wish to consider' appeared to give you the option to consider or not, however, in University speak at the time the words 'you may wish to consider, meant *you will consider*. Just a thought you may wish to consider, the choice is yours?

You shall have no God before me.

Now to the Israelites the other gods were obvious, here are some of them. Molock, Canaanite god that required child sacrifice. The water bearer; Hapi, god of the Nile. Heckel, was the goddess of fertility, and had a frog's head. Ra the god of the sun. Each of the plagues that God brought upon the Egyptians was a direct response to one of their gods. God showed that he was more powerful.

The golden calf the Israelites built in the desert has given theologians, historians and experts on the Torah many great questions. The golden calf was similar to the bull of the god Apis, and a calf was significant to the followers. However, some experts argue that the Israelites made a golden calf to signify that they wanted a new leader to represent them to God. That Moshe (Moses) was not doing what they wanted. Whatever is the correct understanding of these things the people kept returning to follow different gods and that made their God, Yahweh very angry.

So we are faced with questions, questions and more questions.

Who / what are the gods of today?

How do we know if we are following them?

Does it matter if we are?

In India they have millions of gods, why can't we?

As Christian what does it matter if I have another god in my life?

Why should I have only one god?

Who will check up on me anyway?

Over the remaining pages of the book we will endeavour to shed some light into these questions, we will try and identify these false gods then we can step away from serving them and remove their influence in our lives.

A key point to remember is a person or thing can only have power in our lives if we let them, if we make ourselves available to them.

We have to say to them I want to journey with you, I want to do what you do, only then can they have power or influence in our lives. You may say it's obvious, I wouldn't give anyone power in my life.

Of course you wouldn't, but these false gods are subtle, we generally don't aim to follow them, rather we get taken in by something that appeals to us and gradually we find we are under the influence or power of that thing: we then find that we can no longer 'live without it'.

It has become of paramount importance in our lives. It has got such a stronghold on us it clouds our thinking, it challenges our normal beliefs and values, it gradually, slowly, insidiously makes its way to our inner being, causing us to become dependent on it. We look back and say, how did I get here? You may start as a collector of something innocuous, then over time become a fanatic about that thing, it becomes the only thing that interests you. You spend all your money in getting more. You spend all your time reading about it, looking at it and drawing or photographing it. You may even become known by the name of the item for example, Fred the gun, or Mary the cake, Tom the car.

I'm sure if you asked virtually anyone to tell you about their god's, their response would be to say 'I don't have any'.

It's probably obvious to say there are very few golden calf statues around in the UK, although Milton Keys is known for its concrete cows: I understand that is supposed to be conceptual art rather than celebrating a god.

We all live our lives minding our own business, doing what we want when we want, (work permitting). We laugh when we hear about the extreme and dangerous things people will do for fun, while others laugh at Christians for 'going to church'.

When God made man, the Bible says he made man in his own image,[87] that he might have a relationship with man, to spend time with him. Sadly, many men and women nowadays spend little if any time with God.

Even those who attend church and would call themselves Christians have been known to just attend church but have no personal time with God.

The only time they make for God is one hour on Sunday. One in 168 hours per week.

Not a lot. Even 10%, 16.8 hours per week is not a lot. That's just over two hours per day. If we add up our time at church, quiet times and time doing God's work, I wonder if we would still make 16.8 hours per week? Probably not for most people.

That of course doesn't mean everyone is not having time with their creator, but how much time do people spend reading their Bibles and praying, seeking God and his plans for us.

A recent survey in Christianity Today,[88] says 80% of churchgoers don't read the Bible daily! Yet, according to another recent research report (2015) 'Britons spend more time using technological devices than they do sleeping: Communications regulator OFCOM said UK adults spend an average of eight hours and 41 minutes a day on media devices,

87 Gen 1:27 *'So God created mankind in his own image, in the image of God he created them: male and female he created them'.*

88 http://www.christianitytoday.com

compared with the average night's sleep of eight hours and 21 minutes'! [89]

I wonder how much of the remaining waking hours are spent with God in prayer or Bible study. I would suggest that by taking the time we have left and spending it with family, friends, hobbies, eating/ drinking/ travelling even those who are keen to meet with God are lucky to put one hour aside per day.

People though do seem to find time and money for special things, perhaps the restoration of and old car, supporting the local football team, their pets, shopping, clothes, personal appearance, or partying all these things can become gods.

Our bodies can become our gods, some people are so focused on their own looks they spend all their lives and their money trying to look like someone else or to be like their dream, cartoon character or movie star.

Unfortunately, as they age all their cosmetic surgery doesn't work and invariably the skin stretches, leaving the person looking totally embarrassingly, cringe worthily false. It must be so deflating, it looks like what it is: an old person trying to look young and still growing old.

How about our cars: some men are known to spend more on having a brilliant car than on feeding or caring for their children, the car becomes the God.

To grow in God and to spend more time with him we need to look at how we spend our time and what is most important in our lives, if it is not God and our relationship with him, then we need to change what we do and acknowledge Jesus as our God, giving him our lives and our time.

Then we will be able to say he is our God and King and our actions will start to reflect our words.

---

89 *The Communications Market* 2015 (August)

When Jesus was on the earth the Jewish people knew the 10 commandments, the Pharisees[90] and Sadducees[91] and priests would be constantly reminding the people of them in the temple.

But Jesus was questioned by one of the experts in the law to test him.

Matthew 22:36-40 (NIV) *'Teacher, which is the greatest commandment in the Law?' Jesus replied: ''Love the Lord your God with all your heart and with all your soul and with all your mind.' This is the first and greatest commandment'.*

Jesus reply moved away from the sense of a debate between experts and God to a simple instruction from God. The message was clear: that we needed to focus on the one true GOD and 'love the Lord our God with all our hearts, with all our soul and with all our minds and with all our strength'. It was a different slant. The rhema (spoken word) of the word, God speaking to us personally in the moment.

Jesus was explaining to the people how to love God: it was not just a command there was an application of the commandment.

The first commandments says: *'Thou shalt have no other Gods'*, Jesus says *'thou shalt love the Lord your God with all your heart '*.

In one sense it can be argued that although the statements are different and that the one supports the other: I would suggest that Jesus is calling for a greater commitment from his people.

90 Strict Jewish leaders very knowledgeable about the Law and practice and custom

91 Of the Priestly high born house held alternative views to Pharisees, i.e did not agree with oral traditions

Jesus asks us not just to put creator God first in our lives, but to be proactive in loving God. Jesus is calling us to decide to love God and then show our love for him in a tangible way. Not just by being pew fodder.

We can make something or someone our god above all other gods, but we don't have to or need to love that god.

Here Jesus is challenging us or calling us to a deeper relationship.

Jesus knew in dying on the cross he would open the way for us to have a relationship with our heavenly Father. This was not to be just a relationship of laws and rules, but instead a relationship based on love: true love does not need rules and boundaries for it to flourish, as Jesus shows it is sacrificial. It puts the other person first.

This was the love that God was showing, total sacrificial love so that he could have a love relationship with us, his creation. If we have a true love relationship with God we don't' need the rules. We would be so in love with God we would only do that which made him happy.

Jesus in telling us to love the Lord with all our hearts is indeed doing what he says in fulfilling the law.[92]

We go right back to that early picture of man and God walking together in the cool of the evening, that intimacy of relationship that God had with the first man and woman.

Jesus is saying that it will be like that as we love God with all our hearts, we won't need the law or the prophets because all we do will be out of our love for God, to bless him. We need to ask ourselves do we really love God? Maybe even how much do we love God?

92 Matthew 5:17-20 (ESV) *'Do not think that I have come to abolish the Law or the Prophets: I have not come to abolish them but to fulfill them.'*

Can we honestly say we have fully embraced that first commandment that Jesus gives? That we love God with all our heart.

I would suggest most of us fall short of loving God completely and also it will be good for us to understand the value of the commandments to us twenty-first century Christians.

We need to understand how commandments relate to our new relationship with God, why God gave them to his people?

We need to understand how the commandments helped the Jewish people get the habits rules and practices of Egypt out of their systems, how the commandments helped as they struggled to be free of the habits and responses of captivity.

Today those of us who have come from a background of abuse, sin or captivity to a god, who have lived lives by our own moral mores will find in the commandments, in a possibly somewhat simplistic format, guidelines that will be helpful to us in developing our own new moral code, that is in keeping with our new Christian beliefs.

So let us press on!

So Jesus says that to love God with all our heart and mind and soul and strength is the greatest commandment. Jesus then says the second commandment is that 'you love your neighbour as yourself'. We so need to see that fully implemented in our world. It's so hard to love some of the people that are in our world and yet that is the challenge of the second commandment of Jesus.

However, when God gave Moses the Commandments the second commandment differed from Jesus second commandment

Exodus 20. *'You shall not make for yourself an image in the form of anything in heaven above or on the earth beneath or in the waters below. You shall not bow down to them or worship them: for I, the Lord your God, am a jealous God, punishing the children for the sin of the parents to the third and fourth generation of those who hate me, but showing love to a thousand generations of those who love me and keep my commandments.'*

This was still linked to the first commandment, if a person loved God totally they would not have any other gods. Their focus would solely be on God.

However, the second commandment that God gave Moses is Pretty straight forward talking: 'don't be making an image of anything to bow down to it or worship it'.

Now you might argue that who would bow down to an idol or image?

Well the Egyptians were great idol worshippers they worshipped the bull god (Apis) it was believed that Apis was like a go between; an envoy, broker or arbitrator between man and the main gods.

Pharaoh was seen as a god, so were falcons, serpents, so many things and to many of these gods the Egyptians created idols.

The vast majority would have been made out of Gold, and many of the Hebrew slaves would during their time of captivity, become experts at casting and making idols.

Indeed, when Moses goes up the mountain to talk to God, the Israelites get upset and make a giant gold calf to worship.

This is bad and nearly is the end for the Israelites. After God having responded to their call when they were captives, they called out to their God to save them: God sets up an elaborate plan, gets them out of Egypt, away from danger. The first opportunity they get they go back to worshiping their golden idols.

So God is clear, worshiping idols is not right for them, it will damage them, and drive a wedge between them and God.

God says don't have any idols, but if you have them, 'you shall not worship them or bow down to them'.

Then he gives them a reason why, He tells them a bit about himself, He reminds them he is the Lord their God and he is a jealous God! The Israelites did regard him as their God well enough to call out to him for help when they were slaves and he did help them.

So this benevolent supreme being who has just got them out of captivity confirms that if he is their God, and they wanted him to be, well he was jealous for their affection.

As we look back now on the history of the Exodus a time where God shows his love for his people, his amazing powers to bring a whole nation in excess of two million people and animals out of Egypt, to lead them through the Red sea, to provide food for them in the desert, He reminds them He is their God, He reminds them He did what He said he would do. He is so powerful so awesome there is no god like him in all the world.

Mankind has never seen anyone so magnificent, so powerful, so loving. In his response he tells them he is omnipresent and omniscient.

He makes them a deal you want me to love you I will, I do, but you must reciprocate. It's not a heavy burden, you want me to love and care for you, protect you, provide for you. God says all he wants is for them to love him with all of their hearts. The message from God is the same today thousands of years later.

He is saying, you say you want me so now show me, I am jealous, I am all powerful, I will not be replaced by a lump of wood or metal, that I created.

You shall worship me the creator not the created.

God then gives a warning to those who hate him, it's

tough reading; you hate me and I will punish you and your children, I will punish them for the sins you commit!

This is consequence of wrongdoing or sin.

If you grow up the child of a vicious criminal there is no escape from the way society holds you, you are guilty by association even if you are a really nice person.

God is, I would suggest, saying this here, it is to warn the Jewish people at the time to hold onto their relationship with God, to not turn from him again.

To stay true to him, to 'keep the faith' He would fight their battles but they had to love him and obey him. Or they would be tarnished for life.

But with the warning also came the promise, the Israelites had a choice if they chose to hate God they knew in advance the consequences, however if they chose to love God as he loved them and kept his laws, God promises them that he will /would show his love to them to a thousand generations to those who love him and keep his commandments. That is an amazing promise.

That's some time: we can possibly imagine 10 generations, that's around 200- 300 years (a generation being generally accepted as between 20-30 years)

Maybe even a hundred generations but a thousand generations, many of the people then would not have thought earth could have lasted that long.

Indeed, there has only been 4000 years since Moses that would be around 150 generations. A 1,000 generations is around 25,000 years. Wow!.

Some promise!

As Christians we now have the promise of eternal life,[93]

93 John 3:16. *'For God so loved the world, that He gave His only begotten Son, that whoever believes in Him shall not perish, but have eternal life.'*

we will live with God forever in heaven, our children will have the opportunity to respond to the call of Christ and have this much greater blessing for themselves.

Jesus came and fulfilled the law, he offers everlasting life to those who believe.

We just have to love God: our obedience is a natural result of that love.

Moreover, Jesus gave a second commandment

'And the second is like it: 'Love your neighbour as yourself.' All the Law and the Prophets hang on these two commandments.'

This is not about God or worshipping God, this is about how we live, when we are saved when the spirit of God lives in us then there must be an outworking of that, a sign that we are in some way different. Jesus gives us the challenge in that as we love God so we should love our neighbours.

How can we give the sort of love we give to God to our neighbours without making them our idols? But Jesus is not saying love your neighbours as you love me, that is not right, that wouldn't work.

He is saying love them as you love yourself, this was told to the Israelite people in the book of Leviticus when the Israelite people were dealing with foreigners in their land.

Leviticus 19:34 *'Treat them like native-born Israelites, and love them as you love yourself. Remember that you were once foreigners living in the land of Egypt. I am the LORD your God'*. NIV

I guess if someone is really nice to us we find it easier to love them, but if they are very very generous we could fall into the trap of making them too big in our lives.

Imagine we became friendly with a very rich star, they gave us all we wanted, all we needed and all we desired for us and our family.

They provided for us financially, when danger loomed

they got us out of trouble, when we saw something we wanted they bought it for us, whatever the cost.

They provided the best palace for us to live in, made no demands on us other than we spend some time with them.

Very soon we would start to at the least idolize them, it's quite conceivable that we would start to worship them or their wealth, even if in only a little way.

Being a Christian is not about worldly possessions, it's not about having great riches, being famous, being poor, being a leader, follower, king or pauper.

Being a Christian is about loving Jesus, he first loved us to such an extent he was willing to die for us on the cross, his love was sacrificial.

Jesus in this commandment, tells us that we should love others as ourselves, He is calling us to sacrificially love, to love as he loved, to put the needs of others before our own needs. When we love others there is generally a caveat that I will love them, if they love me or if it doesn't cost me too much.

Most parents love their children, they would do anything for them, until the day comes when they are becoming challenging, wanting to live a lifestyle the parents disagree with, or the parents have to give up what they want to do, so they can ferry the children to this club or other and then they moan. As we love Jesus, loving others as Jesus loved us will be the natural response for us to those around us.

When Jesus said we were 'to love your neighbour as yourself,' this led to the response 'who is my neighbour'?

This is a very simple question to answer when we see it from God's perspective.

Our neighbour is anyone we come into contact with in our lives, irrespective of their colour, ethnicity, gender, sexuality, ability or any other discriminating criteria.

Anyone we meet that has a need, those that we hear about that are without the basics of life.

In our modern world we can reach out to many people, whether it is the victims of an earthquake in some far distant land, the bush fires that kill people and wildlife or destroy property, whether it is the children that suffer hunger through famine or a child in a poor neighbourhood in a distant land. These are our neighbours.

Nor must we forget those in our own country who are suffering, ill health, bereavement, unemployment, accidents, and loneliness, the list goes on.

We as one person can't answer every need but we can love those whom we come into contact with; as Christ loves us: sacrificially loving them and ensuring that whenever it is within our ability to help, support and love those we meet, then we are fulfilling the commandment to love others as ourselves.

We live in a world where a former Prime Minister of the United Kingdom talked about the 'Big Society'. A place where he called for an increase of volunteer workers, to run projects for less able people 'where dormant bank accounts could fund projects and local groups could run, post offices, libraries, etc'. The poor of the world are often described as living in the two thirds world.

There is huge inequality in the world, in individual countries, villages and towns everywhere there are those who have, those who have not and those who try and take from both, but especially the poor.

History is full of accounts of communities and countries that were going OK then a neighbour decided he wanted what they had, attacked them, raped and pillaged and then kept all they had.

Man it appears, has several inherent characteristics that are alien to the verse 'love thy neighbour as thyself'.

Man's response to this command is invariably to ask himself a series of questions including the following:

Why?
Who is my neighbour?
Why should I love them?
What's in it for me?
How do I love them?
When should I love them?
They wouldn't love me.

The Jewish people went to Egypt when there was a famine in their land. Joseph arranged for them to live in the Land of Goshen as guests of the Pharaoh

The Israelites asked for and received a place to stay in return for bringing their skills as shepherds. Initially it would seem that were given land because they had something to offer, that they could bring shepherding skills. However, a bigger reason was because they had God's favour on them.

There was a famine people were helping each other.

But God had told Abraham that his ancestors would live in a foreign land.[94]

What started well for the Israelites ended badly when they became slaves of Pharaoh.

In the wilderness God gave the Israelites the ten commandments because it was necessary to get Egypt out of the Israelites.

94 Then the Lord said to Abram, *'Know for certain that your offspring will be sojourners in a land that is not theirs and will be servants there, and they will be afflicted for four hundred years'*

It should have taken the Israelites about eleven days to go from Egypt to the Promised Land it took them 40 years. All that time God was renewing their minds so that they once again saw the world as Gods people and not as Egyptian slaves.

When we come to faith we have to learn the ways to live as a Christian, many of our past behaviours are and were alien to God, so we need to learn to behave in a way that is pleasing to God.

God is aware that we have not got all things right. He understands that we fail. That we have followed a path that he does not like, that we have strayed[95] from his ways and have done and do things that made and make him angry.

That's why in verse 6 of Isaiah 53 it says God laid on him the iniquities of us all.

Jesus is the 'Him', God put the sins of all of us that call on the name of Jesus upon him and they were nailed the cross with him.

The good thing for the Christian is that in Jesus dying on the cross our sins are nailed to the cross and we can have a new life, because we don't have to drag around with us the baggage of our past life.

But rather we can live a life that is pleasing to God. We can become the person that God wants us to be.

When we come to Jesus and repent, we start to live a life worthy of the call.[96] God convicts us of things in our lives that are not right, practices we do that are not Godly and by his Spirit he helps us to overcome them, some more quickly than others.

95 Isaiah 53:6-8 (NLT). *'All of us, like sheep, have strayed away. We have left God's paths to follow our own. Yet the Lord laid on him the sins of us all.'*

96 Ephesians 4:1. *'Therefore I, the prisoner of the Lord, implore you to walk in a manner worthy of the calling with which you have been called.'*

We lived in captivity in a world where the values, behaviours, practice and customs were not Godly, they were alien to him.

We may be out of the land but as they say about Essex, 'you can take the girl out of Essex but can you take Essex out of the Girl? When we become Christians we have a new name, a new start we are no longer slaves to our old lives. The question is; We are out of "Egypt" but can we get "Egypt" out of us?

'Love your neighbour as yourself.' Is a big area where God is trying to take our old values and practices out of us!

Throughout history, man has stored treasure for himself: he has gone to war to protect it. Equally other men have become jealous of what a person possesses and have tried to steal it, or kill to obtain possession of it.

Sadly, in our world some men have also been enslaved and persecuted because of their ethnicity or skin colour; the fight against this will continue for some time until there is universal acceptance of and behaviour change, affirming that all men are created equal. As the United States of America in its Declaration of Independence states:

We hold these truths to be self-evident: that all men are created equal; that they are endowed by their Creator with certain unalienable rights; that among these are life, liberty, and the pursuit of happiness. Thomas Jefferson 1776 [97]

Occasionally a good person may do something for another but it is rare and generally there is an expectation that the good person will in some way benefit from his or her kindness.

In Japan the giving of gifts is a very important part of the culture. There are many ways that giving a gift can be done,

97 arw.wikia.com/wiki/United_States_Declaration of_Independence

equally there are many pitfalls.

'Often after receiving a gift a Japanese person will send an *O-kaeshi.* That is a gift of a particular smaller value to their benefactor. Sometimes the giving of a gift will leave an obligation, *GIRI* [98] the recipient is expected to return a gift of similar or greater value or 'loose face"

Jesus death for us was a gift freely given with no strings attached, no Giri, no O-kaeshi. It is his Gift to mankind; a once and for all act, he did not do it hourly, weekly, monthly, it was once and for all.

We are saved by his amazing love. He died to set us free, to make us acceptable to God the Father. To reunite us with the Father, that we might become sons and daughters of the King of Kings and Lord of Lords!

That is the type of selfless act that Jesus wants us to follow, to love others, as we would want to be loved, as we have been loved by Jesus.

To love others in a way that puts their needs before ours, it is a tough challenge, but the more often we demonstrate our love for others, the closer we get to being the people God wants us to be.

The closer we become to being the person God made us to be, the closer we become to obeying the commandments.

For many reading this book 'loving your neighbour as yourself' is about starting a new way of life, let us all press on towards this goal to love our neighbour as ourselves.

98 *Giri,* is a Japanese value roughly corresponding to 'duty', 'obligation', or even 'burden of obligation. Wikipedia: The Free Encyclopedia 2015

CHAPTER 14

More Commandments?

In the last chapter we looked at the first 2 commandments and also explored the Implication to us of Jesus's summation of the commandments in Matthew 26.[99]

Now let's look at some of the other commandments and the relevance to the Israelite people as they journeyed away from slavery and the value or relevance to us today.

The third commandment was and is a powerful commandment, with a consequence if we fail to obey the commandment. This is particularly relevant to the new Christian to learn how to live a live without taking the Lord's name in 'vain'.

'You shall not misuse the name of the Lord your God, for the Lord will not hold anyone guiltless who misuses his name'. Exodus 20:7.

So what does this mean to us today? It certainly raises some additional questions for us, some of those are:

How do we misuse God's name?

What does it matter today after all the commandment is thousands of years old?

How do we obey this commandment?

What are the consequences if we fail?

Why is it so important to God that He added a consequence to us misusing His name?

---

99 *'Teacher, which is the greatest commandment in the Law?' Jesus replied: "Love the Lord your God with all your heart and with all your soul and with all your mind.' This is the first and greatest commandment. And the second is like it: 'Love your neighbour as yourself".* Matthew 22:36-40.

Is misusing his name the same as Blasphemy?

There are many people today that use the name of Jesus as a swear word, is that what this is about. Doubtless it is wrong to use Gods name as a swear word. But why?

In ancient times if you took the name of the king in vain, the outcome was simple, Death.

In some religions of the world to take the name of a leader would also result in immediate death. The Greeks and Egyptians took this matter seriously. 'The Greeks were content to punish it with a heavy fine, and ultimately with the loss of civil rights. The Romans, in the more ancient times, inflicted the death penalty. It was generally believed, like in Egypt, Greece and in Rome, that the anger of the gods was especially provoked by this crime, and that a Divine Nemesis pursued those who committed it, and made them suffer for their sin, either in their own person or in that of their posterity'.[100]

It's a heavy thing to say something bad about the King and find you and your family are being hunted down and tortured to death.

The second part of the verse suggests that God will not ignore the misuse of his name, ('for the Lord will not hold him guiltless who takes his name in vain').

God says I will not hold him guiltless that uses his name in vain.

Is this an example of God being like any man who gets a bit upset when someone criticizes his car or football team?

We all know the old children's rhyme, 'sticks and stones may break my bones but names will never hurt me'. Surely calling God names is not going to hurt him?

Those who have been bullied or abused or called names at

100 www.studylight.org/commentaries/ebc/exodus-20.html

school may well know how untrue the above rhyme is.

Names do hurt, words can have the power to destroy, 'the pen is mightier than the sword'.[101]

In our modern world we see people destroyed by a journalistic attack, their names dragged through all sorts of public examination, ridicule and even abuse whether they have been caught in some sort of crime or not.

Sadly there have been many instances where the wrong person has been accused and their lives have been destroyed, by the constant muck raking primarily by tabloid newspapers. A person's name is extremely important to them: how do we feel when our name is misspelt on Facebook, or in a legal document. We don't like it!

However, I don't think that God is bothered by a bit of bad press or the misspelling of his name. The God who created the heavens and the earth is not going to be put off by a bad mispronunciation. So what is it? It must be more than this? Surely?

Perhaps we need to ask a different question?

How about, what does 'to take in vain' mean?

To answer this, we need to explore the original language of the 10 commandments.

Now it is clear as is often the case with the Bible, the text is not quite as simple as it sounds. There are multiple meanings to this phrase to 'take in vain' so let's explore some of them.

The best way to do this is to explore what a small selection of the commentators of the Bible have said. The names of God would provide enough material for a book twice the size of this one. Some of these writers are experts in Hebrew and Greek'.

---

101 Edward Bulwer-Lytton Richelieu: *Or the Conspiracy: A Play in Five Acts*. (second ed.). London. 1839

Ellicott in his commentary for English readers says 'The Hebrew is ambiguous'.[102] That helps?

Mathew Henry although he was a writer and Minister in 17th Century, he is widely regarded as having a great understanding and critical strength. One of his comments is that we are if we follow God and take his name in vain it is hypocrisy.[103]

Mathew Henry further states:

'The third commandment concerns the manner of worship, that it be with all possible reverence and seriousness. All false oaths are forbidden. All light appealing to God, all profane cursing, is a horrid breach of this command. It matters

102 Ellicott's Commentary for English Readers. (7) Thou shalt not take the name of the Lord thy God in vain.—The Hebrew is ambiguous, as is to some extent the English translation. Most modern critics regard the phrase used as forbidding false swearing only: but some think that it forbids also 'profane' or 'vain swearing.' Our Lord's comment in the Sermon on the Mount favours the view that false swearing alone was actually forbidden by the Law, since He proceeds to condemn profane swearing on His own authority: 'But I say unto you' (Matthew 5:34). False swearing is among the greatest insults that man can offer to God, and, as being such, is naturally forbidden in the first table, which teaches us our duty to God. It is also destructive of civil society: and hence it is again forbidden in the second table (Exodus 20:16), which defines our duties to our neighbour. The laws of all organised States necessarily forbid it, and generally under a very severe penalty. The Jewish Law condemned the false witness to suffer the punishment which his evidence was calculated to inflict (Deuteronomy 19:19). The Egyptians visited perjury with death or mutilation. Bibliography Information. Ellicott, Charles John'Ellicott's Commentary for English Readers'. https://www.studylight.org/commentaries/ebc/john-6.html. 1905. In Ellicott's Commentary for English Readers - StudyLight.orgwww.studylight.org/commentaries/ebc

103 By hypocrisy, making a profession of God's name, but not living up to that profession. the-ten-commandments.org/ten-commandments-matthew-henry.html

not whether the word of God, or sacred things, all such-like things break this commandment, and there is no profit, honour, or pleasure in them'.

We could say when we become Christians, ok I will not swear any more then all will be well. But I would suggest that this commandment is more than just a don't swear, this is far deeper and has a major spiritual significance in our walk with God and in our growth as Christians.

God's names are very important to God, the Jewish people had called out to God to set them free, they had said they wanted him to be their God, to protect them to keep them, to provide for them: he had made a covenant with this people to be their God.

It would seem reasonable that God should require not just that they honoured His name, but they did not debase it either.

God of the Old testament, Creator God, God of the Jewish nation has many names or meanings for his name.
Wikipedia[104] lists them as follows:

Adir – 'Strong One'

Adon Olam – 'Master of the World'

Aibishter – 'The Most High' (Yiddish)

Aleim – sometimes seen as an alternative transliteration of Elohim

Aravat – 'Father of Creation': mentioned once in 2 Enoch, 'On the tenth heaven is God, in the Hebrew tongue he is called Aravat'.

Avinu Malkeinu (help·info) – 'Our Father, Our King'

104 Names of God in Judaism. https://en.wikipedia.org/w/index.php?title=Names_of_God_in_Judaism&oldid=680039315

Bore – 'The Creator'

Ehiyeh sh'Ehiyeh – 'I Am That I Am': a modern Hebrew version of 'Ehyeh asher Ehyeh'

El ha-Gibbor – 'God the Hero' or 'God the Strong' or 'God the Warrior'

Emet – 'Truth'

Ein Sof – 'Endless, Infinite', Kabbalistic name of God

HaKadosh, Barukh Hu (Hebrew): Kudsha, Brikh Hu (Aramaic): (Arabic) – 'The Holy One, Blessed Be He'

HaRachaman – 'The Merciful One'

Kadosh Israel – 'Holy One of Israel'

Melech HaMelachim–'The King of Kings' or Melech Malchei HaMelachim 'The King, King of Kings', to express superiority to the earthly ruler's title.

Melech HaOlam–'The King of the World'

Makom or HaMakom – literally 'The Place'

'The Omnipresent' (see Tzimtzum)

Magen Avraham – 'Shield of Abraham'

Ribono shel `Olam – 'Master of the World'

Ro'eh Yisra'el – 'Shepherd of Israel'

Tzur Israel – 'Rock of Israel'

Uri Gol – 'The New LORD for a New Era' (Judges 5:14)

YHWH-Yireh (Adonai-jireh) – 'The LORD Will Provide' (Genesis 22:13–14)

YHWH-Rapha – 'The LORD that Healeth' (Exodus 15:26)

YHWH-Niss'i (Adonai-Nissi) – 'The LORD Our Banner' (Exodus 17:8–15)

YHWH-Shalom – 'The LORD Our Peace' (Judges 6:24)

YHWH-Ro'i – 'The LORD My Shepherd'

YHWH-Tsidkenu – 'The LORD Our Righteousness' (Jeremiah 23:6)

YHWH-Shammah (Adonai-shammah) – 'The LORD Is Present' (Ezekiel 48:35)

Rofeh Cholim – 'Healer of the Sick'

Matir Asurim – 'Freer of the Captives'

Malbish Arumim – 'Clother of the Naked'

Pokeach Ivrim – 'Opener of Blind Eyes'

Somech Noflim – 'Supporter of the Fallen'

Zokef kefufim – 'Straightener of the Bent'

Yotsehr Or – 'Fashioner of Light'

Oseh Shalom – 'Maker of Peace'

Mechayeh Metim – 'Life giver to the Dead'

Mechayeh HaKol Mohye alkol– 'Life giver to All' (Reform version of MechayehMetim)

Wow that is some list: many Christians today are familiar with some of the names, but as you read the list you realise the amazing breadth of God's power and outreach. God is not limited to one or two areas but he is truly omniscient, omnipresent, omnipotent.

Do the names of God matter today to the Christian?

The names of God matter today to both Jew and gentile for many reasons, to a Jew it is important for them to understand the special place they have in God but also to understand the full nature of God's love to them. For both Jew and Gentile, the names of God describe to us who He is and tells us something about what he has done and will do. They shew us something of his power, slendour and majesty.

These names underpin the basis of doctrine and belief: additionally, having and believing the many names of God has given courage and fortitude to help the Jewish nation in the many times of trouble and persecution they have suffered.

The Levites quoted in Psalm 137:4 asked the question *'How shall we sing the Lord's song in a strange land'?*

They were referring to the fact that not only were they in a foreign land they were captives and afflicted.

In some foreign lands it was illegal to practice their faith.

However, David in Psalm 18:49 says: *'Therefore I will give thanks to You among the nations, O LORD, And I will sing praises to Your name'*. Irrespective of other people and their views and ways. God chastised the Jewish nation for being stubborn, yet it is that stubbornness that helps them respond to God in affliction and distress.

For the Jew their history is vital, they are also as a nation very good at remembering all that God has done for them and the differing names for God help them to focus on what God has done and on ways to praise him.

For the Gentile, all who believe in Jesus Christ who are not born a Jew. Honour the same Lord: God the Father.

Paul says in Romans 11:17 [105] that we have been grafted into the vine: into God's family, the Jews were God's chosen nation but because of their disobedience in not acknowledging Jesus as Saviour we who were gentiles: who were not born of a Jewish family were offered the free grace of salvation, we

105 *'But if some of the branches were broken off, and you, although a wild olive shoot, were grafted in among the others and now share in the nourishing root of the olive tree'*. Romans 11:17

were made heirs of the Father (Creator God) and joint heirs with the son Jesus Christ the Righteous.

Therefore, we as Christians have full access to the Father (Romans 8:17),[106] God the Father who we also call the God of the universe, the God of Creation, our Heavenly Father: (that was how Jesus told us to pray) we have access to all that God has created and made available to mankind.

To avail ourselves of all the gifts and provision God has for us we need to know Him. Not just know of Him.

As a child you grow up and learn about your parent's day by day, the good and the bad. The things that are important to them, the things that make them happy, sad, violent, loving, afraid caring. You learn how they deal with an emergency, their ability in a crisis: in many family's parents can be given a nickname based on how they dealt with a situation. It may be that the tough dad enjoys boxing, is a martial artist but cried about a little kitten or some such thing and the family call him softy, 'gentle giant' or something similar, not to be unkind to him but rather because they know more about his true character.

So the names of God give us the opportunity to find out more about the God we love and praise, he is not just a jealous God: according to the Bible he is slow to anger quick to praise.

When we read his names we see that among his many names and their meanings: he is a caring, strong, present, merciful God who provides for his people and those who love Him. Can you add to the following list?

106 Romans 8:17 AMP: '*And if [we are His] children, [then we are His] heirs also: heirs of God and fellow heirs with Christ [sharing His spiritual blessing and inheritance], if indeed we share in His suffering so that we may also share in His glory.*'

- He is a God who provides
- He is a God who Saves
- He is the strong one
- He is Master of creation
- He is a shepherd of his people (you and me now)
- He is infinite
- He is our Banner
- He is present
- He is Merciful
- He is the Holy one
- He is our Righteousness
- He is the Clothier of the naked
- He is supporter of the fallen
- He is the Maker of peace
- He is life giver of the dead
- **And my favourite: He is Straightener of the Bent.**

'On a Sabbath Jesus was teaching in one of the synagogues, and a woman was there who had been crippled by a spirit for eighteen years. She was bent over and could not straighten up at all. When Jesus saw her, he called her forward and said to her, 'Woman, you are set free from your infirmity.' Then he put his hands on her, and immediately she straightened up and praised God.' Luke 13: 12-13
Yes. God is concerned about every one of us.

Many of us during life get a little bent from all the trials we go through.

When we become Christians we are immediately adopted into his family, we have the same rights and privileges as a free natural born Jew. We too also carry the cross that Christ told us about. When we have a challenge or crisis in our lives we need to look to God and see how He would deal with the situation and then seek him that He will be our all sufficient one in every circumstance of our lives.

When we take the name of God in vain and profane his name we are robbing ourselves of the chance to understand who God is. Worse still we exclude ourselves from calling to him for help, a) because we don't know him, b) because we have little knowledge about him, c) because the aspect of his nature we need to help us we have not honoured. Take His name Jehovah Jireh, God our provider, if you don't know that this is one of his names you won't go to him when you are in need.

When we were children we used to play with the words of hymns and carols or scriptures, as you get older when you're trying to be serious, maybe sing the words of the carol at a special service the funny incorrect words spring to mind long before the correct words.

When my son was very young I was made redundant, we had no savings we received a small weekly benefit, one week we received a utility bill for almost the total amount of the benefit. I asked the utility company if I could pay the bill over a few weeks as I had a poorly child and no job. They refused, so on receipt of the benefit cheque on the Friday, I cashed it and paid the bill, that left us on Friday evening with no money and no food: my wife and I made the decision to pay the bill knowing we would have no money for food but trusting on God to be our Jehovah-Jireh: to be our provider.

We told no-one just God.

The following morning, I woke up and found three bags of groceries on the door step, enough to keep us for a week.

To this day 35 years later I have no idea who was God's hands and feet. But boy did my wife and I praise God for his provision. I still remember that morning, and opening the bags of groceries and thinking, how did this happen? I don't know today, but I do know how precious a moment that was and how God got us through the time of unemployment. I'm, so pleased I knew God was also my Provider.

He, God, will not let you down, give Him the chance to act before you try and sort it out yourself. We did not have mobile phones in those days, we did not call anyone or put it on Facebook, it wasn't invented.

We prayed, we asked God to honour us and provide for as we did what was right we paid the debt we had. My wife and I took 'render unto Caesar that which is Caesar's to mean for us, to pay our debts. We prayed that God would be our Jehovah-Jireh and he was.

When things are going well for you and you have all you need and want, when it is clear that 'someone up there is smiling on you', give him praise and Glory for his provision for you. We should also give to others out of our abundance, whether that is in time, money or love.

When your earthly parent or someone gives you a gift you say thank you.

Give them a big hug and spend time together enjoying the moment. God will enjoy you saying thanks and spending time with him. That is all he wants is for us to spend time with him. It's not a lot to want is it?

The Hebrew and Greek languages often have more than one meaning for a word.

Get to know the names of God their full meanings and how this can help us to understand Him and get closer to Him.

'You shall not misuse the name of the Lord your God, for the Lord will not hold anyone guiltless who misuses his name'.

If you misuse his name you rob yourself of his greatness and majesty, and you reduce the likelihood of you knowing any of his names and how they will impact on your situation. Why would we want to do something that God does not like?

If someone you love says to you I don't like you calling me this name, please call me this name: you would of course change what you call them to make them happy, why not do the same to God?

How do we obey?

Simple, we should not use the name of Jesus or God as a swear word. Using Jesus' name as an expletive or expression of frustration is not a phrase that a Christian would want to use, especially as we are told not to take or misuse the name of the Lord. Nor would it be right if we took one of the many names of God and twisted that name or used it as an expletive.

There are many examples in modern language that misuse or warp God's name, we need to avoid using them. We need always to consider our speech especially when we invoke or involve the Lord in our dialogue.

Guard our tongues and minds Matthew 15:18 tells us. *'But the things that proceed out of the mouth come from the heart, and those defile the man'.* Then the explanation follows in verse 19. *'For out of the heart come evil thoughts, murders, adulteries, fornications, thefts, false witness, slanders'...* What is in our hearts and minds flows out in our words: Jesus says, therefore we need to guard our hearts. As the writer of Proverbs says. *'Watch over your heart with all diligence, for from it flow the springs of life'.*[107]

107 Proverbs 4:23

Paul in his letter to the church in Rome urges them to not be conformed to this world but be transformed by the renewing of their minds.[108]

The more we learn about who God is, the more time we spend with him and the more we grow close to him, the less likely we are to misuse his name.

What are the consequences if we misuse his name?

We as Christians are grateful that Jesus intercedes to the Father for us, all the time.

If we make a slip of the tongue and say something we immediately regret or get our words mixed up I don't believe God will do anything other than forgive us.

If we misuse God's name and mean it and don't repent then we will be judged, what that will mean will be up to God! It will I suggest be probable that we will remove ourselves from God and his plans, if we don t listen to his voice he won't force himself on us. I would suggest that the consequence if we don't repent is that we will no longer dwell with him in heaven and therefore spend eternity separated from God. Not a nice thought.

Why is it so important that God put a consequence to it?

Firstly, God is concerned about his name and how people see Him, when someone misuses his name it can bring his name into disrepute and He does not want that. The explanation given by the Virtual Jewish Library includes the following statement:

'In Jewish thought, a name is not merely an arbitrary designation, a random combination of sounds. The name conveys the nature and essence of the thing named.

108 Roman 12:2 *'And do not be conformed to this world, but be transformed by the renewing of your mind, so that you may prove what the will of God is, that which is good and acceptable and perfect'.*

It represents the history and reputation of the being named'.

We could also consider the concepts of Chillul Ha-Shem and Kiddush Ha-Shem. An act that causes God or Judaism to come into disrespect or a commandment to be disobeyed is often referred to as 'chillul ha-shem,' profanation of The Name. Clearly, we are not talking about a harm done to a word: we are talking about harm to a reputation. Likewise, any deed that increases the respect accorded to God or Judaism is referred to as 'kiddush ha-shem,' sanctification of The Name.

Because a name represents the reputation of the thing named, a name should be treated with the same respect as the thing's reputation. For this reason, God's Names, in all of their forms, are treated with enormous respect and reverence in Judaism. [109]

There is also a large amount written by scholars looking into the culture and customs at the time the commandments were recorded, exploring their implications impact and ramifications.

Simply put, in many ancient cultures and faiths it was popular at the time to confirm a deal or agreement by ending or starting with the words, in God's name I pledge this, or make a threat using God's name.

God addresses this in Leviticus (Lev 19: 12) *'Do not swear falsely by my name and so profane the name of your God. I am the Lord'.* NIV

Seldom today in the western world do you hear people doing that but in distant times this was a popular way of

109 *Jewish concepts*, Jewish virtual Library, 2016 aiceresearch@gmail.com

showing to others how strongly you felt about a deal, contract or threat. When you invoked God's name you added a 'power' to the threat

You made people fear you more, maybe causing them to believe that God heard you and would support your cause.

God did not or does not enter into any pledge agreement or contract lightly, when he decided to set men free from their own sin and guilt he made a new covenant with man, Jesus blood was the blood of the new covenant. He gave his own Son to die on the cross, because God so loved the world. This was a huge cost to Almighty God.

God cannot and will not go back on his promises he is unable too.

But man can and does. How many times have we made a promise to someone or even to God and said I will do this or that and then failed.

God cannot fail, he cannot break a promise, that is one of the reasons why he is without sin, why we can trust him, why our salvation through Christ on the cross is forever and why we can be called children of God because he has adopted us!

His name is precious to him, because it encompasses so much of his character and power. Praise God.

'OMG'

We live in a world where superficial emotion and feelings are paraded daily before our eyes. 'Oh My God', says the 'wannabe' celebrity, with ready-made tears. Or the person out clubbing, all for no apparent reason other than it stirs emotion in others and makes them appear dramatic, artistic, sincere?

The celebrity sort of shallowness, where one celebrity says of another 'I love them loads, their work and everything.'

Yet somehow in the follow up statements they highlight

the rifts and differences between them and the other person. Almost slandering or libelling them in the process. They then give reasons why they would never work with that person again.

There are many people who publicly state they have no faith and yet in moment of emotion or 'crisis' or 'happiness' put their hands over their faces and say, OMG.

They don't even pronounce all the three words, just say OMG.

It is shallow it is false, it is without substance and it tries to make God their tool their deity to follow them. But it also attempts to convey a sense of purity and sincerity in the person: that when something happens to them that is major, they try and appear humble, moved rather than just saying that's great, that's bad, I never expected that.

If they were truly devout believers of God they would react differently and not use his name to look good, or emotional on TV. They might just say Praise God, or thank you Lord you are with me, or Lord Help.

Proverbs says, *'The tongue has the power of life and death, and those who love it will eat its fruit'*. We must watch what we say, there are times when we all just speak out without thinking however we need to learn that to take the Lords name in vain is wrong, if we love the Lord we will not want to do anything that would upset, annoy or offend him.

Finally remember Jesus said:

'I tell you, on the day of judgment people will give account for every careless word they speak, for by your words you will be justified, and by your words you will be condemned.'
Matthew 12: 36-37 ESV

When we come to that day of Judgment we look for God's mercy and grace, let us keep from disobeying the commandment that God takes so seriously.

CHAPTER 15

Sabbath day

'Remember the Sabbath day, to keep it holy. Six days you shall labour, and do all your work, but the seventh day is a Sabbath to the Lord your God. On it you shall not do any work, you, or your son, or your daughter, your male servant, or your female servant, or your livestock, or the sojourner who is within your gates. For in six days the Lord made heaven and earth, the sea, and all that is in them, and rested on the seventh day. Therefore, the Lord blessed the Sabbath day and made it holy'. Exodus 20: 8-1, ESV

Today we live in a fast paced 24-hour day world that is open and active seven days a week 365 days a year. My previous job required me to be on-call, 24/7. Not uncommon nowadays. We live in world that is noisy, loud, fast paced, tempting, constantly offering us, great deals, ways to improve our situation, how we look, how we feel.

Temptations, incentives and promotions are always before us, we can go to Instagram or Youtube and see influencers promoting this product or that, from baby wear to make up: clothes, sanitary wear and so on. Telling us this food is better for us than another one, this betting chain gives us a better deal than its competitor; car A. has more features than car B, so therefore car A must be right for you.

The UK recently had a vote in Parliament to extend the Sunday trading rules, to give shops and businesses the opportunity to open for longer. It did not get through the House of Commons and the Government was defeated. Although there is an argument that shop workers will earn more and be better off, it is also worth noting that 90% of shop workers were against the proposal.

Whatever the rights or wrongs of the debate, we can still buy virtually anything on-line 24 hours a day 365 days per year and get it delivered to our door the next day.

The value of people's lives has diminished. Terrorists have shown no mercy in the ways they have attacked innocent people and families and children.

Children are trafficked as slaves, pornography is easy to access and to promote.

A world where more and more people are struggling to understand their gender, where society is funnelling some of them into grasping at short term 'feel good' solutions.

Society is getting very good at finding solutions that 'scratch the itch' but do not deal with underlying problem.

The pressure of the fast pace of life is we conform to it, we have to make quick life changing decisions, we don't take time to stop and reflect, we think 'on the hoof', how many people miss lunch, eat a sandwich at their desks?

Fast foods are so good now some people have lost the art of cooking.

I can ring up a company and have a cooked meal delivered to my door within an hour of my call. The quality of the food is amazing. Nothing appears to be 'closed' to us if we really want it.

Many people on the way to or from work go directly to the gym, bar, swimming pool, or go cycling or shopping, they no longer go straight home, or directly to work.

For others the day starts with a round of golf, a jog, or a dog walk.

Its all, available, there is nothing to stop you being active 24 hours a day seven days a week. Equally there is less time for reflection, to go to church and in some cases to meet with one's family. Man was designed and built to have a certain amount of relaxation and sleep in a day. We are still trying to work out the best work life balance, how much sleep is necessary? What is the correct number of hours we should work?

Per week? Per day?

The government says we should work 37.5 hours per week and no more than 48 hours per week

This law is sometimes called the 'working time directive' or 'working time regulations'.[110] However we can if we wish too '*opt out*' from the Directive (generally at the 'guidance' of our bosses) or sign to be exempted from this law

This should be an exception but for more and more employees it is becoming the norm.

For many years I worked 60+ hours per-week, and at times, due to the pressure of work, had to work 11-12 days continually at over 12 hours per day!

When I was working in business I had to be up at 6.am to leave the house by 7am, be at work before 8am. It was very hard to put a quiet time in place, before I left, but the alternatives were not easy. On an average day, from the moment I arrived at work till the time I left between 6-7pm, it was constant pressure and issues, often no time for lunch let alone a 'tea break', by the time I got home between 7-8pm I was tired, stressed needed to turn off, the thought of reading the Bible was not high on my agenda. Especially if I had a meeting to attend in the evening.

So there was no option but to take time in the morning to be with God, even if it meant getting up a bit earlier. However,

110 https://www.gov.uk/ http://www.legislation.gov.uk/uksi/2003/1684/contents/made

those days when I did have a quiet time before I went to work always seemed to be better days. 'The mind of man plans his way, But the LORD directs his steps'.[111]

Now as a minister I have to ensure I get up earlier each day to ensure I get a quiet time. I can have an extra hour in bed, but if I don't spend time with God, gradually I would get further away from Him and become dry and of little use.

When we start the day with God and lay before him our plans and ideas, when we submit our plans to the Lord, we give him the opportunity to intervene in our lives, the chance not only to change the wrong thoughts we have, but also to allow Him to convict us of unwise plans, for him to intervene in meetings, circumstances that are beyond us or threaten us. It is for each of us to decide how much time we give to God and when. There is not a suggested time table in the Bible. We are all wired differently with different needs, hopes, expectations, challenges and pressures, so there is no right or wrong.

God does not demand us to relate to him or to spend time with him but whenever we do it is us that gains.

How many times has man gone ahead with his own plans and seen them fail yet when God is involved things go well for the believer.

Sometime we can look at a balance sheet and compare what God gave for us and what we give to God!

So we ask?

Is the balance of our lives right?

How do we work out:

God time

Work Time

111 Proverbs 16:9 NIV

Family time
Playtime
Sleep time

Many successful men and women diarize time for their wives/husbands and families. It is very easy to go from one meeting to another at work, and be caught in the pressure to forget our families and our 'down time', but we need to be disciplined to ensure we have a good work life balance.

It is just as hard for a full-time mum or primary carer, where do we plan the time for rest, for us?

As a full-time carer for my wife her needs were first in all that I did and planned. Whether that was in helping her with the activities of daily living (washing, bathing, dressing, feeding sorting and managing her medications) helping her in her social life (very limited), being a chauffeur, confidante advisor: her needs came first. Then the needs of the children and the house.

However there came a time when I felt God tell me that I was not taking time for me and if I continued in that way I would become seriously ill and even die! So I started to consider how I could find time for me in my wife's routine, where I could find time for God in the midst of incredibly stressful and difficult times.

When you care for someone 24 hours a day in addition to being the parent of young children your day is very much prescribed for you by the regime of the person you are caring for. We did not have day/night carers so I was on duty 24 hours per day 7 days a week.

I slept on the floor, invariably I was woken by my wife 4-5 times a night.

I never got a full night's sleep, nor did I get a breakfast when I wanted.

My wife's needs for a special diet had to be prepared before the children: her breakfast was first, the children second and then me. But I learned that my wife needed times in the day to rest, so I chose some of those times to take a break. I would spend some time in prayer and Bible reading and other times I would just have a 'cuppa' and read the paper.

There is time in each of our days that we can reclaim, we just have to look for it, even seek divine wisdom and then having found the time use it wisely, you may not need for all the rest time to be in prayer, in fact I would suggest, at times of intense pressure it will be good to split your free time; take a quiet time with God and then pause and be still; relax with a 'cuppa' before returning to the challenges you face.

It is a privilege to care for someone it is also an amazing personal challenge, when we do it in our own strength we tire and become less value to the person we are caring for. But if we find time to spend with God, we will find we are better equipped as carers and are less frazzled by the events of life.

Whatever your situation If you take time for God you will not regret it.

Not only will you be closer to him you will find he will lead and protect you,

Psalm 91 says

> *Whoever dwells in the shelter of the Most High*
> *will rest in the shadow of the Almighty.*
> *I will say of the Lord, 'He is my refuge and my fortress,*
> *my God, in whom I trust.'*

And later in v 14-16

'Because he loves me,' says the Lord, 'I will rescue him:
I will protect him, for he acknowledges my name.
He will call on me, and I will answer him:
I will be with him in trouble,
I will deliver him and honour him.
With long life I will satisfy him
and show him my salvation.'

It's a great scripture to rest on.

So we work hard and our play has now become ever more challenging, exacting and dangerous, i.e. Base jumping, scuba and cave diving, street luge.

Many people will argue the Jews have got it wrong about taking one day a week off. Orthodox Jews will still today do no manner of work on their Sabbath. They are limited in how far they can walk, what they can carry and what food they can prepare.

Whether you support the Jewish people and their laws and practices or not there is certainly some merit in listening to what God says especially for the Christian it's a necessity.

The Sabbath or seventh day is holy, you shall refrain from doing any work on the seventh day.

It would seem reasonable to argue that if God can make the heavens, earth and all that dwells therein in six days surely, we can do all we need to do in six days and that we should follow God's example and take one day a week off.

Now I know some will argue that with the statement that God took seven days to create the heaven and earth, because he is outside time etc.

However, we can still take the learning from the scripture, whether God called it days or time period: God took a period of time to rest: the Bible says: So God blessed the seventh day and made it holy, because on it God rested from all his work that he had done in creation. Genesis 2:3

Now in ancient times the Commandments were great teaching, God was showing his people that they needed to take one day off from work per week. God says that he completed the work of creation in six days and then he took the seventh day off, so if God could, so can his people. It is a very special thing in Israel and in other places to celebrate Shabbat. A whole day off, a time to reflect on God and to fellowship. What a great teaching for today. Are we courageous enough to go against the tide and follow the teachings of the Lord?

To tell people in Moses time about Sabbath rest was very important, this was a world where slavery was rife, people were very poor, lived off the land. One day was very much like another, they slept, worked the land and if they were lucky ate.

Maslow[112] had not been born and his views on self-actualisation had not even been dreamed about.

Mankind was all about existence, unless you were one of the very special people, i.e. King or wealthy merchant and landowner, your focus was on getting enough food for each day. If you were fortunate to be in the service of the above well off people, you would be fed, but you worked whenever they said. No 37.5 hour week then.

There were no employment laws, you worked when the boss said, you ate what they gave you, when and if they gave you food, maybe even the scraps off their table, and you slept when you could.

112 Maslow, A.H, (1943) *A Theory of Human Motivation*, https://en.wikipedia.org/wiki/Abraham_Maslow

If you were a land worker, it was all you could do to barely eke out a living.

But here is God saying to his people, one day (the seventh) a week you must rest and spend time with me!

God knows especially as he made us and designed us that we are naturally a spiritual people, we need time to rest and to develop our spirituality.

So God said one day a week don't work but rather take time to focus on me, when you do that you will feel better, refreshed and rested and that spiritual part of us will feel fulfilled.

This was a word for all people throughout the ages not just for the two million Israelites in the desert. It started with them, but God knew they were going to become successful as a nation and many of them were going to have plenty, at that point many of them would forget him and his laws and suffer the consequences of ignoring God.

God knows that we are a people of Mind Body and Spirit. We will be fulfilled, we will be refreshed and we will be renewed. When I was researching my first degree I found research evidence that Nuns who were engaged in regular spiritual activity lived longer; FMRI scans taken during worship demonstrate it causes positive brain stimulation: it is good for you. Lynda A. Tracy, Laudemont Ministries, in her article: *Biblical Worship Is Good For You*, cites the interesting work of Levin and Vanderpool.[113] I am convinced worship is good for people and extends their life.

God wired us up, he knows what will strengthen us, what will help us run the race and help us make the finish line.

113 J.S Levin and H.Y Vanderpool, *'Is Frequent Religious Attendance Really Conductive to Better Health'*, Social Science and medicine Vol 24. No,(1987), Pp 589-600. www.laudemont.org/a-bwigfy.htm

God knows how we are wired, what our bodies are capable of, what we need in terms of food, rest, sleep.

Whether we listen to the theological arguments, whether we fully understand them. Equally, whether we understand God's voice, it seems sensible to consider the benefit to us of taking rest, of making one day a week, special.

As a Christian, part of every day is (or should be) spent in time with God whether in prayer, worship, fasting, meditation, contemplation, listening to or reading his word.

However, what God requires is that we keep one day a week Holy unto him; both to honour him, but also to give our bodies and minds a chance to recover and be refreshed. If not, we run the risk of burn-out, of overreaching ourselves and our skills and potentially overstraining our bodies and minds. For some people to the point of no return

That can be unsafe for all: in certain circumstances it will put our physical health in real danger, or become such a drain emotionally that we will fail to cope. The impact on our physical bodies of not taking rest and relaxation (R&R) can be devastating.

When I was caring for my late wife full–time, I felt God say to me, that if I did not take time for me and carried on just working and working I would die!

Quite bluntly, then God helped me realise my body would not be able to keep up the pace I was driving it at and maybe, just maybe I did not need to keep going at that pace.

At that time our Pastor James Glass, a great man of God, he told me the same thing, but with a lot more gentleness and compassion, I had to care for me as well as for my dying wife and the children.

It was a revelation and I have since then (with the occasional fall) made sure I take time for me and quality time to be with God both daily and weekly.

God told me first, he then brought James alongside me to help me find out how to follow God's plan. God knows the benefits to us of a day off per week and spending time with him, we should follow the maker's instructions and we will be healthier. Q. I wonder if today's increase in depression and poor mental health is a reflection of a society with a declining church attendance?

There is much more that can be said on this subject but I would encourage you dear reader, to see what the Bible says about the Sabbath day and rest.

CHAPTER 16

You shall not murder

Exodus 20:13 NIV

This is a hugely controversial subject: It is one of the commandments regarding our duties toward other men. Whilst I don't think anyone generally has a difficulty with the principle of this commandment. Most people live their lives thankfully never taking another life. I know murder still happens, but most people live their lives without intentionally or unintentionally killing someone else. When people get angry they generally manage to have some level of self-control and avoid killing someone. It is dangerous to generalize but I hope you will have patience with me in this case. The difficult moral question is, does this commandment only refer to unlawful killing, or does this commandment refer to accidental killing or killing in a war zone, or mercy killing?

'You shall not Murder' it is not as simple as it sounds at first reading. We need to look at this verse in more detail to fully understand what God is saying. To consider this from a cultural and contextual point of view. When we read the history of the Jewish people there are many battles, wars and persecution, killing of tribes and nations: reflecting on them can make it a bit difficult to understand this simple law.

God is a God of love his laws are to value the sanctity of human life. In the Old Testament[114], Deuteronomy 19:3, Jewish law included an instruction to set aside cities for people to live

114 Deuteronomy 19:3

in who had accidentally murdered someone. After a trial and assuming they were found to have committed the killing by accident, the accused person could be sent to live in these cities and would be safe from pursuit.

Consider, a person is accidentally killed; the person who committed the act is genuinely remorseful. There is no malice aforethought; the perpetrator did all in their power to resuscitate the victim. The death penalty for them seems wrong.

Would it be right to argue that to take their life would be morally wrong: if it was an innocent killing?

To argue that the Perpetrator should be given a second chance.

This appears to be what the Bible is saying: it was an accidental killing, therefore, the city of refuge would make sense.

Another reason for sending a person to a city of refuge is it may stop one death leading to a revenge killing leading to a feud.

Jewish culture and law is about saving life obviously in war they will fight to kill. In the 12th century the Jewish Scholar Rabbi Moses ben Maimon[115] (known as Maimonides) collated 613 verses of laws from the Torah the following is a section relating to *Thou shall not kill.*

482. Don't commit murder (Exodus 20:13)
483. Don't accept ransom for life of the murderer (Numbers 35:31)
484. Exile an accidental murderer (Numbers 35:25)
485. Don't accept ransom from him (Numbers 35:32)

115 Sefer Hamitzvot

486. Don't kill the murderer before trying him (Numbers 35:12)
487. Save the pursued at the cost of the life of the pursuer (Deuteronomy 25:12)
488. Don't show pity for the pursuer (Numbers 35:12)
489. Don't stand idly by when you can save a life (Leviticus 19:16)
490. Set aside cities of refuge for those who commit accidental homicide (Deuteronomy 19:3)
491. Don't cause loss of human life (through negligence) (Deuteronomy 22:8)
492. Build a parapet (in roof of house) (Deuteronomy 22:8)
493. Don't mislead with advice which is a stumbling block (Leviticus 19:14)
494. Help a man remove the load from his beast which can no longer carry it (Exodus 23:5)
495. Help him load his beast (Deuteronomy 22:4)
496. Don't leave him in a state of confusion and go on your way (Deuteronomy 22:4)

    (by Rabbi Moses Ben Maimon, known as Maimonides 1135-1204)

God made mankind in his image he does not want us killing each other although in specific circumstances he allows it although it must grieve his heart to see it. We read in the book of Genesis[116] that *'Whoever sheds the blood of man, by man shall his blood be shed, for God made man in his own image'*.

The consensus of opinion from the majority of scholars of the Torah and the Old testament appear to interpret this

116 Genesis 9:6 (ESV)

scripture as meaning that if a man kills another man unlawfully, the magistrate or person in power has the right to demand the perpetrators life in payment for the life he has taken.

I believe that God does not want a man to take another man's life except in vary particular circumstances: however, if a man takes another person's life there will be consequences.

You shall not kill does not prohibit a soldier taking life in a time of war, the situation is different, two sides (armies) fighting for a common piece of land or town. Generally, war is started by an unjust or unreasonable view taken by one side or leader of a nation. There is a risk to all involved, all the soldiers know that they may face death or maiming on the field of battle, that they may have to take a life, that what they will engage in will be a violent, dirty, filthy horrendous time, when they will need to put aside their previously held views and values including any belief they held regarding the sanctity of human life. Soldiers and Officers alike have to be trained to kill. To lay aside that vestige of decency, to not take hold of any political or moral high ground: the training is unpleasant and at times difficult to watch, however in a time of war to know there are trained soldiers and Police officers willing to step up to the plate to protect the population is a real strength to the people.

Soldiers have to learn, to realise that unless they can subdue the enemy, normally by killing them, they will be killed. This training is tough, some don't make it, others can show delayed reaction to doing something that is intrinsically against their will.

Invariably engaging in war does not leave the victor unscathed, we are reminded of the proverb 'to the victor belong the spoils'. In fact, many soldiers suffer for years with recurring nightmares about the battles they have fought, the lives they have taken, their fallen comrades; or the conditions they lived in whilst conducting war and for some a sadness about lives of the enemy that have been lost.

There is much documented work on Post Traumatic Stress Disorder that many soldiers face. I have worked with former soldiers who are still paying a high price for the engagement in war. More recently many soldiers who fought in the Gulf war, but who returned home without a physical injury, had terrible problems readjusting and fighting with the 'demons' the war had left them with. This was called the Gulf War Syndrome.

Killing is not a good option: God knows the impact it has on a person to take another person's life even if it is a justifiable homicide.

So whenever someone kills another person there will be consequences, most of us seldom experience dead bodies in our lives even when a loved one dies naturally we are ushered away and even if we see them in the coffin or Chapel of Rest it still can be very disturbing. To be the person that caused the death of the induvial is potentially destroying for the perpetrator.

I was a witness at a very tragic road traffic accident in which two young people were killed instantly.

We were first on the scene, I spoke to the emergency services on 999 about what I was seeing and checking the bodies for signs of life (there was none). It was challenging and for months afterwards I got flashbacks and horrible dreams and thoughts, and I had had no involvement in their deaths, I was purely a witness. Death is both untimely, it reminds us of our own frailty, and violent death is challenging and horrible to see.

For many in our emergency and health services they face horrendous situations and see death; for some this is on a daily basis and although some staff appear to be unmoved by what they see invariably at some point what they have seen and experienced will come back and impact them and will bite them hard.

The commandment says we must not kill, there appears to be a valid exception in times of war, if we take the Old Testament as our guideline then the Lord certainly supported the Israelite nation as they fought numerous wars.

So that raises the question, are there any other circumstances where it is acceptable to take the life of another person?

One such incidence is quoted in Exodus 22:2-3.

'If a thief is caught breaking in at night and is struck a fatal blow, the defender is not guilty of bloodshed; but if it happens after sunrise, the defender is guilty of bloodshed'.

We need to read this verse with caution, this is not a 'get out of jail free card'.

It would be incumbent on the home owner to prove that it was not their intention to kill the intruder, rather that they were endeavouring to restrain or prevent them from leaving until help arrived. This dispensation only is available through the hours of darkness. Considering the book of Exodus is reputed to have been written around 1250 years BC, some 3500 years ago the relevance of this 'rule' to today's laws is amazing[117].

117 You can use reasonable force to protect yourself or others if a crime is taking place inside your home. This means you can: protect yourself 'in the heat of the moment' - this includes using an object as a weapon . *stop an intruder running off - for example by tackling them to the ground. There's no specific definition of 'reasonable force' - it depends on the circumstances. If you only did what you honestly thought was necessary at the time, this would provide strong evidence that you acted within the law. Read guidance from

So when can we justify killing someone. We all have to work through all the different scenarios on our own. Just because someone else says its ok doesn't mean we have to agree with them.

We all have to find our moral position, to be confident that the views we have are our own and we are responsible for them. If we act upon them and get into trouble, we need to know why we acted as we did.

Some questions.

How do we face God if we have killed one of his created beings?

What will he say to us?

As we have considered there are very few circumstances where it is ok to take the life of another person. A very difficult issue is when we see people suffering because of chronic ill health, and they ask us to help them die. Especially if they are someone we love. Should we? Can we?

Can we decline their request?

What a moral maze!

When my wife was terminally ill we discussed this subject, I was caring for her we talked about euthanasia. Her suffering was great and it was for a long time over nine years. The morphine seemed to have limited effect. She wanted to escape the pain, I wanted her to escape the pain. The doctors wanted her to be free of the pain. Except for one local Doctor who was worried that if he gave her more morphine medication she would become addicted. Surely the relief of pain has the

the Crown Prosecution Service. You do not have to wait to be attacked before defending yourself in your home. However, you could be prosecuted if, for example, you: *carry on attacking the intruder even if you're no longer in danger *pre-plan a trap for someone – rather than involve the police. www.gov.uk/reasoable-force-against-intruders

priority. (She was terminally and as it turned out in the last year of her life). I reminded him she was 'terminally ill, but still he would not help. Thankfully her London specialist overruled them and was able to help her.

My wife and I talked long about euthanasia and researched the subject in real depth. We wanted to do what was right in God's eyes, my wife was adamant and I was fully with her, that her days were in God's hands. It was not right for her to die by her own or my hands. Even though her suffering was great and very hard to watch, her prayer was, let God's will be done. She knew the following verse and took strength from it.

But as for me, I trust in You, O LORD, I say, 'You are my God.' My times are in Your hand: Psalm 31:14

We both trusted that God was in control, that his will would be done. We didn't understand it, we for sure didn't like it. They were horrendous times for her and for the family but we knew we could not go against God.

We prayed much and God intervened in many ways. Some people argue that euthanasia is suicide, others that it is a very positive way to care for an individual or for a person to decide for themselves.

I would suggest that before you go this route you spend much time in prayer research and studying the scriptures. Before you act you are convinced this is the way forward. Ensure before you take any action that you have sought help and counsel and are without doubt about your proposed course of action. If you have a faith seek the counsel of your Faith Leader, as a Christian you should seek the guidance of your Pastor, Vicar or Priest.

I think most people would support a police officer shooting a terrorist who is armed and shooting and killing people and is killed to stop the slaughter.

There are times when it appears perfectly right to take the life of another person, the difficulty is that the person that does that will invariably suffer some kind of trauma.

However, the subject gets more complex for the new Christian, Jesus refers to the very act of being angry as being as bad a murder!

Jesus says[118]

'But I say to you, that whoever is angry with his brother without a cause shall be in danger of the judgment: and whoever shall say to his brother, Raca, shall be in danger of the council: but whoever shall say, you fool, shall be in danger of hell fire'.

Many people have suffered violent crimes at the hands of other people and years later are suffering mental scars from their times of trial.

What a terrible tragedy it is when a child is bullied at school to a point where they commit suicide rather than face the bullying anymore. Although the bully didn't actually hold the gun they must at some point face judgement.

How do we feel about the victim of sexual abuse and or rape who commits suicide because they can't live with the pain and guilt, yet they are innocent?

Jesus wants us to live at a higher level, we are the intelligent species, we should be able to see the hurt our words and actions can do to other people,

Jesus tells us that we must consider what we say and do that, we should control our tongues and our actions.

If people do all things in love, if we control our tongues we may save lives rather than allowing an unguarded word to get beneath others skins causing them damage.

We have nicknames for many people, we see now on Twitter and on Facebook the way that some people are damaged by 'Trolls'.

118 Matt 5:22 American King James Version (AKJV)

Bullies are people who are being hateful to others, they are trying to kill them intellectually and emotionally and sometimes literally.

Bullies attack all sorts of people and all ages. What is especially sad is when your church leader or other professional you trust turns out to be the bully.

Some church leaders say 'hurt people hurt people' so true: but it does not justify hurting people. It is very easy to use the phrase to become a type of self-justification.

When people who are hurt then hurt others it doesn't make it right. When the people causing the hurt are leaders, pastors, teachers, it's worse because we often look up to these people to lead guide and protect us.

Bullies/abusers: this sort of harm is evil in origin leading to some victims committing suicide because of these terrible attacks. To take away a person's innocence as is often the result of abuse and bullying is to kill a part of them, they will often feel terribly rejected and alone, hated, terrified, with no-one to turn to.

Bullies are very crafty, making the person think it's their own fault they get hurt.

If we read Genesis 3 we read the story of the fall of mankind. In the first verses the serpent (Satan), says to the woman, 'did God really say you must not eat from any tree in the garden'?

This is not a direct challenge but a very subtle way of bringing doubt into the woman's mind. The woman's response is very accurate and direct as we read in verse 3. 'but God did say, *'You must not eat fruit from the tree that is in the middle of the garden, and you must not touch it, or you will die.''*

Eve fully understood the rules that God had laid down, if you eat of a certain tree you will die.

Eve is repeating what God has told her and her husband Adam.

God is specific the tree has a name; the Tree of the Knowledge of Good and Evil.

Satan's response is very clever because he talks about death of the body, but one can argue he ignored the greater and as turns out for mankind the more serious death: the death of the spirit. The death of innocence, the death of freedom.

When Eve ate the apple and then her husband did the same their relationship with God changed, they felt ashamed of their nakedness, yet they were husband and wife so moments before must have been happy naked in each other's company and in the garden. They would have been at peace walking in the garden naked with God walking with them. It was not so much being naked that was the problem: rather it was they had a different thought process about the body, they had lost their innocence.

After they ate the apple Adam and Eve were ashamed to be in the presence of God: yet he created them, he made them and obviously they had been naked with him when they walked together in the evening.

After eating the apple there were huge consequences for Adam and Eve: they were no longer allowed in the garden, they had to leave the Garden of Eden. What a disaster for them and for us.

So much changed, they had to work and toil for a living, grow plants for food and also learn to kill animals for food: learn to make clothes; the woman would experience pain in child birth. There was enmity between serpents and mankind. All for one moment of sin.

When we sin, we fall short of the glory of God it separates us from him, if it wasn't for Jesus dying on the cross and rising up on the third day, we would be without hope.

People are hurt and damaged in many ways, with varying degrees of impact. If we are attacked, we cannot tell beforehand how we will react. Some become angry and seek revenge, others feel the weight of the attack, the degradation, the humiliation, let alone the pain. Additionally they may experience pain and emotional distress as their bodies recover from physical injuries or their minds from trauma.

Take the child that gets run over and injured in a genuine accident and recovers well: after their body recovers the child is no longer the innocent child they were before: they have been exposed to the harsh side of life: they are changed.

When someone's innocence is taken away violently or abusively a part of them dies, it is dead, finished, it can't be replaced or returned. However, much therapy they receive it won't be possible to restore it. They can find a new normal. Only God can help them have perfect peace and live through and with the loss.

If you are someone that has been the victim of such a loss, it may help to talk to a church leader or Chaplain, if you are unable or your church leader is unwilling, I offer this prayer that may help:

Dear Heavenly Father, you know all the things I have suffered in my life and the manner in which they have affected me. You know too the ways I have responded to these things both the good ways and the bad ways. I pray you will forgive me for those times I have responded badly, and I pray you would heal me in mind body and spirit for the damage that has been done to me at the hands of other people.

Lord, I pray too that you would heal me for the damage I have done to my body mind and spirit as I have struggled to cope with these painful experiences.

Lord, I pray too that you would free me from all ties and hurts and that from this moment on I would be the person you want me to be and that the past wrongs would no longer direct my footsteps. I pray Lord you would heal, restore and bless me in your service and I would be a delight to you. I pray too Lord that you will have mercy on those who have caused me pain.

I ask these prayers in the name of Jesus.

Amen

God bless you

CHAPTER 17

You shall not commit adultery

Exodus 20:7 NIV

The story is often told of the vicar who wakes up one morning and low and behold his bike is gone. It has been stolen!

He is very angry about this and decides to take it out on the congregation of his church. He will give the congregation what for when he preaches at the next Sunday service.

He will take them through the 10 commandments, and when he gets to Thou shall Not Steal the 8th Commandment he will really blast them! However, on Sunday all is going well with his sermon, the congregation are looking appropriately contrite and then when he gets to the 7th Commandment 'thou shall not commit adultery', he remembers where he left his bike!

It's a cheap joke of which there are many variants. We joke about the vicar committing adultery, it once was shocking, today, as a society we take marriage vows less seriously now than perhaps we once did. Today there is more temptation and opportunity to 'play away'. National stars and celebrities are caught with non-spouses in compromising situations. There is both desire to be faithless and the freedom to commit the acts. Sadly, the jokes about the vicar committing adultery have become for many real-life situations with a number of people in the church and families being hurt.

Adultery is not new it was an issue from the beginning that's why there's a commandment about it. It was relevant when Jesus was alive just as it is relevant today.

One might argue having sex is in itself not an issue, but that is the very nub of the problem, sex in itself for sex sake is against the Bible.

It's not having sex that is the sole problem it is breaking a relationship in a permanent way. Or not entering into a relationship. The sexual act was an integral part of marriage a different, special, loving, fun and physical way for a husband and wife to be fulfilled.

The Bible says 'Therefore shall a man leave his father and his mother, and shall cleave unto his wife: and they shall be one flesh'.[119]

So firstly a man must leave his father and mother this is saying to the young man you leave your old life behind, the ways you acted, the games you played all the old life must be left behind.

It's time to take on responsibilities no longer will your parents care for you, no longer should you expect them to provide a roof over your head and no longer can you indulge in the things you used to do. When Genesis was written about 4000 years ago girls and indeed women were often looked on as possessions, not able to make their own decisions. Whilst this is still the case in some countries, thankfully many countries now see women as equal.

In our 21st century Western world women are emancipated they have free choice so this verse applies to men and women equally. When they choose to get married they must leave the past behind, the drinking, the partying: together they become one flesh. They have to take on responsibility and be there for each other, not quite them

119 American Standard Version (1901) Genesis 2:24

against the world but almost.

In the eyes of God, when a couple get married they become one flesh, the act of intercourse consummates the marriage and also joins them together in a way they should never have experienced before. They become one flesh, they become a very close special unit. It is one of the most precious acts a man and woman can share.

The consequences of committing adultery and breaking a marriage vow are both irreversible and catalytic.

Paul says in 1 Corinthians 7:

'Now concerning the things about which you wrote, it is good for a man not to touch a woman. But because of immoralities, each man is to have his own wife, and each woman is to have her own husband. The husband must fulfill his duty to his wife, and likewise also the wife to her husband. The wife does not have authority over her own body, but the husband does: and likewise also the husband does not have authority over his own body, but the wife does'.

Firstly, the phrase for a man to touch a woman means to have a sexual relationship with a woman, this is not allowed unless with in marriage.

The couple become so close they receive comfort pleasure and satisfaction from each other's bodies. Paul reminds couples that they have an obligation to the other to give of their body to their partner, neither can demand but neither can withdraw their body from their partner. Of course, a couple may decide to abstain from full sex for a joint reason for a short time, but they should still give of themselves to each other in other ways in order that neither feels rejected and the weaker one doesn't go off in search of sexual fulfilment.

In his commentary of 1 Corinthians 7 David Guzik makes several good points, it is certainly well worth reading his commentary:

1. The affection due her is an important phrase: since Paul meant this to apply to every Christian marriage, it shows that every wife has affection due her. Paul doesn't think only the young or pretty or submissive wives are due affection: every wife is due affection because she is a wife of a Christian man!

2. Paul also emphasizes what the woman needs: not merely sexual relations, but the affection due her. If a husband is having sexual relations with his wife, but without true affection to her, he is not giving his wife what she is due.

3. Affection also reminds us that when a couple is unable – for physical or other reasons – to have a complete sexual relationship, they can still have an affectionate relationship, and thus fulfil God's purpose for these commands.

4. On the same idea, also the wife to her husband – the wife is not to withhold marital affection from her husband. Paul strongly puts forth the idea that there is a mutual sexual responsibility in marriage: the husband has obligations towards his wife, and the wife has obligations towards her husband.[120]

There are many stereotypes and stories related to marriage and sex, especially the 'not tonight I have a headache' response from the wife.

Now if the wife or the husband has a 'headache' in a loving relationship that is fine, but when one of couple pretends to be unwell and not able to make love to their spouse then that is wrong. It's better to have a brief discussion of the real reason and sort it out, it may still mean they don't have

120 1 Corinthians 7: 3-6 David Guzik *Commentary on the Bible*

intercourse that time but it will be a joint decision, and they can still take time for a certain amount of intimacy. A partner can feel rejected when the spouse says 'not tonight I have a headache' and they know their spouse does not have a headache! It's vital that a couple discuss these type of situations so that they don't become a problem.

If one partner regularly uses an excuse to not engage in sex with their 'other half' or the reasons for refusal become more extreme, the other partner may start to build up ill will towards their spouse; they may start to look outside of their marriage for the comfort and attention they feel they are missing.

This may lead to an adulterous relationship. None of this is justifiable, but it may be understandable. In our modern world there are many sexual and erotic temptations before men and women so a healthy sex life within marriage is very important.

If one of the couple is ill it may be difficult to experience full intercourse, but it can be great fun trying to find ways of mutual sexual pleasure, or mutual intimate pleasure.

When a couple get married, they marry before God and in front of a congregation.

They bring together their minds, bodies, spirits and emotions, to become one flesh. Making love for the first time to someone that you are truly, madly, deeply in love with, and want to share the rest of your life with, is for the majority of couples, an unbelievable experience.

Maintaining an active sexual relationship between husband and wife within marriage is very special, and a vital part of the relationship. Bound together in love, that is eternal, a safe place for children to grow up in. That's the theory, but if either or both of the couple has had intercourse before their marriage, this may well impact their marriage.

The Bible is clear the first time a couple should have intercourse is after they are married, not before, but after. There are several reasons for this that should be obvious, some are:

- To consummate the marriage.
- Their chosen person should be very special.
- They should have kept themselves for this person.
- So they can prepare themselves for a lifetime together without the pressure of a sexual union.
- To protect the sanctity of marriage. Marriage is special, sexual intercourse is a major part of marriage, but it isn't the only part. Having sex before marriage is like building a house on a part of the foundations.

Once you engage in a sexual relationship you open yourself up to a total exposure to the other person, they may not be interested or wanting that sort of commitment, they may just want some fun, or release, but not the responsibility of marriage. That is why you should only have intercourse within the sanctity of marriage. All within the framework of marriage where all the foundations are in place and the relationship is balanced. Where the commitment is 'till death us do part'. God gave us ways to live that ensure that no-one is harmed and no-one does what God says is wrong. These are reasons why sex before marriage is wrong according to God and the Bible.

- Because God says you shouldn't. Exodus 22:16 - And if a man entices a maid that is not betrothed, and lie with her, he shall surely endow her to be his wife .

- To stop temptation to sleep around 1 Corinthians 7:2 'But because of the temptation to sexual immorality, each man should have his own wife and each woman her own husband.'
- There is a mystery of the first time of making love to someone that you are truly madly deeply in love with. An active sexual relationship between husband and wife within marriage is very special.
- Adultery is wrong and has huge consequences for the relationship. More often than not leading to pain, separation and divorce.

However, if the couple are widows/widowers and are marrying then there is no reason for them not to have a full and enjoyable sex life within their new marriage.

The story of King David and Bathsheba[121] in the Bible is graphic and shocking and the consequences are catastrophic. It starts by saying that it was spring-time, a time when Kings go off to war, but King David who was a great warrior for some reason didn't go off to war.

So he is in his palace, he should have been out in the fields with the soldiers. He got up from his bed and went to the roof and saw a woman bathing. (This raises loads of questions at this point but for time I will just complete the story).

David sent his staff to find out who the woman was, her name was Bathsheba and then King David tells his staff to call her over and she went to bed with him: Bathsheba becomes pregnant and tells David, he then arranged for her husband who was a senior soldier in his army to be called home and spend time with his wife.

121 2 Samuel 11

But the soldier (Uriah) was an honourable man and wouldn't sleep with his wife while his fellow soldiers were at war and in danger, David even tried to make him drunk but Uriah held on to his views. Now David really does get it wrong.

David sent him back to the frontline with orders he should be at the worse place for the fighting and that he should be left to be killed by the enemy. He was.

The consequences for David and Bathsheba were huge.

God was very angry with King David and King David paid a very high price for his adultery and for the arranging for the killing of Uriah.

The story of David and Bathsheba has been well covered by Rabbis, Theologians, Historians and Bible commentators. I don't propose to spend time in exploring this event, sufficient to say as background, that Bathsheba was the granddaughter of one of David's most trusted advisors, and had probably seen the king on many occasions and he had probably seen her growing up. They were known to each other. Bathsheba was carrying out a purification, bathing after her period, which means she was not already pregnant by her husband. It seems King David did not recognize her, but saw well enough an attractive young lady bathing. From what I can understand there was nothing pre-planned, neither did it appear Bathsheba could see the King watching her nor is it noted that there was any intention on her behalf to seduce the King.

So what caused King David to get into so much trouble?

David was where he shouldn't have been, he should have been at war, there was a major battle going on, he was the leader of the army, he was a mighty warrior, yet he stayed at home. Why?

Then we wonder why was Bathsheba bathing on the roof in view of the king? In those days bathing for a woman would have been a very private time, and would have taken place where she felt safe from others in her household. Also bathing may just have been handwashing or face washing, not having a shower. Not like our modern world where people selling showers and baths will advertise young ladies posing provocatively using their products: films show naked women in showers or baths; today there are so many opportunities to see women bathing. But still generally it is private.

David then responds to the lusts that seeing Bathsheba bathing triggered by getting his staff to find out who she is and then bring her into his bed and committing adultery with her. David could have looked the other way, bit tough but he was the King, a role model, he was a Godly man used to hearing God's voice. I wonder did he hear God speak to him and say ignore what you are seeing? Don't react? Or did his lust overwhelm everything he knew?

Did Bathsheba have a choice? In those days if the King called, you went. The King could have what he wanted.

Both David and Bathsheba suffered for their sin, the child Bathsheba conceived died.

David's household became embroiled in war, 3 of his sons were killed. One of David's sons seduced David's wife.

It was a terrible time for Bathsheba and for King David. The pain that followed the night of passion was horrendous. The greatest price was paid by Uriah, (Bathsheba's husband) an honourable warrior for King David, who David ensured was killed in battle.

Today when people commit adultery, the whole family on all sides suffer; many experience years of excruciating emotional pain and torture. Especially the children.

Whilst many of the victims of adultery may not be sent out to war, many feel as though they have died, their life has been taken from them.

Was Bathsheba trying to get the favour of the King? Some commentators blame Bathsheba for trying to seduce the King, others place the blame squarely with David, for taking advantage of Bathsheba. Was she flirting? We don't know her age, but maybe she thought she was just having a game? Did she want her 'flirting' to end up in the King's bed? Probably not her plan? The outcome from the time of passion was terrible. Eventually there was healing for them as God restored David who when shown the error of his ways truly repented: God later referred to David as a man after my own heart

But the cost of their adultery was enormous.

Today, the young people who go to some of the Mediterranean resorts with the idea to drink as much as they can for as long as they can, and have sex with as many different people as possible make themselves very vulnerable.

It sounds tempting when you are young and carefree, it's tempting too for the over forty singles as well. Especially when you have a very limited moral code.

But the number of people who suffer from these holiday 'relationships' is large, additionally it's a bad foundation for building long-term relationships and marriage.

There is the risk of sexually transmitted disease, together with the potential damage to health of excessive drinking and drug taking.

There is a vogue amongst some of the younger generation to have people purely to have sex with.

Someone to meet with to have sex: someone they may never have met before, or at best they have had a couple of drinks with. The rationale being that neither partner is expected to 'feel 'anything from the intimate time together, it is purely to release their sexual needs.

Over recent years there has been a change in the attitude of many young people, with better contraception they are taking more risks, playing more sexual games.

On a night patrol as a street Pastor it is clear that many young women are out there to experiment, to drink, play drinking games, and find young men for 'fun'

They often dress erotically and with no thought to decency and their own well-being.

Sadly, Street Pastors, Paramedics and other groups who work the night time economy have been presented with young girls, barely clothed, sometimes naked, drunk, unconscious, vomiting or lying in their own vomit or just 'out of it' in an alleyway or in the gutter, either because they have been thrown out of the clubs, or because they have collapsed on the way home.

Those working in the night time economy both paid and volunteer all have their stories of young ladies who they have had to rescue. So sad.

We live in a challenged and 'free 'society. For some it is a great place, for others it is a dark place where the experimentation is dangerous and sometimes fatal.

If your younger life has been spent having many sexual partners it's very difficult to become faithful to just one person in a marriage, even to be faithful to one person for life.

But every generation of society is encouraged to live life to the full, a quick kiss and cuddle is not anything to be concerned about, we walk a tightrope, we can live life to the full as a married couple; I was talking recently to a lady who had been married nearly 40 years and her and her husband were still having loads of fun together. We need to know if we are married we can't play sex games outside the house unless it is with our loved one, i.e. wife or husband.

CHAPTER 18

You shall not steal

Exodus 20:15 NIV

This is an obvious commandment adopted by most religions, although how people define stealing is interesting.

Simply put don't take what is not yours! For years many businesses have lost a lot of money through staff taking home items of office equipment that do not belong to them, from a pencil all the way to a computer.

OfficeZilla blog states 'The U.S. Department of Commerce reports 'sticky fingers' activity at work costs companies $50 billion per year'.

To give some idea what that is: that's the equivalent of nearly 35% of the UK's £ 110 billion spend on the NHS! [122] Or it would pay for UK's annual spend on medication for over two years.

So 'taking the odd pencil never did anyone any harm' is obviously not right.

Yet to take a pencil or pen seems quite normal, for example you use it to complete a piece of work, put it in your pocket or handbag and forget it. Next time you need a pen or pencil you just get another one from the cupboard.

It is such a small thing a pencil, it wasn't our intention to steel it, we needed a pencil to do our work, then we forgot it. Is God really interested in such a small thing?

We need to keep ourselves free from all sin even the smallest sin affects us. As we Journey on our new Christian

122 Uk.Gov.NHS

life, we want to be sure that all we do pleases God, if the pencil belongs to our employer unless he has said take what you want, take it home; to take it home is theft. Theft is sin, therefore we can't do it.

The danger is not in the 'little sin' it is in allowing any sin in our lives, we open ourselves to a greater sin. We tend to argue along the lines that a little thing can do no harm, but we fight against an enemy that prowls around like a roaring lion looking to devour or deceive us. He doesn't mind how far short of 'God's glory' you fall, just that you fall.

If we give him an opening however small he will walk right into it, he will use it as a way of ruling us, of leading us away from God, Satan is very good at doing this he is a great deceiver, we must continue to focus on Jesus in all areas of our lives. If we have part of our mind ignoring Gods word, it will grow and became a cause for major sin.

Romans 8: 7-8. *'For the mind that is set on the flesh is hostile to God, for it does not submit to God's law: indeed, it cannot. Those who are in the flesh cannot please God'.* NIV

CHAPTER 19

You shall not give false testimony against your neighbour

Exodus 20:16 NIV

Well, you might say, I don't get to go to court often to tell about my neighbour so I don't have to worry about this commandment.

Oh that it was that simple. It is not as obvious as that, yet we are all tempted and often fail and find ourselves giving false (testimony) witness against our neighbour.

How often do we listen to gossip and add our thoughts to the debate, invariably they are not supportive or complimentary comments about the person?

We are to remember when we discuss others that we should not be defamatory about the person.

'Oh I love a bit of gossip, do tell' is a line that has been used many times in plays and comedies and in real life.

We all love to hear gossip, that's why there are so many magazines and tabloid papers that survive on gossip, especially about celebrities, pop stars and WAGS of famous sports stars.

The number of Sundays over the years where the headlines have been along the lines, 'Bishop or MP or pop-star involved in three in a bed romp'. Or, 'church organist ran off with my wife'.

Or 'MP photographed dressed as a baby and being whipped by a pro'!

It seems that not a Sunday goes by without someone important being named and shamed in the press for some misdemeanour or other. Journalists believe they have a right to tell the public: that what they write is in the public interest. Irrespective of whether innocent people get hurt in the following journalistic melee. I am not a journalist so I don't understand the pressure they are under to produce a headline or a story nor indeed their passion for telling the sordid details of others failures and challenges.

Would they be happy to be on the front page of their paper for their own private sin?

But whatever the rights and wrongs about journalistic responsibilities, the Bible teaches we should not bear false witness against our neighbour and that is the key point. Gossip is bad and the problem with gossip is generally the story gets embellished along the way.

Is it wrong to tell someone that a person is guilty of a crime? Whatever your opinion surely, it is wrong when the message changes and the story escalates as the message goes from person to person, the alleged guilty person often goes for example from being a petty burglar, to someone who was always a thief, comes from a family of thieves and also is well known locally as a child molester and rapist, and the police have been chasing them for years.

Invariably these latter points are made up along the way, they are damaging to the individual and very hurtful to their family, yet we see it happen often.

Gossip is destructive, it generally involves a character assassination of a third party and from then on, that person is not only dealing with the consequences of any sin they have committed but also trying to clear their name for the wrongful and hurtful gossip that has been spread abroad.

In Church gossip is very destructive and dangerous. It is important that as Christians when someone starts to gossip we tell them that we will not listen and that they should desist. We need to guard our tongues as Psalm 141:3 ESV says: *'Set a guard, O LORD, over my mouth: keep watch over the door of my lips!'*

It will make a happier church and save some people much pain.

CHAPTER 20

Covid-19 a plague today in our 21st century world?

Is there a link with the Plagues in Egypt thousands of years ago and Covid-19 today?

This book was on its way to the publisher, I had finished it; I thought.

As I work in a hospital I was aware of the start of Covid-19 and how it was impacting our world; I kept thinking about the plagues the Egyptian people suffered, because Pharaoh, would not let the Israelite people go.

I wondered, maybe I should add another chapter to the book before it was printed?

A chapter reflecting on Covid-19 and the possible similarity to the Plagues in Egypt and to consider some of the questions that are being asked about God and this plague / pandemic.

I wondered too, what, can we learn from the scriptures, also what if anything is God saying to us? People have asked me many questions about this pandemic including:

Is Covid-19 from God?

Is Covid-19 a plague?

The Free dictionary gives some good and relevant definitions of what is a plague;

- A highly infectious epidemic disease, especially one with a high rate of fatality; a pestilence. (n)
- A widespread affliction or calamity seen as divine retribution. (n)

- To afflict with any evil.
- To be a widespread or continuous problem or defect. (v)
- A virulent, infectious disease that is caused by the bacterium *Yersinia pestis* (syn. *Pasteurella pestis*) and is transmitted primarily by the bite of fleas from an infected rodent, especially a rat. (n)
- Something that causes persistent hardship, trouble, or annoyance:
- Any highly infectious, usually fatal epidemic disease?

www.thefreedictionary.com/plague Copyright © 2003-2020 *Farlex, Inc*

Covid-19 is not a plague as it is not caused by the bacterium Yersina Pestis or transmitted by the bite of a flea. However, it is plague like, in the way it is affecting so many millions of people around the world.

For the first time in living memory we have been assailed by a world-wide pandemic; affecting millions of people. Some would argue that as a percentage of the total world population those affected by Covid-19 is a small percentage. However, the impact to people with Covid-19 is awful and to the families whose loved ones are suffering and dying, it is a nightmare.

It is also a huge challenge to the health services around the world and is an ongoing challenge to several countries across the world. It may be with us for years to come! For those countries that have instituted a lock down, the impact on the community is huge both financially and emotionally, this whole event has threatened the infrastructure of nations. It will take a long-time to recover from Covid-19; for example, some commentators are saying it will take airlines 3 years to recover even if air travel immediately returned to where it was before the lockdown.

Much has been written in the past about the possibility of such an event, films have been made and TV series recorded and shown to a people who thought it would never become a reality.

Yet today, here we are in lockdown. At the time of writing, cases of Covid-19 are still rising in the UK and in other places in the world. China, Italy and Spain are seeing the rate of new infections slow and reflecting that possibly they are over the worst? I was completing the final edit of this book as the lockdown started in the UK.

In the hospital where I work, I found myself caring for Covid-19 patients and their families and supporting the health care workers who work so tirelessly and diligently in a pressured, humid, challenging and at times unreal environment. It seemed to me there were some parallels to the pre-exodus time in Egypt nearly 4000 years ago and for us now.

Can we as Christians learn anything from history that will help us in our current situation?

Maybe we should consider some questions that are being voiced?

Is God speaking to us?

Are we hearing God's voice at this time?

Would we know if we heard it and does it matter to us at all?

We need to explore these questions; imagine if God is speaking to us and we are not listening, we may be missing out on the answer to our prayers, the solution to our catastrophe?

In the book of Numbers chapter 22 we read the story of Balaam's donkey. Balaam, a non-Israelite prophet has been asked by Balak the King of Moab, to curse the Israelite people. So, Balaam goes on his donkey to meet with Balak. On the way the donkey suddenly goes off the road and into a field. Balaam is angry with the donkey but what Balaam has not seen is, that standing in the road in front of them is an Angel of the Lord, standing with his sword drawn. The donkey saw the Angel of the Lord and understood, he would not pass the Angel, yet Balaam did not see the Angel.

It was not until the donkey started to speak that Balaam's eyes were opened. Have we in our modern world become like Balaam, going on our way, not seeing what God is putting before us? Nor hearing what God is saying to us?

Before the Israelites were released by Pharaoh and set on their journey to the promised land, there were 10 plagues.

Plague of blood
Plague of frogs
Plague of lice or bugs
Plague of flies
Plague of pestilence, (only affected the live stock)
Plague of boils,
Plague of thunder, hail and fire
Plague of locust
Plague of darkness
Plague of death of firstborn.

As I was reading about the plagues that led up to the Israelites exodus from Egypt, I started to wonder and attempted to draw parallels with what is happening to us today and wondered are there lessons to be learnt from the exodus and living during a pandemic?

I have added this chapter in that it may help some Christians at this time. Many people who are naturally anxious about the pandemic are asking questions including:

Did God give us Covid-19?
Why did God allow this pandemic?
If Covid-19 is not from God then where is it from?
Is this the end of the world?
How do we hear God's voice at this time?
What is God's saying?
Is God speaking?

I will try and explore these and other such questions, so hopefully something in this chapter will be helpful.

Countries have experienced serious pandemics before, if we study statistics we would see we were due a pandemic; with one projected approximately every 100 years. The last major pandemic was the Spanish pandemic in 1918. Therefore, we were due one?

Yet we live in an advanced world where we can travel to the moon, we can transplant people's hearts, where we are able to control the spread of major diseases. So even if we were due a pandemic, we had nothing to fear? We had got the plans in place and the tools to deal with it, hadn't we?

For centuries governments and people have feared the bubonic plague in its various guises. Not since the bubonic plague, which was known as the Black Death in the 14th Century has there been such a world-wide impact.

It is estimated that with Black Death in excess of 75 million people died, some estimates claim a figure of 200 million deaths. The outbreak was primarily in Asia, Africa, Europe and the UK. It is hard to be sure of the full impact of this plague as there were few records kept in those days and very poor communication especially outside of key towns and cities. Unlike now where we have access to World Wide web, mobile telephone and satellite links.

In England in 1665 during the Great plague, London was the worst affected place in the UK, with an estimated 100,000 deaths. The plague is believed to have started in China or the Far-East and quickly moved to other countries especially Europe which was also badly affected.

Somehow that resonates with us now, we are told Covid-19 started in a market in Wuhan in China; since then the UK and Europe have been badly affected. How sad and scary it was when we started to hear about the impact of Covid-19 on Italy and Spain. Then it started to grow in the UK.

It seemed strange when our government imposed this lockdown; encouraging people to work from home, that made sense even if a little unreal. Then the government started to talk about unnecessary businesses shutting, cafés, restaurants, cinemas, libraries, estate agents; travel being restricted, flights being cancelled for the duration of the lockdown. Our national sporting events were cancelled no football, horse racing, tennis, golf and motor sport. We couldn't even go to the gym or swimming pool. The government promising billions of pounds of aid to businesses and to those who have lost their income because of Covid-19.

Lockdown also means we can't visit our loved ones; even loved ones who are seriously ill or dying, we are not allowed to go to be with them in hospital. Hospital staff are trying to connect loved ones with those who are sick and dying, using iPads. As a Hospital Chaplain it is very moving to be part of that.

How unreal it is too that churches, the place of sanctuary even in war time, cannot open for normal services; that no more than 2-3 people can be in the church at the same time. As Christians we know that the church is not the building, the church is the people. But throughout history even in war time, some may say especially in war time, church congregations continued to meet. It is impossible to be sure at this time the impact that Covid-19 will have on the church in the long-term. We are fortunate during this pandemic to have tools like Zoom, WhatsApp and YouTube, to stream a live service to people's homes or have a prayer group over Zoom. How valuable is all this modern technology that is available to us?

Many people take part in these 'services' and draw strength and comfort from them, but some, for a variety of reasons will not. Not everyone has the internet, others are unable to load the programme/app on their computer, phone or tablet. Equally, there are those who generally don't like this style of communication.

The lack of people physically attending church may cause a downturn in financial contributions to churches, not everyone can do on-line banking, nor want to post cash.

It is interesting to note that Daniel Defoe writing about the Great Plague of 1665 said this about the church. *"Wherever God erects a house of prayer, The Devil always builds a chapel there; And 'twill be found upon examination the latter has the largest congregation."* (Daniel Defoe, History of the Plague in London Published May 29th 2003 by Penguin Classics (first published March 1722).

There was sadly some truth in Defoe's comments before this pandemic.

Is Covid-19 as Defoe says, 'the Devil building a chapel there'?

For many centuries the church was sacrosanct, a place where a refugee could go and be safe, where they could know that no-one would try and harm them there.

Sadly, we have seen some atrocities over the decades where people in church have been gunned down, or bombs have been placed in their church or place of worship. This is for sure not God's plan.

Churches are responding in many ways to Covid-19, some extending their involvement in the local community, others trying to support the vulnerable members of their church. Many churches used to remain open each day for people to quietly sit, meditate and pray. Because of the potential risk of passing on infections that is no longer a good idea.

Equally, parish Priests and Ministers of Religion were advised to stay away from the sick and dying in hospital and therefore many are no longer going into hospital to visit their dying parishioners so they don't become a risk to themselves and those they visit. Some minsters have ignored this advice and risked a visit.

In most cases Hospital Chaplains who have been trained and fit tested for PPE, visit patients and minister to them; if chaplains are not available staff will try and give emotional support depending on the volume of patients, and the severity of their condition. It is without doubt not the same as a family or pastoral visit, but it is a great help to patient and relative alike, who otherwise would remain out of communication with their loved ones at such a traumatic and sad time.

In the great plague nearly 500 years ago the disease had horrendous symptoms, including fever, breathing difficulties, buboes (swelling of the lymph nodes in the groin, or under the arms) black skin and gangrene like skin. It was obvious who had the plague.

Covid-19 is often subtle in its presentation; it doesn't produce buboes or gangrene like skin; it mimics other types of flu and colds and fevers yet with far more devastating consequences for many who contract the disease. It is possible that someone suffering from hay fever can be misdiagnosed as suffering from Covid-19 until their swab test results come through. Equally a person can have Covid-19 and have no symptoms!

For staff as they care for a high risk Covid-19 patient there are a number of questions they have to address about the risk to themselves, to their families or to colleagues or other patients on the ward. Not least if this patient has no obvious symptoms, are they a risk to me? The only way to proceed is to act as if they had the disease.

In 1665 the risk to those who were trying to care for those infected was incredibly high. They had little if any type of effective PPE (personal protective equipment). Today during this Covid-19 pandemic the debate rages about whether there is sufficient PPE? Is sufficient equipment available to all those working in health? What is the right type of PPE for this patient or carer? Should the general public use PPE when shopping, walking in the street or along the beach? Should shop staff use PPE?

We learn that PPE fitting is important, many people walk around wearing masks that have huge gaps at the side or around the nose, they will probably be ineffective, there needs to be a good seal. I had to shave off my beard and moustache so that I could wear PPE to have the best chance of it being effective.

We hear on the news about emergency mortuaries being set up in refrigerated containers, it is not ideal however it provides a good temporary response for the higher level of deaths we are experiencing with Covid-19. Recently, sadly the UK number of deaths from Covid-19 passed 13,000. In July 1665 in the great plague it was reported that 13000 people died in London in July alone. As I write the number of Covid-19 deaths in the UK has now exceeded 30,000!

In 1665 they did not have sophisticated mortuaries as we do now, nor even the opportunity of refrigerated containers. Indeed, it is reported that in the great plague horse drawn and hand drawn carts were pulled or pushed through the streets, the people pulling the cart calling out, 'throw out your dead'.

There were not sufficient graves, so people were buried in mass graves outside the city or village. When I was boy there was (and still is) a green area that was supposed to be a mass grave from the plague and to this day no one is allowed to disturb the ground or build on it. Children play happily on the grass today although I was never that sure it was a good idea?

At times of crisis people naturally look to all manner of sources to try to get an explanation for what is going on. They look to medical science to understand the virus, to find a good screening tool, to find a cure, or another method for reversing the effect. Some people turn to old wives' tales, others to alternative types of therapy and medication. Some people prefer the 'ignore it will go away plan', or yet others go with the 'why worry were gonna die anyway so let's party', idea.

Peoples rhetoric gets interesting and with our modern technology there are plenty of platforms on which to pontificate. During a recent news interview one respondent was fervent in decrying selfish people who broke the lockdown, yet another was angry with the government for taking away 'our human rights'.

Many people seek a higher power to blame rather than themselves or the government, whilst there are those who have a strong belief structure in a higher power and follow their god.

For the Christian it is certainly time to seek God, to know that our days are in his hands; that when we become Christians we offer to him our souls and bodies.

We seek him to lead us and guide us as we attempt to do his will, in our lives and trust him with our lives. He has the power to guide protect and save us.

He is in control of our lives and we trust Him, for the Bible tells us in Jerimiah 29:11

'For I know the plans I have for you declares the Lord, plans to prosper you and not to harm you. Plans to give you a hope and a future'.

This pandemic has caused high levels of anxiety and fear throughout the countries of the world. Sadly, many families now have lost a loved one or know someone directly affected by Covid-19.

We have news bulletins every 15 minutes. Daily we hear about the numbers of people with the disease, the numbers who died the day before and the plans of the government to support the people, and also details of the situation in other countries. Then several times an hour in the headlines we hear it all again together with the opinions of politicians, 'experts' medical staff, professors; so many people crystal ball gazing with varying degrees of success.

Because of the availability of the news broadcast we hear every few minutes, we learn the number of people who have died in our town, village or city. How many people are confirmed as having the disease, how many are out of work, what the chances of us becoming infected are, the number of celebrities that have the disease or have died. Constantly before us we hear about the businesses that are closing down, the failure of governments, we seldom focus on what is going well except once a week when people gather outside their homes and clap and celebrate the staff in the NHS.

We can't ignore Covid-19 if we want too, we have been put into lockdown and some groups have been isolated so far for maybe twelve weeks! Who knows how long there will be some form of restriction on movement and public meetings.

This pandemic appears to have caught us all off guard, there has been an amazing response from our emergency and medical teams. But it seems as if we have been playing catch up. Covid-19 has not respected rank or position, wealth or status. There was a real sense of shock when the UK Prime Minster, Boris Johnson was admitted to hospital with Covid-19 and was kept in ITU. He later spoke that plans were being made in case he did not recover. Thankfully he recovered, but for other families the reality is the pain of loss.

There have not been calls for mankind as a whole to call out to God, individual churches are calling for days of prayer, Easter passed without a united UK wide National Day of Prayer, equally as far as I am aware there has not been a call for a world-wide day of prayer. When the church unites in prayer it is a very powerful weapon, the united call to God has a great impact.

This is a world-wide pandemic

The situation in Egypt in 1400 BC only affected the Egyptian and Israelite people. The Bible says that the Israelite nation, God's people, were being held as slaves by the Egyptians and were being treated badly; they called out to God to set them free. God chose Moses to be his messenger, to go to Pharaoh (the King of Egypt) and tell him, God says 'set my people free'. Pharaoh refused, God warned Pharaoh that if he did not do what God wanted and set the Israelites free He, God, would punish Pharaoh and his people.

Pharaoh did not believe that God was any more important

or powerful than his wise men or magicians or indeed than any of the many gods that were worshipped in Egypt at the time. Pharaoh, had the Israelite nation within his land when he was born, he inherited them, they had come to Egypt over 400 years before his birth.

Around that time there was a famine in the land of Egypt; an Israelite man Joseph, had heard God's voice, obeyed God and did what God said to save the people who lived in Egypt and nearby lands from starvation. Genesis chapters 41-47

It was an awesome thing that God did through Joseph.

However, after that the Israelite nation settled in Egypt, they prospered greatly and their numbers grew over the hundreds of years that followed the famine.

Successive Pharaohs began to worry that the Israelite nation was becoming a threat to their kingdoms. The terror of the famine had gone. The Israelites were made slaves; all their possessions were taken by the Egyptians and their treatment became bad, then very bad, then terrible, etc.

The Israelites called out to God and he answered them.

When Moses went to Pharaoh and told him that God wanted him, Pharaoh, to let the Israelite people go, Pharaoh was not interested, he got his magicians to replicate some of the things that Moses did, in particular Moses, at God's instruction threw down his rod and it became a snake, Pharaohs magicians did the same thing, must have been scary standing and suddenly all around you were snakes, slithering about.

Then, Moses snake ate all the other snakes, impressive! But it wasn't the game changer that was needed. Pharaoh still would not let the Israelites go!

As we read earlier there were 10 plagues, all but one was aimed at Pharaoh, his advisors and magicians and the gods they served. They were not directed at the Israelite people.

God told Pharaoh, 'let my people go', if you don't you will be punished.

Everyone knew that God had caused the plague, that it was targeted, at Pharaoh and his people, but even more important and vital to understand, God said to Pharaoh via Moses, let my people go and there will be no consequence.

In war, a powerful ruler who is attacking a foreign city will often give the King of that city and its inhabitants a chance to surrender and live, to be treated reasonably well, even as prisoners.

God said this to Pharaoh, 'He said let my people go'.

God did not want or need to harm Pharaoh or his people, if Pharaoh had said at the beginning 'yup they can go', we probably wouldn't have heard much about it nor would there have been such suffering. But, Pharaoh was stubborn and arrogant.

I have not heard of anyone who has reported hearing the voice of God saying 'I'm sending Covid-19? I am punishing mankind, I am sending a plague. There would not be any doubt if Covid-19 was from God.

As Christians when we come to Jesus, when we give our lives to God and start our new life, there are things that God wants us to change. God doesn't treat us harshly we just know some things are right and others are not.

As we love God we start to want to spend time with him doing what he wants us to do. We want to be like Jesus, many have worn the wrist band, 'what would Jesus do?'. When God shows us that an aspect of our lives is wrong or bad for us we generally try and change that part of us. Somethings are incredibly hard to change, I was a 60 a day cigarette smoker, I didn't want to change. But God made a way. I was set free.

Some people have attitudes that are not very nice and it can be very hard to change those ways. We have the Holy Spirit to help us but even so we fail many times, Paul in

Romans 7:15 puts it so well.

'For I do not understand my own actions. For I do not do what I want, but I do the very thing I hate'. (ESV)

How strange that people committed to God should still do the things they know to be wrong. Thankfully John helps us when he says:

'My little children, I am writing these things to you so that you may not sin. But if anyone does sin, we have an advocate with the Father, Jesus Christ the righteous, He is the propitiation for our sins and not for ours only but also for the sins of the whole world'. 1 John 2: 1-2. (ESV)

In addition to our own weaknesses we have an enemy, Satan. Peter tells us in 1 Peter 5:8: *Be sober-minded; be watchful. Your adversary the devil prowls around like a roaring lion, seeking someone to devour.* (ESV)

So, If Covid-19 is not from God and not from man, then where is it from?

You may have noted that one of the dictionary definitions of a plague is;

'To afflict with any evil', many people believe that the source of Covid-19 is from an evil power?

For the Israelites in Egypt they were suffering terrible torture and deprivation, Pharaoh had told his slave drivers to treat the Israelites harshly. They were doing this and the Israelites called out to God and he heard. They did not suffer the plagues that God sent on Pharaoh and his people.

This pandemic does not seem to be sparing a particular nation; it is affecting most people groups in most countries, there does not seem to be a nation that is totally free.

The disease has spread around the world partly because of our world-wide travel, a number of people in our world no longer live in their native land or land of their birth.

Immigration and emigrations have brought millions of people to lands where they have better opportunity.

For the last few years some countries including Turkey, Greece and some EU member states, have been almost overrun by the refugees from the persecution in their own lands like Iraq, Iran and Syria.

The Israelites had God on their side, the Bible says they called out to God. It appears that they called out to God as a nation. We as a nation and a people need to be united in calling out to God for Him to end this disease.

The people of Israel were slaves for hundreds of years, we need to endeavour to ensure we don't leave Covid-19 as our legacy to the next generations. We don't leave our children as slaves to a world broken by Covid-19.

I don't know when you will read this book, but I encourage us all to seek and serve God with all our hearts, soul and minds. As Jesus taught us.

When we see people of all ages dying from Covid-19 in such numbers and when the person that dies is a loved one or a friend of ours we ask a straight and simple question:

Why?

Why did they die?

Why did they get this horrible disease?

I have been asked many times in the hospital why did this person die?

Did God do this?

If you can ask the question did God do this? Then the answer has to be no.

The God of the Bible would not leave you in any doubt if he were punishing you/us, if he had caused Covid-19. We would know. He would not leave any room for doubt, we would know.

God told Moses to tell Pharaoh that if he did not let the people go there would be a horrible consequence. There would be a plague. God was not silent and then started the plague, he warned Pharaoh and his people. He gave Pharaoh time to reconsider.

Therefore, I do not believe Covid-19 is a God given plague, He would have left us in no doubt.

He has allowed it and sadly we don't understand why it has happened.

We can academically explain how a plague can start, how a disease can spread, how maybe one ethnic or age group may be more vulnerable to a disease or virus, or how the disease can spread in some areas and not others. Why one family member gets covid-19 and another doesn't.

We can also probably explain why a group of people at an event have different reactions to Covid-19, some contracting it with minor symptoms and others with extremely severe symptoms.

Equally we can probably academically explain why if there are two people with the disease, why one lives and one dies?

If God had started this we would know, we would not need to try and work out why this and that. So, I believe we should be talking to God, as Christians we should be interceding for our world, nation, for our leaders, towns, friends and families. We need God now more than ever.

The plagues were not random, when Moses threw down his staff and it became a snake the wise men and magicians in pharaoh's court all managed to copy what Moses had done, their staffs became snakes. There the likeness ended when Moses' snake 'ate' all the other snakes. These wise men and magicians called on their gods.

God did not want people to believe that their gods were as

powerful as he was so each of the plagues was targeted against one of the Egyptian gods.

Not only was God giving Pharaoh the chance to change his mind he was demonstrating to Pharaoh and his people their gods were fake. If God was behind this Covid-19 pandemic we would be very clear what God's purpose was, why he was targeting people and what he wanted from us.

However, God is a God of Love; The Bible tells us that God loves those he created even though he hates what we do wrong, our sin. We read in Genesis 9: 12-17 about the covenant (promise) God made with mankind and all living creatures. How special it is when we see the rainbow, we know God is with us. God cannot renege on his promises.

> *And God said, "This is the sign of the covenant I am making between me and you and every living creature with you, a covenant for all generations to come:*
>
> *I have set my rainbow in the clouds, and it will be the sign of the covenant between me and the earth.*
>
> *Whenever I bring clouds over the earth and the rainbow appears in the clouds,*
>
> *I will remember my covenant between me and you and all living creatures of every kind. Never again will the waters become a flood to destroy all life.*
>
> *Whenever the rainbow appears in the clouds, I will see it and remember the everlasting covenant between God and all living creatures of every kind on the earth."*
>
> *So, God said to Noah, "This is the sign of the covenant I have established between me and all life on the earth."*

God wants a relationship with us but he has not created the havoc, distress and pain we are seeing. God wants a relationship of love with his people; for the Christian we have that brilliant example of how God sees the new world in Revelation 21.

> *Then I saw "a new heaven and a new earth," for the first heaven and the first earth had passed away, and there was no longer any sea. I saw the Holy City, the new Jerusalem, coming down out of heaven from God, prepared as a bride beautifully dressed for her husband. And I heard a loud voice from the throne saying, "Look! God's dwelling place is now among the people, and he will dwell with them. They will be his people, and God himself will be with them and be their God. 'He will wipe every tear from their eyes. There will be no more death' or mourning or crying or pain, for the old order of things has passed away."*
>
> *He who was seated on the throne said, "I am making everything new!" Then he said, "Write this down, for these words are trustworthy and true."*
>
> *He said to me: "It is done. I am the Alpha and the Omega, the Beginning and the End. To the thirsty I will give water without cost from the spring of the water of life".* (NIV)

The Bible tells us God wants to dwell with man whom he created, 'to wipe every tear from their eyes' God does not want people to suffer. As Christians we believe that our days are in God's hands, that our names are written in the Lambs' Book of Life.

If God wanted to tell us we are doing something wrong, he can tell us and does in many ways. He does not need to strike us down with a disease.

However, that does not mean that there are not consequences of our sin or that God does not take away from us things that are harmful to us. In the same way a parent will stop a child putting their hand in the fire or move the child away from the object that is threatening them, or move the object from the child.

We can and must as Christians learn to hear when God is telling us that something is harmful to us and give every effort to refrain from doing that thing. The Bible says repent, we need to feel so sad and bad about what we have done wrong that we don't do it again. Repent means for the Christian to turn around, turn away from what you have been doing. It is tough and we can only succeed with the help of the Holy Spirit.

When the plagues happened in Egypt there is a debate about their impact on the Israelites. We read in Exodus 8, God says 'I will put a division between my People and your people'. Some have interpreted this to mean that the Israelite people were spared the plagues, others have argued that this is quoted after the first three plagues therefore the Israelites faced the first three plagues.

What is clear is for much of this time of plagues the Israelites would have known what was happening, they would have been told by their leaders and maybe even by the slave drivers and yet they were not affected, or the plagues had a much lesser effect on them in their camps; they must have watched and heard about all that was going on with awe and a certain amount of anxiety and fear.

We need to note that the final plague would have affected the Israelites if they had not obeyed God and sacrificed a lamb and painted the blood over their door posts.

That is why today the Jewish nation celebrates Passover. For the Christian, Jesus is the sacrifice for our sins, this is why we often refer to him as the Lamb that was Slain for us!

When we see today people suffering and dying from Covid-19 we are filled with many feelings. Our hearts go out to those who are suffering from horrible symptoms, we are especially saddened for those who are unable to contact or see their families. We weep for the families whose loved ones have died because of this awful pandemic and for those who were unable to be with them at the end.

We think of staff that are daily caring for sick and dying patients with limited thought for themselves.

Then for ourselves, we are concerned, anxious, worried, frightened; are we at risk? Did I touch anyone that had Covid-19? Or a surface that was contaminated? Did I get too close to someone or breathe in their germs??

The Israelites may well have wondered about many of these questions, they had an answer that God was in control, he had challenged Pharaoh to let the people go and God was going to ensure that the Israelite people would be free.

We too as Christians have that promise during Covid-19 and whatever crisis we face that God is in control, we read in Psalm 121, that God neither slumbers nor sleeps, he is there for his people 24 hours a day. He is with us and he wants us to talk to him and tell him about our lives. God did not create mankind as robots, programmed to do what he says when he says, rather he gave us free will to do what we want when we want, indeed if we keep going against God's plans, he hands us over to the things we want rather than keep nagging us.

People have told me they pray for others, for the world or for peace but they are unable to pray for themselves as it seems wrong. Maybe selfish? That is such a shame as God wants us to talk with him. Praying is just like talking with God; Jesus gave us a prayer to pray to the Father in heaven to help us start our prayer time or give us words to say. When said with another person it is very powerful and moving especially if one of the those is very unwell. We read the prayer Jesus taught us in Matthew 6 (ESV):

> *Pray then like this: "Our Father in heaven, hallowed be your name.*
>
> *Your kingdom come, your will be done, on earth as it is in heaven.*
>
> *Give us this day our daily bread,*
>
> *and forgive us our debts, as we also have forgiven our debtors.*
>
> *And lead us not into temptation, but deliver us from evil.*
>
> *For if you forgive others their trespasses, your heavenly Father will also forgive you,*
>
> *but if you do not forgive others their trespasses, neither will your Father forgive your trespasses".*

Covid-19 is affecting us all differently, the plagues in Egypt affected everyone differently. We are all wired differently and we all respond in a unique way to every situation and stimuli. We need other people to support us when we are suffering, this illness can limit the amount of support we all get, we can feel isolated, partly because we are but even more so because when we are unwell things can seem worse.

For many people and families and church groups Zoom and other similar apps have helped people keep in touch and feel supported. Some church leaders have made sure every member of their congregation is spoken to every week, for others its every month, yet others even longer.

There is little excuse for people not to be contacted as we have modern methods of communication. In Egypt and in the Great Plague people were reliant on messengers to carry news and information. In the great plague people with the plague were locked into their houses and big letters and signs were marked on their doors. Warning people to keep away. There was no Zoom or internet then.

Once inside they weren't expected to come out, even those who were self-isolating were not advised to come out, but writers at the time said that they had not stored up sufficient provisions to cope with being isolated and had 'popped out' for food.

We have seen during this time the way some people appear to have gone crazy in the amount of food and supplies they have stored. It would make sense to have two weeks supply in case one got the virus, but some have exceeded this by a long way, they will still be going through their stores in 2021!

So why has God allowed Covid-19?

Some of the things that happen to mankind are consequences of actions taken in the past when we did not understand or know, what we know now. For example, if we build our house on the beach there is a probability we will at some time get flooded.

Sometimes we do not care for ourselves and become vulnerable, we have free will and God does not force us to do what is right.

Sometimes the answer to 'why has God allowed this to happen'? Is, 'I'm sorry I don't know'. This is such a tough question when asked by someone who has just lost their loved one.

We know human beings are frail or vulnerable and sometimes it helps to reflect on the frailty of the person. It is better to say we don't know, rather than just trying to dredge up some important sounding words we hope show our love and support and comfort for the person; but rather to be honest and say we don't know. Often the person does not expect an explanation but instead they are seeking someone to listen to them and journey with them as they realise the enormity of their loss and allow their feelings to emerge.

When a tragedy or international crisis occurs, trained first responders go immediately to assist, charities gear up their response to get the aid on site asap. Experts, and professionals from all fields and specialities arrive to support the local first responders, emergency services, carers and experts, to save, protect and ultimately rebuild the devastated area. At the same time in many areas specially trained Chaplains go in with those responders to support the first responders and others and to share hope with those who are suffering.

With Covid-19 hospitals are helping hospitals, counties are helping counties, countries are helping countries. Charities are helping in as much as they are allowed.

As I write this chapter I am in touch with a colleague in the USA who is part of a charity team responding to another natural disaster happening at the same time as Covid-19; Sharing Hope in a time of crisis.

The Egyptians had no one to help or support them, their wise men couldn't. Pharaoh was not immune to the plagues yet remained determined to keep the Israelite people as slaves; slaves that were being brutalised.

The Egyptians had magicians and gods made of gold or wood, the Israelites had a living breathing God to answer their prayer to set them free.

During this pandemic we hear that there have been increased incidences of domestic abuse during the lockdown. In some cases, the stress of living together in lockdown has caused people to boil over and lash out; not acceptable. Sadly, in some family's where domestic abuse is the way of life some wives and children have been bullied and battered by their 'loved 'ones. We know too of families where older people or husbands have been abused.

There are helplines to ring, if you can go out, get away from the abuse tell someone, there are people and groups who want to help. You may not feel it is a safe to speak; if you are experiencing domestic abuse, call out to God, even if you don't know him, he knows you and he will respond. He loves you and he won't let go of you if you want him to be there for you. There is an answer. If you know or suspect someone is being abused and you are unable to help them, tell God he will help them.

God is a great God, the Bible is full of tales of his greatness, the New Testament tells stories of God's greatness, that Jesus healed people of their sicknesses and diseases. Reports of people being raised from the dead; the blind gained their sight the deaf their hearing.

At the time of the Exodus, it is estimated that God led in excess of 2,000,000 people and their animals away from the slavery and brutality that the Israelite people were suffering at the hands of Pharaoh and the Egyptian people.

That was an amazing miracle, the people cried out to God and He heard their cry and He responded. God appointed Moses to go to Pharaoh but Pharaoh wouldn't listen and so on one night, the Passover, the Israelites were given specific instructions to follow so that they remained safe when God passed over the Egyptian land to strike down the Egyptians.

The Israelites were told to follow God's plan to eat a special meal, wearing clothes ready to travel and were then to leave Egypt immediately and start on their journey.

The Israelites as instructed by God, painted the blood of the sacrificed lamb on the door of their house or tent, so that their first-born would not die, it was called the Passover and since that time the Jewish people have celebrated the Passover. There was a lamb that was slain for every household so that they could daub the doors and lintels in the blood. The Passover Lamb.

For the Christian today Jesus is the Passover lamb, He shed his blood and died on the cross that you and I are free from God's wrath over our sin, that we can be reunited with God the Father through the glorious death and resurrection of Jesus Christ the Son of God, our Saviour. Paul in his letter to the church at Corinth reminds us;

> *'But Christ has indeed been raised from the dead, the first fruits of those who have fallen asleep. For since death came through a man, the resurrection of the dead comes also through a man. For as in Adam all die, so in Christ all will be made alive'.*
> 1 Corinthians.15: 20-22,

God led the Israelites until they came to the Red Sea, there the Israelite people were faced with major crisis. In front of them a mighty stretch of water that they had no chance to cross, behind them the mighty Pharaoh and his massive armies.

Yet God had a plan, Moses stretched out his hand and the waters of the sea stood still, long enough for the Israelite nation, over 2,00,000 and their animals to cross over. Yet when the Egyptians tried to cross the waters started flowing again trapping the Egyptians.

God had demonstrated his mighty power, again.

Some ask, 'will God not move now in power and deal with Covid-19'. I don't know.

It may well be argued that God is holding back the real power of this pandemic; like he held back the Red Sea; that Covid-19 should, could and ought to be worse than it is. But, God is hearing the cry of his people and restricting the impact of this disease.

Why has He not stopped this disease entirely? The Bible says that we live in a fallen world, a place where many people have chosen to ignore God, indeed many people declare there is no God. It is a world where people worship idols and false gods, a place where Satan rules for a little while longer. In Luke 10, we read after the disciples had gone out praying for people, Jesus saying, 'I saw Satan fall like lightning from heaven'. We know too when Jesus died on the cross he defeated Satan and all the powers of Evil.

The Bible tells us that Jesus will return as King of all creation. The Bible also tells us that as the time for Jesus to return approaches, there will be all manner of events in the skies and on the earth, including plagues. Many people believe we are close to the second coming of Jesus. When we read the Bible there are many verses that paint a picture for us of the time when Jesus will return; there will be a new heaven and a new earth a place without hate, a world of love. I discuss this in more detail in other chapters. However, I have included a couple of verses to start painting the picture.

> *But realize this, that in the last days difficult times will come.* 2 Timothy 3:1

> *''And upon the earth distress of nations, with perplexity; the sea and the waves roaring; Men's hearts failing them for fear, and for looking after those things which are coming on the earth: for the powers of heaven shall be shaken'.* Luke 21:25-26

> *'And I will grant wonders in the sky above and signs on the earth below, Blood, and fire, and vapor of smoke'.* Acts 2:19

We live in a time of claim and counter claim, where one person tells us that his or her view is correct. Recently we have heard people making statements about Covid-19 that sound at best far-fetched; people with strong held views and beliefs, that have been disturbing others.

We have seen how some have been silenced or at least had their platforms taken away when what they are saying is causing some level of public disorder.

At the same time journalists have been examining and reality testing the statements prominent people have been making, or looking at different aspects of Covid-19.

The BBC recently published an interesting article in its Reality Check series, regarding the number of people who had died in London because of Covid-19:

> *The number of people killed by coronavirus in London in the four weeks to 17 April has narrowly surpassed the number of civilians killed during the worst four-week period of aerial bombing of the city during the Blitz in World War Two.*

> *Figures held in the National Archives, and collated by the Commonwealth War Graves Commission, show that 4,677 people were killed during the Blitz and buried in London cemeteries in the 28 days to 4 October 1940.*
>
> *Registered deaths in London attributed to Covid-19, in the four weeks to 17 April this year, have now reached 4,697 according to a BBC count based on data from the Office for National Statistics (ONS).*
>
> *The first of those four weeks – the week ending 27 March – came before the sharp rise in Covid-19 deaths took place. So, figures released next week are expected to show a four-week tally considerably higher than that recorded during the Blitz.*
>
> By Chris Morris & Oliver Barnes, BBC Reality Check. bbc.co.uk – © copyright 2020 BBC

The story of the exodus tells us the Jewish nation prayed to the Lord. It doesn't say this family, or this group prayed, or that group prayed, rather the nation prayed. What we don't know is if we as a nation or a world pray fervently will we see Covid-19 removed by God? I don't know. I'm confident God will make a major powerful response.

However, what we do know He is able, He is omniscient (knows everything), omnipresent (in many places at the same time), omnipotent (has unlimited power).

If we believe He can, we need to show Him that we want Him to intervene, to act on our behalf. God gave us free will in our lives, He has said he would not overrule our free choice, He would let us decide for ourselves. Therefore, if we want God to intervene, we must individually and collectively tell him that.

Being a Christian does not mean we won't have problems in our lives, we will.

There will be storms, there will be trials, but we will not be alone, God promises to be there for us.

We read in the book of Mark about the disciples after a long day, are in the boat when the storm comes, a furious storm that makes even the hardened fishermen among them really very scared; water is filling the boat.

This storm makes them terrified, but Jesus is asleep in the stern of the boat, so they wake him. He asks them why they are afraid. Then He calms the storm.

The disciples were with Jesus, they were as close as you can get, yet the storm came.

As Christians we are not free form storms of life; Christians, suffer just as anyone else does, also Christians can and have suffered persecution. However, we have within us the power of the Holy Spirit, we can pray and God will respond to our crisis, to our storm. We need to 'let go and let God'. He will be there for us.

Therefore, let us as a people put aside all intellectual expertise, academic knowledge, our own wisdom, all hope for profit; our arrogance and pride and admit we cannot solve this pandemic and with all humility ask God in, to stop Covid-19, I and many others believe He will.

He has been intervening as we have individually been asking him to.

Let us collectively as a nation ask him to deal with Covid-19. He will.

It is just a tiny prayer but a huge step forward for mankind.

I hope we manage to make one united prayer, that God will not only intervene and stop it but remove Covid-19 from the face of the earth.

CONCLUSION

I pray this book will help you on your journey with the Lord as you learn to be more like Him and become the person he created you to be.

The journey to faith, believing in the Lord Jesus Christ is different for everyone:

We are all unique creations, we all broadly speaking face the same challenges, troubles, fun and enjoyment. We are each wired differently and therefore we often respond contrary to others in the situations we face.

The Bible says in John 3:16. *'God sent his only begotten Son to die for us, that whoever believes in Him will not perish but have everlasting lives'.*

When we believe that Jesus is the Christ, the Son of God, and have surrendered our lives to him and been baptised, we have a new name that the mouth of the Lord Himself shall give us. *'The nations shall see your righteousness, and all the kings your glory, and you shall be called by a new name that the mouth of the LORD will give'.* Isaiah 62:2

Jesus wants us to do more than just live or survive. He wants us to do more than He did when He was on earth! We can pray for the sick, see the dead raised to life; let us expect to see miracles.

In John 14:12 Jesus says *'Truly, truly, I say to you, whoever believes in me will also do the works that I do: and greater works than these will he do, because I am going to the Father.'*

That is the hope we have in God, based on the words of Jesus. His Son.

We are Christians, followers of Jesus Christ, Son of God, second Person in the Trinity. Jehovah, Messiah.

We go forward in life learning to be like Christ Jesus, to be imitators of him, he also said that if we were to follow him we should do what he does. This makes real sense, when we go to a teacher to learn a new skill or idea, we will copy what they do, Jesus wants us to copy him.

The Israelites stopped copying God and got into all sorts of danger, suffering, pain, separation and slavery.

As we have read it took over 40 years to get the Israelites into the promised land.

The journey time to walk would have been just a couple of weeks.

The Israelites should have reached the boundaries of the promised land in a few short weeks, I'm sure that God's plan for them was to go into the promised as soon as they were free. But there was a problem, the Israelites had been in Egypt too long and they had become too like the Egyptian people. In addition, they had become slaves, used to being subservient and beaten, in a land that was not their own.

It is possible that some of the Israelites would not have spoken Hebrew. Most of the Israelites who left Egypt on the Exodus would have been the last of several generations of slaves. Some were goldsmiths, shepherds, menial workers or personal servants, that's all they knew.

The Israelites were a very mixed bunch, and before they could enter into the promised land they had to be free of all the ways of Egypt, for some this meant learning about their ancestors, learning about God, or learning Hebrew, for others it meant to be willing to do what God wanted them to do when He wanted them to do it and not following their own will.

Life changing things like this don't always happen immediately, they needed time to understand what change was needed and time to implement the change.

Some people can go a lifetime and be unable or unwilling to change.

A generation of Israelites died in the wilderness as they prepared for the promised land: for those who died in the wilderness their promised land was heaven.

I remember assessing a man for a Christian residential rehabilitation programme: a man who had been in prison for over twenty-five years, I accepted him onto our programme and he was released from prison. He was delighted he was *free*. My team and I were so pleased for him as he enjoyed being free.

We talked about how the world to him had changed beyond his comprehension, how it was amazing for him to choose when he got up and when he went to bed.

He could go for a walk totally free. He was very happy, he knew God and believed that one day he would go to heaven. One day only about two weeks after his release he died, it seemed a shame that he died so soon after his release, but I know he got what his heart desired: he died a free man!

Today when we turn to Jesus we need time to understand what changes we need to make to be more like Jesus.

It's not just about us fancying change, it is about God leading us by his Spirit

This book will have given you some ideas and hopefully challenged you.

As you walk into the future God has for you, be open to change, look for the areas in yourself where you have become more like the world (Egypt in the story) and seek God to help you change them. He is not calling you to become something you are not, rather he is calling you to be the person he made you to be: that will be great!

The Israelites stubbornness was a huge problem for them. There was an aspect where it was a strength of character, that stickability, that determination to keep going to the end.

We see that today in the Israeli people. They are determined, dogged, they have survived as a nation throughout history, through the most horrendous persecution; atrocities that are almost too painful to reflect on.

When we come to faith, we make that journey to the promised land, over time we change from a person that did not have godlike ways or values, to someone who does what God wants and becomes someone whom God is pleased in and someone who reflects Gods love.

Hopefully the book will have helped you find some of the issues to watch out for as you Journey with Jesus. It is possible to get "Egypt" out of the new Christian because we don't do it on our own,

I pray you will go from strength to strength and be more like him every day.

Thank you for reading this book.

God bless you.

Paul

CONTACTS

The following is a list of contact details for charities that offer support to individuals needing support. It is a small representation of the charities that freely offer support, many of them with local active branches. If you are still unsure where to get help or support, a good place to start is the Citizens Advice Bureau; also, your local library usually will help you find out who to contact. Alternatively, your GP, Medical practice or Care Manager will also be able to advise you. If you want help for spiritual issues your local Pastor, Minister, Vicar or Faith Leader will also want to help.

ADDACTION
Substance Abuse Support
020 7251 5860

ALZHEIMER'S
Research UK
0300 222 1122

AGE UK
0800 055 6112

CRUSE
Bereavement Support
0808 808 1677

CAP UK
Christian Financial Support
01274760720

CARE for the Carers
01323 738390

CICRA Children with
Crohn's and Colitis
020 8949 6209

BACP
Counselling changes lives
01455 883300

CHILDRENS TRUST
01737 365 000

DIABETES UK
0345 123 2399

DOMESTIC ABUSE
National Domestic Violence helpline
0808 28000247

CHILD LINE
0800 1111

EPILEPSY SOCIETY
01494 601 400.

MARIE CURIE
End of Life Care
0800 090 2309

MACMILLAN
Cancer Support
020 7840 7840

MEN'S ADVICE LINE
0808 801 0327

MIND
info@mind.org.uk
0300 123 3393

NATIONAL LGBT AND
DOMESTIC ABUSE
HELPLINE
0800 999 5428

NSPCC
0808 800 5000

RELATE
0300 003 0396

RESPECT FOR
PERPETRATORS OF ABUSE
0808 802 4040

SAMARITANS
116-123

SALVATION ARMY
020 7367 4500

TALK TO FRANK
Honest information re drugs
0300 1236 600